THE CLASSICAL HERITAGE IN ISLAM

ARABIC THOUGHT AND CULTURE

This new series is designed to provide straightforward introductions for the western reader to some of the major figures and movements of Arabic thought. Philosophers, historians, and geographers are all seminal figures in the history of thought, and some names, such as Averroes and Avicenna, are already part of the western tradition. Mathematicians, linguistic theorists, and astronomers have as significant a part to play as groups of thinkers such as the Illuminationists. With the growing importance of the Arab world on the international scene, these succinct and authoritative works will be welcomed not only by teachers and students of Arab history and of philosophy, but by journalists, travellers, teachers of EFL, and businessmen — in fact any who have to come to an understanding of this non-western culture in the course of their daily work.

Also available in this series:

Ibn Khaldun Aziz Al-Azmeh
Ibn Rushd Dominique Urvoy
Moses Maimonides Oliver Leaman
The Arabic Linguistic Tradition G. Bohas, J.-P. Guillaume, D. E. Kouloughli
Al-Farabi and his School Ian Richard Netton
Naguib Mahfouz Rasheed El-Enany
Avicenna Lenn E. Goodman

Forthcoming:

Ibn Arabi Ron Nettler

The Classical Heritage in Islam

FRANZ ROSENTHAL

Translated from the German by
Emile and Jenny Marmorstein

ROUTLEDGE
LONDON AND NEW YORK

Translated from the German
Das Fortleben der Antike im Islam

First published in English in 1975
by Routledge & Kegan Paul Ltd

First published in paperback in 1992
by Routledge
11 New Fetter Lane, London ECP 4EE
29 West 35th Street, New York, NY 10001

Reprinted 1994

Printed in Great Britain by Redwood Books, Trowbridge, Wilts.

British Library Cataloguing in Publication Data
Rosenthal, Franz, *1914–*
The classical heritage in Islam. — (Arabic thought and culture)
I. Title II. Series III. [Das Fortleben der Antike im Islam. *English*]
297.1975

ISBN 0–415–07693–5

CONTENTS

INTRODUCTION

I. TRANSLATION TECHNIQUE AND TEXTUAL CRITICISM

II. BIOGRAPHY AND CULTURAL HISTORY

III. THE CLASSIFICATION OF THE SCIENCES AND METHODS OF RESEARCH AND TEACHING

IV. PHILOSOPHY

VI. MEDICINE

VII. GEOMETRY, ARITHMETIC AND OPTICS

VIII. GEOGRAPHY AND ASTRONOMY

IX. MUSICOLOGY

X. MECHANICS

XI. THE OCCULT SCIENCES

XII. LITERATURE AND ART

PLATES

FIGURES

PREFACE

The heritage of classical antiquity affected Islam to its core by virtue of the influence it had on religious disciplines, theology, mysticism and law. It did not leave Arabic philology, grammar, literary studies and the art of poesy altogether untouched. The following pages scarcely refer to any of these intellectual and literary activities. They are confined to the the direct and obvious links between the two cultures which mostly concern other branches of learning. Nevertheless, despite this limitation, the material that merits consideration remains very extensive. Hence, the choice of texts offered here is in a way arbitrary. I do not wish to claim—as many compilers of anthologies tend to do—that the texts chosen contain all that is best and most important on the subject. By using other passages, it would be quite feasible to provide a selection equal in scope and similar in content. However, I hope I have selected what is relevant and typical. If not superior to other, possible anthologies, this one should at any rate be of equal merit.

Special emphasis has been laid on permitting ample breadth in the choice of typical passages. The samples include literary renderings, paraphrases, commentaries and imitations, as well as independent Islamic elaborations. They consist of complete works, long chapters, collections of fragments and brief individual observations. They are taken from early authors, authors of the Golden Age and later writers who imitated or completed their works. No systematic chronological plan has been adopted, since it would be meaningful only within a much wider framework. As far as possible, themes of general interest were given priority (which raised special difficulties with regard to the exact sciences, where a concern with detailed problems naturally predominates). The excerpts are often lengthy, for they are intended to convey a coherent picture and to demonstrate that discussions that appear long-winded and clumsy to us had a definite place in medieval Islamic writing. No use has been made of the divine right of translators to avoid difficult and dubious passages by substituting dots. Where dots are found in the passages translated here, they usually signify the omission of irrelevant material. They may also mean that Arabic *qāla* 'he said' in its various forms, which is used to indicate the interruption or continuation of a quotation, has not been translated.

The following pages aim at stressing the influence of classical antiquity on Islam. They seek to convey an impression of the extent and quality of Muslim acquaintance with the cultural heritage of classical antiquity and to show how that cultural heritage was reflected in the minds of Muslims and how it affected them. Inevitably, since we deal more with adoption and borrowing than with independent achievement, a rather one-sided view of Islamic intellectual life will emerge. Let it therefore be expressly stated here that no matter how fundamental and undeniable the degree of dependence, the Muslim acquisition, adaptation and development of the heritage of classical antiquity constitute an independent and, historically, an extraordinarily fruitful achievement.

Like his Arab colleagues of more than a thousand years ago, the modern translator, on completion of his work, feels a strong desire to pour out his heart regarding the many difficulties which his task has caused him. From obstacles due to unreliable manuscripts and, frequently, even less reliable printed editions to the insoluble dilemma of the choice of the right word and of a consistent terminology, there are innumerable difficulties about which a great deal could be said. However, only one point should be emphasized here: while it is true that one can really understand an Arabic translation from the Greek only if in each case the Greek expression corresponding to a given Arabic word or phrase is identified, nevertheless, it would be altogether inappropriate here to render our Arabic texts on the basis of reconstructed Greek equivalents (especially in those cases where no reconstruction is required because the Greek original is available). *Entelecheia*, for instance, has been elegantly rendered in Arabic by *kamāl* (or *tamām*) but while one should be aware that *kamāl* frequently represents Greek *entelecheia*, it would be absurd, for our own purposes, to translate *kamāl* as 'entelechy' instead of 'perfection'. The ideal—unattainable like every ideal—is to render an Arabic text in the way it might have been understood by a medieval Arab scholar familiar with the literature on the subject.

The reader will notice, perhaps with regret, that very few explanatory notes have been added to the translated passages. Bibliographical information and biographical notes have also been kept as brief as possible. The reason is that any interpretation of some length, even of the less difficult texts and even if it is not exhaustive, would unduly expand the framework of the present volume. Proper commentaries on some of the texts could fill large volumes. A few notes, indications of sources, and the like, have crept in, though, perhaps because of the author's lifelong scholarly habits. They are not systematic or exhaustive. However, the translated texts as they appear here, are neither obscure nor unintelligible in themselves, even though a thorough understanding requires a more detailed exposition. It might have been desirable to reprint the original Greek text, wherever available, for comparison. This would also have taken up too much space and might have necessitated the omission of some important and not easily accessible material. Hence, much further work is needed on the part of the reader, if he wants to derive full benefit from this book. Perhaps he will make better progress on his own than through the best efforts of the author.

Occasional minor deviations from the Arabic text as transmitted have usually not been noted. Sometimes pointed brackets ⟨ ⟩ have been used to indicate necessary restorations of textual omissions. The transliteration of Arabic words and names conforms to widespread usage.

I owe a great debt of gratitude to my friends, G. E. von Grunebaum and R. Ettinghausen, to the former for encouraging me to compile this volume and to the latter for his constant readiness to help me in the choice of illustrations. Professor C. Colpe, who, during his stay in New Haven, kindly offered to read the proofs of the German original, contributed valuable improvements to it.

Above all, I feel grateful to the numerous libraries in many parts of the world which most generously placed their manuscript treasures at my disposal and gave their consent to the publication of the illustrations.

Franz Rosenthal

A NOTE ON THE ENGLISH TRANSLATION

A translation like that on the following pages which has passed through so many languages presents particular problems. I have considered it my duty to try to soften the impact of the last shock, the one caused by the translation from German into English, by comparing the result of the Marmorsteins' conscientious labour with the Arabic texts in most, but not all, cases. This will no doubt have increased stylistic incongruity, but it has also given me the opportunity to correct a number of mistakes and to change my mind frequently on debatable points of which there are many. The reader will also find a very few additions, mainly of a bibliographical nature. However, the present book remains, for better or worse, a faithful translation of the German *Fortleben der Antike im Islam*, with all its imperfections.

Franz Rosenthal
1973

TRANSLITERATION SCHEME

Letter	*Transliteration*	*Pronunciation*
ا	appears here only when the a vowel is lengthened, e.g., ā	
ب	b	as in English
ت	t	as in English
ث	th	as in 'thing'
ج	j	as in English

ح	ḥ	compressed h (not found in European languages)
خ	kh	guttural as in the Scottish 'loch'
د	d	as in English
ذ	dh	as in 'there'
ر	r	lingual r
ز	z	as in English
س	s	sharp as in 'sun'
ش	sh	as in English
ص	ṣ	emphatic sharp palatal s
ض	ḍ	emphatic dull palatal d
ط	ṭ	emphatic dull palatal t
ظ	ẓ	emphatic dull palatal z
ع	ʿ	explosive guttural sound, tonal counterpart to ḥ
غ	gh	rattling guttural between gh and r
ف	f	as in English
ق	q	dull guttural k
ك	k	as in English
ل	l	as in English
م	m	as in English
ن	n	as in English
ه	h	as in English
و	w, ū	as in English
ي	y, ī	as in English
ء	ʾ	strong vocal inflection

INTRODUCTION

1. HISTORICAL AND IDEOLOGICAL MOTIVES

In the time of the Prophet Muḥammad (ca. 570–632) neither Mecca nor Medina were entirely cut off from the outside world, as it was once widely assumed, nor were they centres of a flourishing cultural life, as is frequently stated or implied nowadays. The very limited impact of contemporary higher civilization upon Central Arabia shows itself in the absence from the Qurʾān of references to medicine or physicians, which in view of the religious tradition behind it would have almost been mandatory. Scientifically untrained native healers can be assumed to have existed, and a genuine physician might on occasion have strayed into Central Arabia, like the one encountered in contemporary Nessana on the far northwestern border of the Arabian desert.[1] Such a physician would not, of course, have been an eminent scientist. Neither he, nor anyone else, would have brought a great deal of learning from the outside world to the cities which were soon to become the holy places of Islam. On the other hand, their inhabitants had an opportunity, through the caravan trade, of getting acquainted with the cultural life of their age in Nessana as well as in the larger settlements of Palestine and Syria. That they made use of that opportunity is attested by our sources, meagre as they are.

All cultural links of this kind lead to areas where the civilization of classical antiquity—that is to say Hellenism and, in so far as it reached the East in Greek garb, Roman civilization—had left its mark. Indeed, we can assert that culturally speaking the western part of Central Arabia formed part of the ancient Hellenistic world—a very remote part, it is true, and one that was largely untouched by the loftier of its intellectual attainments. Memories of the pre-Hellenistic ancient Near East naturally persisted, renewed and reinforced in various respects by the successful advance of Christianity, Gnosticism and Judaism. The higher civilizations of South Arabia and of the Persian Sassanian Empire were also strongly influenced by Hellenism. The triumph of Hellenism, as described by H. H. Schaeder,[2] is a fact which is being confirmed again and again by fresh discoveries.

However, at the beginning of the seventh century, this was a Hellenism which had largely dispensed with the Greek language, since Christian missionaries, and, in their wake, those of the Gnostic sects, appealed from the outset to the uneducated, the great mass of the people, and insisted on using the indigenous languages for literary expression. Moreover, it was a Hellenism which no longer actively embraced the whole culture of classical antiquity, but was largely restricted by the new religious outlook to a rather narrow selection. The first wave of Islamic conquests (632–41) secured for the Arabs dominion over thoroughly hellenized Syria and Egypt and the comparatively strongly hellenized western part of the Sassanian Empire. They were probably hostile to, and at first certainly did not appreciate, the opportunity thus offered them of taking over the culture of classical antiquity, at the fringe of which they had been living all the time. Religion and language separated the Arab Muslims from their neighbours. Their first task was to gain victory for these two distinctive features of the new age. Inherited cultural affinity constituted an obstacle, even a danger, for the realization of this task. However, the pre-eminence of the achievements of the higher civilization was apparent on every level and inexorably demanded that the new rulers acquire them. When the Umayyad dynasty (660–750) came to power and Damascus instead of Medina became the capital of the Islamic Empire, these conflicting tendencies made themselves increasingly felt. The Arabs were favourably inclined towards the superior culture and used what it had to offer; yet they dared not admit their dependence on it (this is why Arabic literature ignores castles like Quṣair ʿAmra). More than half a century passed after the death of the Prophet before Arabic became the official administrative language, and even then, undoubtedly, cultural victory was still not secured for Arabism—

quite apart from the fact that the Umayyad rulers during the second wave of Islamic conquest (ca. 670–711), which culminated in the conquest of Spain, were involved in serious hostilities with Byzantium (which was not the case to the same dangerous degree later in the heyday of the Islamic Empire). Hence it was only natural that the Umayyads could neither foster nor tolerate official study of Greek culture, and it is therefore not surprising that there was no large-scale translation activity under their rule. The situation of the ʿAbbāsids, when they came to power in 750 and moved the centre of the Islamic Empire eastwards to Iraq, was quite different in this respect. They no longer needed to disapprove officially of the acceptance of foreign cultural values.

What Arabic tradition has to say about the earliest translation activity substantially supports this view. According to it, Greek alchemical writings were translated into Arabic by a certain Iṣṭifan (Stephen) at the request of the Umayyad Prince Khālid, a son of the Caliph Yazīd (680–3), who died in the first decade of the eighth century. The general situation would appear to have been assessed correctly by this report. Like medicine—where we encounter a highly dubious claim to the effect that Māsarjawaih, elsewhere associated with the poet Abū Nuwās towards the end of the eighth century, had already translated Ahrun's Syriac Medical Encyclopaedia at the beginning of that century[3]—alchemy is a science of immediate practical use and, accordingly, was one of the first achievements of Hellenistic culture to arouse Arab interest. Anyone wishing to make a translation required a patron, perhaps a member of the ruling house, since the caliph himself was unable, for political reasons, to support such activity. Hence the tradition concerning Khālid is not unlikely in itself. However, we are dealing here with a branch of knowledge in which falsifications were the norm rather than the exception. Therefore, we should do well to relegate the precise story of Khālid's alchemical translation activity to the realm of legend. Most probably, while actual translations into Arabic were occasionally made (and published?) in the Umayyad period, people then were normally content to obtain useful information if needed for private purposes, either orally or in writing, directly from scholars of Greek (and other foreign) literatures, of whom many were still around at the time. Practical usefulness was the leading consideration, irrespective of whether it was a question of medical or alchemical knowledge or, perhaps, of information about Judaism or Christianity which could be applied towards a better understanding of the Qurʾān. In recent years, the voices in favour of the historical reality of a rather extensive translation activity in Umayyad times have become more insistent, and it has been argued that most, if not all, of the claims for pre-ʿAbbāsid dating put forward in manuscripts and literary testimonies must be taken at their face value.[4]

The ʿAbbāsids came from the Persian East. This fact, in conjunction with the increased cultural confidence of the eastern half of the Empire in the face of Greek influences, explains why translations from the Persian and from some Indian scientific material are among the earliest known to us. Even the Muslims' first acquaintance with Aristotle was attributable to the interest of the Sassanians of the sixth century in Greek learning.[5] Besides, as I have already stated, the ʿAbbāsids no longer stood in that cultural-political opposition to Hellenism which had been unavoidable for the Umayyads. Yet, it was another factor that proved decisive here. The political movements of the preceding century had relied on differences of opinion on matters of dogma in order to justify their existence and provide ideological guidance for their adherents. Similar processes had taken place earlier in Christianity, where they had fostered the growth of a theology that was philosophically sophisticated, extremely rich in content and frequently concerned with fundamental questions. From it, the Muslims received at a very early date the impetus for penetrating discussion of theological questions to which the Qurʾān merely alludes without pursuing them to the end, such as, for example, the nature of God or free will. Moreover, in order to be able to defend their religion against the arguments of Christian theologians, Muslims were obliged to familiarize themselves with Christian theology and to attempt to transform it according to Islamic ideas. Thus, it appears likely that the ʿAbbāsids based themselves ideologically on the Muʿtazilah—not an organized group but a number of individual thinkers and their followers, to whom can be ascribed the chief merit of introducing into the realm of Islamic culture the philosophical treatment of theological problems based on ideas and methods originally found in Greek philosophy.[6] It is most probably no accident that the Muʿtazilah should have flourished during the decisive years of Graeco-Arabic translation activity, that is, from the last decades of the eighth century until the reign of Caliph al-Maʾmūn (813–33) and his immediate successors. Rather, Muʿtazilah influence on the ʿAbbāsid rulers ought to be regarded as the real cause of an official attitude towards the heritage of classical antiquity that made impressive provisions for its adoption in Islam.[7]

Neither practical utilitarianism, however, which made an acquaintance with medicine, alchemy and the exact sciences appear desirable to Muslims, nor theoretical utilitarianism, which prompted them to occupy themselves with philosophical–theological problems, might have sufficed to support an extensive translation activity, had not the religion of Muḥammad stressed from the very beginning the role of knowledge (*ʿilm*) as the driving force in religion and, thereby, in all human life.[8] Admittedly, Qurʾānic *ʿilm* has the religious connotation of acknowledgment of the premises of religious existence and acquaintance with the religious duties of the Muslim, and the word soon came to refer specifically to 'knowledge' of Islamic religious doctrines and obligations. However, *ʿilm* never lost its wide and general significance. Thus the interest in knowledge for its own sake, in systematic learning *per se* and in the sciences as expressions of man's thirst for knowledge, was greatly and effectively stimulated. Without this central position of 'knowledge' in Islam and the almost religious veneration extended to it, the translation activity would presumably have been less scholarly and less extensive. It would probably have been confined to the absolutely essential anp immediately useful to a much greater degree.

2. THE TRANSLATORS

Historical forces require the presence of men capable of acting in concert with them. It is one of the great problems of history where the priority lies in each case in the causal chain connecting personal and impersonal factors. In the early centuries of Islam, the driving forces existed, and the material resources were therefore available. Only men with the abilities needed for accomplishing the actual task of translation had to be found. Fortunately, they were available among the minorities of the Islamic Empire, above all among the Aramaic-(Syriac-)speaking Christians whose ancestors had themselves once absorbed Greek literature into their own language. Though the educated among them, their physicians and clergy, clung firmly to their native tongue, in the course of time they felt unable to resist the pressure of the changing cultural climate around them and had to reconcile themselves to living with the Arabic language. Almost all translators were Christians of various churches. A doubtful exception is Māsarjawaih who according to tradition was of Jewish origin and who is regarded as an early translator from Syriac. Among the heathen Ṣābians from Ḥarrān, the name of Thābit b. Qurrah (ca. 834–901) can be mentioned. Born Muslims acted only as patrons who ordered, and paid for, translations done by more or less professional translators and in some instances even provided translators with regular salaries for their services. The famous representatives of Greek knowledge among the Muslims of the ninth and tenth centuries, al-Kindī (died after 870), his pupil as-Sarakhsī (died 899), al-Fārābī (died 950), Abū Sulaimān al-Manṭiqī as-Sijistānī (died ca. 985), al-ʿĀmirī (died 992) and, of course, all those of later times, knew neither Syriac nor Greek. Frequently all the information we have about the translators is just their names, and we have to draw from them sometimes uncertain conclusions as to their Christian origin. Staunch Islamic opponents of all Greek culture made much of the fact that its interpreters were infidels. For its protagonists, however, this was irrelevant since, in the words of al-ʿĀmirī, the translators worked on behalf of Islam and within its sphere of influence, thereby acquiring the right of citizenship in Islam.[9]

There seems to have been a direct line to the Muslim world for the transmission of Greek philosophy that originated in Alexandria. It appears to have contributed little to actual translation activity, however, at least in the earlier period (cf. chap. II, no. 12). Of special importance, on the other hand, was the Nestorian medical academy in Jundīsābūr (etymologically perhaps 'Good is Sābūr's Antiochia', in Greek script Gue [= We] Antioch-Sābōr) in Khūzistān, southeast of Baghdad, where, among other learned physicians, the Bukhtīshūʿ family played an outstanding role. As physicians at the caliph's court from the time of the second ʿAbbāsid ruler, al-Manṣūr (754–75), they were in a particularly favourable position to work as translators and, perhaps, even to influence the general direction translation activities were to take. Of the two professions providing translators, physicians and clergymen, the former were more respected and clearly better situated financially and socially than the latter. The physicians from Jundīsābūr, however, felt limited to translating Greek works on medical matters from available Syriac versions. As frequently happens, it was an outsider, the great Ḥunain b. Isḥāq (808–73) from al-Ḥīrah on the Euphrates, who contributed decisively to breaking the hold of the Syriac language on Greek medical literature, though even before him, at least in other disciplines, certain texts may already have been translated directly from the Greek. In general, it can be said that the concentration of translation activity in Baghdad and the eastern Nestorian region had the result that the number of translators familiar with Syriac alone greatly exceeded that of those who knew Greek or were bilingual. Syriac was the translators' mother tongue. Greek they had to learn—and at that time an understanding of the language of the classical writers required special and intensive study. From Ḥunain's time onwards, it was widely recognized that translators had the obligation to make use of all available aids for their task. They tried to get hold of as many Greek manuscripts as possible. They also compared them with Syriac translations wherever such existed, in order to gain a better text and a better understanding of the Greek original. Conditions were not always ideal. It could happen that no Greek manuscript could be found, or a translator knew no Greek and hence Greek manuscripts were of no use to him. In those cases, a translation from Syriac was obviously preferable to none at all. There are many instances of translators themselves informing us about the background of their translations. In the absence of such information, we must always reckon with the possibility of an intermediate Syriac stage, but where the language of a translation does not provide evidence for a Syriac intermediary, there is no reason why we should not assume a direct translation from the Greek.

Linguistic problems caused special difficulties for the translators. Greek and Arabic have entirely different word formations and syntaxes. The Indo-European system of compound formation is basically foreign to the Semitic Arabic language, and so is

Greek syntax with its fairly free position of words and sentence subordination. Above all, ideas new to speakers of Arabic required the coining of an adequate Arabic terminology. The translators from Greek into Syriac had helped themselves in the simplest manner. They took over many Greek words or formed highly artificial new words. They also tended towards a slavish imitation of Greek syntax, to which Syriac, long used to foreign influences, lent itself more readily than Arabic. The procedure was acceptable as long as scholars translated for scholars. Most of the translations into Arabic, however, were ultimately intended for caliphs, government officials, highly literate theologians and educated laymen. Hence the Arabic language and style of translations had to satisfy as far as possible the great demands made by these classes of society. Under these circumstances it might have been a certain advantage for translators that Arabic was often their second language so that they had no personal stake in literary Arabic and thus approached the problem of word choice and style relatively unbiased. Most early translations were rather clumsy, and it could happen at any time that a translator with a mind of his own followed his personal taste. However, Ḥunain and his school, in which his son, Isḥāq b. Ḥunain (died 910) and his nephew Ḥubaish were prominent, succeeded in coining an authoritative terminology and attaining a high and genuinely Arabic quality of linguistic expression. Although the medieval Arab reader not especially trained in the language of Graeco-Arabic translation literature found much in it that seemed strange and hard to understand (and the same applies to the modern student of it), it is none the less true that Ḥunain and his school provided a true home in the Arabic language for a wealth of foreign ideas and that the coining of a good scientific terminology in Arabic is primarily, though not, of course, exclusively, due to his efforts.[10]

The zenith of translation activity in the ninth century was naturally followed by a pronounced decline in the tenth. The most important works had already been translated, and only a gleaning remained to be done. Though it was not as difficult in the eastern part of the Islamic world as it was in Spain to find men who knew Greek (cf. chap. VI, no. 8), the chances had substantially diminished of exerting political pressure on Byzantium to yield rare Greek manuscripts, for which by then it had become the most likely source. And the Christians living under Muslim domination had adapted themselves to their cultural environment, their own cultural tradition having been greatly weakened. Yet, just at that time there developed an extremely fertile exchange of ideas with Muslim philosophers, in which men like Abū Bishr Mattā (Nestorian, died 940), Yaḥyā b. ʿAdī (Jacobite, 893–974), Ibn Zurʿah (Jacobite, 943–1008) and Ibn Suwār (Nestorian, 942 till after 1017) participated on the Christian side. Apart from their own translations, they devoted themselves above all to the adaptation and utilization of earlier translated material (cf. chap. I, no. 10). They were usually important scholars, that is, philosophers and theologians, in their own right—in contrast with the ninth-century translators, who only rarely, as in the case of Ḥunain and Qusṭā b. Lūqā (ca. 820–912), were creative scholars. After the tenth century there were no more translators of classical works who exercised an influence on Muslim civilization. Within the Christian communities, many works of special interest to them continued to be translated.

3. WHAT WAS TRANSLATED?

In 1886, M. Steinschneider (1816–1907) submitted to the Académie des Inscriptions his prizewinning work, 'Arabische Übersetzungen aus dem Griechischen'. In the course of the next ten years it was published in various places. A reprint bringing together all parts appeared in Graz in 1960. Though the work is dated, it remains of great and lasting value as a comprehensive bibliography of work carried out in the field of translation literature up to roughly the end of the last century. It can also be maintained that by and large all that is essential and fundamental is contained in it. Until superseded by a fresh presentation, it remains quite adequate as an impressive survey of the extent of the Graeco-Arabic translation literature. For preliminary information about work done in recent years one can consult the surveys of F. Gabrieli[11] and J. Kraemer,[12] for example, as well as the collection of R. Walzer's essays, which appeared under the title *Greek into Arabic* (Oxford, 1962).[13] Here we must confine ourselves to a few general remarks. Other authors are mentioned in connection with the translated texts, where further references to the scholarly literature can be found.

The translation activity depended basically on the syllabus current in the old schools which had somehow managed to survive the victory of Islam. They were concerned with medical, philosophical and monastic education. They no longer cared for rhetoric, since it served direct political ends and had had a proper place only in independent pagan or Christian states. Nothing of Greek poetry, tragedy, comedy or the historical literature was translated into Arabic. All this had been included in the school curriculum as part of rhetorical training. On the other hand, didactic poems like the 'Golden Words' of Pythagoras, the gnomic verses of Pseudo-Menander, the 'Phenomena' of Aratus, or the astrological work of Dorotheus found their way into Arabic as part of a school tradition familiar to the translators.[14]

The works of ancient philosophy, medicine and the exact sciences were taken over almost in their entirety, to the extent that they had survived into the late Hellenistic period, which means that our knowledge of Greek works in these fields does not substantially differ from that of the Arabs. Occult sciences like alchemy were in a way specialized branches of the exact sciences. They were cultivated by the same type of scholars but more privately and not so much in their official capacity.

Works that had become classics were naturally the ones most studied in the schools. However, they had to be adapted to educational requirements, and changing times necessitated certain changes in emphasis. Furthermore, many a great author appeared long-winded, so that abridgments and paraphrases were deemed more suitable for conveying the contents of his work. This happened to Plato, whose writings the Arabs preferably knew through adaptations dating from the time of middle Platonism. In the case of some authors, commentaries written on their works provided more information and had become more meaningful than the original text. This was the case with Aristotle's *Logic* which was translated literally and is preserved for us in literal form, but was by preference studied from commentaries. To a certain extent, this holds true for the entire body of Aristotelian writings, all of which, apart from the *Politics* and parts of the *Ethics*, appear to have been known in Arabic. Doxography (such as the 'Placita

Philosophorum' of Pseudo-Plutarch) and gnomology, two related forms of literary activity particularly congenial to the spirit of classical antiquity in its decline, transmitted a fairly large store of significant Greek ideas to the Arabs. Often, the original text of eminent authors proved hard to understand, and paraphrases and elaborations were easier to master. This happened to the famous Neo-Platonists, Plotinus and Proclus. In medicine and in the exact sciences, however, it was essential to adhere rather closely to the original text; hence more literal translations predominate (to be paraphrased and interpreted by the Arabs themselves later). Although primarily concerned with Galen's medical works, Ḥunain insisted on a complete presentation of the great physician's *œuvre*. As a result, some of Galen's philosophical and ethical writings, which are now lost in the original, have survived in Arabic. On the other hand, Plutarch's ethical writings, which would have been appreciated by Muslims as much as they were, in fact, in the West, became known to the Arabs only very fragmentarily through Syriac intermediaries, no doubt because manuscripts of works that were not included in the ordinary curriculum of the schools for some reason or other, usually historical or traditional, were difficult to obtain. A systematic search for rare Greek works was indeed undertaken in the time of Ḥunain, but it was an extremely difficult and laborious task to which the men of the Middle Ages, owing to their whole outlook on matters of the mind and the spirit, were generally unequal.

As has been mentioned, the Arabic translators drew upon the same late Hellenistic stock from which most of our own knowledge of classical antiquity derives. However, they were considerably closer to it in time. Accordingly, Arabic translations often represent Greek manuscripts older than those preserved for us, and they deserve therefore the special attention of philologists, even if it is true in textual criticism that the older manuscript is not always the better one. Of particular importance is the fact that works or extracts from works lost in the original have been preserved in Arabic and that the possibility of new discoveries still remains. The proud list of names of writers part of whose work has been preserved only in Arabic includes Theophrastus, (Pseudo-?) Euclid, Hero of Alexandria, Pappus of Alexandria, Rufus of Ephesus, Dorotheus of Sidon, Galen, Alexander of Aphrodisias,

Nicolaus of Damascus, Porphyry and Proclus. To these may be added later physicians such as Philagrius and Palladius, Magnes of Emesa and the veterinary surgeon Theomnestus of Magnesia as well as the anonymous[15] philosophers to whom we owe the adaptations of Plotinus and Proclus, and the unknown authors of the original versions of the Graeco-Arabic gnomic collections. Some pseudepigraphical writings, for example, the exchange of ideas between Aristotle and Alexander, must also be included among the regained texts of classical antiquity. A great deal of pseudepigraphical material, though not the work of the eminent men to whom it is ascribed, nevertheless reflects Hellenistic works and is significant for cultural history. Seen in its totality and despite its great interest for us, this rich harvest for classical philology which we owe to the efforts of Arabic translators is of only minor significance, the by-product of a great event of world history.

4. THE HISTORICAL SIGNIFICANCE OF THE MUSLIM ADOPTION OF THE CLASSICAL HERITAGE

As stated earlier, the Arabian environment in which Islam had its roots was in contact with Hellenistic civilization. This generated in Islam a certain affinity with classical culture. Soon there came the translation activity bringing Islam and Greece together in a consciously creative act. The heritage of classical antiquity was revived with the aid of scholarly research. The result was a new outlook on life, giving Islam an intellectual direction that, owing to insufficient original preparedness, it would not have taken on its own. Thus was born what we call Islamic culture. True, the translators and those who profited from their work had no express intention to regain and give new life to the spirit and essence of classical civilization (or what might have been assumed to be its spirit and essence). Nor was their effort influenced by the negative motive of undermining Islam and doing away with its way of life and fundamental beliefs. On the contrary, the principal aim of all but a very few of the Muslims concerned with the Greek heritage was to breathe a new life into their religion. Yet, the process that took place in the Muslim empire between the eighth and tenth centuries is much closer in spirit and character to the European renaissance than any of the movements to which it has been the fashion to apply the term 'renaissance' during recent decades. If we were to characterize it in one word, we might meaningfully—and fully conscious of the significance we attach to the word—call it the renaissance of Islam.

Speculation as to the course of world history had certain events not taken place or otherwise occurred is by and large a waste of time. It can be suggested, however, that with regard to certain events it is relatively easy to imagine what might have been the outcome had they never taken place or been different, whereas with regard to others it is entirely impossible. Islam's adoption of the classical heritage is among the latter. It is altogether impossible to imagine how Muslim civilization and world history would have developed without it. Perhaps the spiritual power of original Islam, combined with the prevailing political and economic conditions, would have sufficed by itself to lend permanence to the empire of the Arab conquerors and to make it the force in world history that it actually was. The historian is bound to consider this unlikely. Be this as it may, Islamic rational scholarship, which we have mainly in mind when we speak of the greatness of Muslim civilization, depends in its entirety on classical antiquity, down to such fundamental factors as the elementary principles of scholarly and scientific research.[16] More than that, the intellectual life of Islam in its most intimate expressions bowed to the Greek spirit.

> Whether the Qurʾān is from eternity
> I do not enquire.
> Whether the Qurʾān was created
> I do not know.
>
> . . .
>
> The drinker, whatever the case,
> Has a fresher glimpse of God's face.
>
> (Goethe, *West-östlicher Divan*)

Before becoming familiar with Greek thought, the devout Muslim (let us hope he was not a 'drinker'!), would not have recognized the dispute about the created or uncreated Qurʾān and about all the essential religious thought of Islam as the problem it was. And only after the Muslim mind and the Muslim spirit had been shaken up by the Graeco-Arabic renaissance could the Islamic mystic, under Hellenistic, Gnostic, Persian and Indian influence, look God as squarely in the face as he so frequently did. However, in Islam as in every civilization, what is really important is not the individual elements but the synthesis that combines them into a living organism of its own. Islamic research has to raise the fundamental questions—and attempt to answer them—of which creative ideas were basic to Islam, how the Muslims dealt with the Greek heritage, how they then harmonized it with the other cultural elements that were theirs by innate genius or tradition and, finally and most important, what was the new and original thing that evolved out of their creative endeavours. The indisputable fact remains, though, that Islamic civilization as we know it would simply not have existed without the Greek heritage.

It was significant for the development of modern Europe that the coming of Islam made final the break with classical antiquity in the West and that in subsequent centuries Europe was confronted with the material prosperity of Muslim civilization and considered it an ideal worth either emulating or fighting. But more than anything else, it was the intellectual life of medieval Europe that profited from Muslim achievements in the realm of science and scholarship by means of translations from the Arabic. A very few works were translated for the purpose of acquainting Christianity with the real character of the enemy of its religion. Most of the works that found their way to the West and there strengthened the much weakened ties with classical antiquity were the fruits of the Graeco-Arabic translation activity, the result of the process that saw to the survival of classical antiquity in Islam.

The following pages are meant to give a rough impression of the extent of classical knowledge in Islam. They cannot do justice to its full significance.

I

TRANSLATION TECHNIQUE AND TEXTUAL CRITICISM

Wherever translations were attempted, it was realized that translators had to contend with language problems difficult to solve or, rather, insoluble. The Arabic translators, and particularly the Christians among them, were familiar with the fact that many Syriac works were translations from the Greek, and they were aware of the great difficulties those works presented for the understanding to readers ignorant of Greek. The speakers of Syriac also knew the Bible with its complicated linguistic and textual history, and their scholars had considered the problems connected with it and occasionally expressed their opinions on the subject. Hence, it is not surprising that the Arabic translators on their part should have realized and clearly noted what was involved in the task they were engaged in, though it must be admitted that they showed comparatively little interest in the theoretical discussion of translation technique. A slavishly literal method of translation might have appeared particularly suitable for scientific purposes (and it was later much used in the West, particularly in translations from Arabic into Hebrew), but the dangers inherent in it were recognized and briefly illustrated. The impossibility of translating poems—an indisputable fact, even if it is still disputed here and there—was noticed and proved.

We know that throughout its history, Islam has always had to contend with two major linguistic problems: an inner Arabic problem resulting from the great difference between the Arabic language of literature and religion on the one hand and the language of the people on the other, and a multilingual problem caused by the variety of languages spoken by Muslims and members of religious minorities. The tension created by the uneasy coexistence of literary and colloquial Arabic proved extremely fruitful for the development of Arabic philology. Much less scholarly attention was paid to the multiplicity of languages. There must have been an extraordinarily large number of Muslims speaking two or more languages. Nevertheless, this seems to have been regarded simply as a practical problem of which little notice was taken, though foreign grammars and dictionaries were occasionally compiled. But wherever scholars and writers had to deal with translations, they were well aware of the many linguistic problems connected with them.

Not only language and style created difficulties for the transmitters of the Greek heritage. They also had to accomplish much preliminary philological work before they could even begin translating. We easily forget that Arabic translators did not possess standard text editions like those at our disposal as the result of the splendid modern philological endeavour spanning many centuries, which we tend to take for granted. The Greek of the works they translated was a dead language and known to be very different from the speech of contemporary Byzantines. Since they were mainly scholarly works, it was a technical language, demanding specialized language competency in the various disciplines. There were not many manuscripts. A work often had to be translated on the basis of a single manuscript. The available text was sometimes corrupt and, of course, never as easy to read as a modern printed edition. It was well known, thanks to a long tradition of manuscript and textual criticism, that there were textual variations between manuscripts. In the manuscript age, however, it was almost impossible to devise a fairly reliable technique for the handling of variant readings. Thus it was essential to work to the best of one's ability towards the establishment of an intelligible text by collecting and collating Greek manuscripts and referring to existing Syriac versions. If, as it also happened, several Arabic translations, differently translated or in different recensions, were available, these could then be compared with a view to achieving a better understanding of a given work.

The translators' efforts led to the formation of a rich technical vocabulary, which alone made it possible for all those new ideas to be assimilated. They also created a highly developed philological method. This method soon declined from the zenith which, continuing an old tradition, it reached at an early stage, but it left its lasting imprint on Islamic scholarship. Naturally, the language of the translations remained difficult to understand in many cases. We must assume that, apart from written commentaries, there was an oral tradition of teaching. It would appear to have continued to exist for centuries and to have helped those who wished to apply themselves to 'foreign' learning in their study of works produced with such great effort and methodological strictness.

The two methods of translation

1. Aṣ-Ṣafadī, *al-Ghaith al-musajjam* (Cairo, 1305), I, p. 46, still quoted by the late ʿĀmilī, *Kashkūl* (Cairo, 1380/1961), I, p. 388; cf. *Isis*, XXXVI (1946), pp. 253 f. Cf. also chapter IV, B, no. 3 (p. 100).

The translators use two methods of translation. One of them is that of Yuḥannā b. al-Biṭrīq, Ibn an-Nāʿimah al-Ḥimṣī and others. According to this method, the translator studies each individual Greek word and its meaning, chooses an Arabic word of corresponding meaning and uses it. Then he turns to the next word and proceeds in the same manner until in the end he has rendered into Arabic the text he wishes to translate. This method is bad for two reasons. First, it is impossible to find Arabic expressions corresponding to all Greek words and, therefore, through this method many Greek words remain untranslated. Second, certain syntactical combinations in the one language do not always necessarily correspond to similar combinations in the other; besides, the use of metaphors, which are frequent in every language, causes additional mistakes.

The second method is that of Ḥunain b. Isḥāq, al-Jauharī and others. Here the translator considers a whole sentence, ascertains its full meaning and then expresses it in Arabic with a sentence identical in meaning, without concern for the correspondence of individual words. This method is superior, and hence there is no need to improve the works of Ḥunain b. Isḥāq. The exception is those dealing with the mathematical sciences, which he had not mastered, in contrast with works on medicine, logic, natural science and metaphysics whose Arabic translations require no corrections at all. On the other hand, Euclid has been improved by Thābit b. Qurrah al-Ḥarrānī, as have been the *Almagest* and the *Intermediate Works*.[1]

2. Moshe b. ʿEzrā, *al-Muḥāḍarah wa-l-mudhākarah*, according to the modern Hebrew translation of B. Halper, *Sefer Shīrath Yisrāʾel* (Leipzig, 5684/1923), chap. 8, p. 132.

If you wish to translate anything from Arabic into Hebrew, adhere to the intended meaning and do not translate word for word, since not all languages are alike.

Poems are untranslatable

3. An anonymous extract from the *Ṣiwān al-ḥikmah* of Abū Sulaimān al-Manṭiqī as-Sijistānī, according to Istanbul MS Murad Molla 1408, fol. 35a; cf. *Isis*, *loc. cit.* As J. Kraemer has demonstrated (*Zeitschrift der Deutschen Morgenländischen Gesellschaft*, CVI [1956], pp. 295–316), the 'Homeric poems' quoted subsequently are, in fact, a translation of the *Monostichoi* of Menander.

Stephan has translated part of the Homeric poems from Greek into Arabic. It is known that poems lose most of their special splendour in translation and that the ideas expressed in them become largely corrupted when the artistic form of the poetry is altered.

4. Al-Jāḥiẓ, *Kitāb al-Ḥayawān* (Cairo, 1323–5), I, pp. 37 f.; (Cairo, n.y. [1938–45]), I, pp. 74 f. Cf. *Isis*, *loc. cit.*

Only the Arabs and people who speak Arabic have a correct understanding of poetry. Poems do not lend themselves to translation and ought not to be translated. When they are translated, their poetic structure is rent; the metre is no longer correct; poetic beauty disappears and nothing worthy of admiration remains in the poems. It is different with prose. Accordingly, original prose is more beautiful and appropriate than prose renderings of metric poetry.

Arabic–Hebrew–Spanish

5. Moshe b. ʿEzrā, *al-Muhādarah wa-l-mudhākarah*, in B. Halper, *Sefer Shīrath Yisrāʾel*, chap. 3, p. 65; Arabic text, ed. P. Kokovtsov, in *Vostochnyya Zametki* (St Petersburg, 1895), p. 216.

When I was a young man in my native land, I was once asked by a great Islamic scholar, who was well versed in the religious disciplines of Islam and most kind towards me, to recite the ten commandments for him in Arabic. I realized his intention: he, in fact, wanted to belittle the quality of their language. So I asked him to recite to me the first *sūrah*—the *Fātiḥah*—of his Qurʾān in Latin [that is, it seems, Spanish], a language he could speak and understood very well. When he tried to render the *Fātiḥah* in the above-mentioned language, it sounded ugly and was completely distorted. He noticed what was in my mind and did not press me further to fulfil his request.

Technical terminology

6. Ḥunain b. Isḥāq in a note from his Syriac translation to Ḥubaish's Arabic translation of Galen, *Über die medizinischen Namen*, ed. M. Meyerhof and J. Schacht, in *Abh. Preuss. Akad. d. Wiss.*, phil.-hist. Kl., 1931, Arab. text, pp. 17 f., trans., p. 32.

Ḥunain b. Isḥāq says: In the following passage Galen quotes Aristophanes. However, the Greek manuscript, from which I translated this work into Syriac, contains such a large number of mistakes and errors that it would have been impossible for me to understand the meaning of the text had I not been so familiar with and accustomed to Galen's Greek speech and acquainted with most of his ideas from his other works. But I am not familiar with the language of Aristophanes, nor am I accustomed to it. Hence, it was not easy for me to understand the quotation, and I have, therefore, omitted it.

I had an additional reason for omitting it. After I had read it, I found no more in it than what Galen had already said elsewhere. Hence, I thought that I should not occupy myself with it any further, but rather proceed to more useful matters.

Manuscripts and textual criticism

7. Ḥunain b. Isḥāq, 'Über die Syrischen and Arabischen Galen-Übersetzungen', ed. G. Bergsträsser, in *Abh. f. d. Kunde d. Morgenlandes* (*AKM*) XVII (1925), II, pp. 4 f., no. 3. Cf. also Bergsträsser, *Neue Materialien zu Ḥunain Ibn Isḥāq's Galen-Bibliographie*, in *AKM*, XIX (1932).

Galen's book on the sects [*Peri haireseōn tois eisagomenois*] . . . was translated into Syriac before me by a certain Ibn Sahdā from al-Karkh, who was a weak translator. When I was a young man of twenty or a little older, I translated it for a physician from Jundīsābūr named Shīrīshūʿ b. Quṭrub, from a very faulty Greek manuscript. Later, when I was about forty, my pupil Ḥubaish asked me to correct the translation. Meanwhile a number of Greek manuscripts had accumulated in my possession. I collated these manuscripts and thereby produced a single correct copy. Next, I collated the Syriac text with it and corrected it. I am in the habit of doing this with everything I translate. A few years later I translated the Syriac text into Arabic for Abū Jaʿfar Muḥammad b. Mūsā.

8. *Ibid.*, pp. 17 f., no. 20.

Galen's *Book on the Method of Healing* [*Therapeutikē methodos*]: . . . The first six books of this work were translated into Syriac by Sergius when he was still a very weak translator. After he had acquired experience as a translator, he translated the remaining eight books and produced a better translation than that of the earlier books.

Salmawaih urged me to correct the second part of Sergius's translation for him in the hope that this would be easier and better than the production of a new translation. So he sat down opposite me with part of the seventh book, he with the Syriac text and I with the Greek text, and we collated it. He read the Syriac text aloud and whenever I noticed something that conflicted with the Greek text, I drew his attention to it and he would then begin to correct it. Yet in the end, this became too much for him, and he realized that an entirely fresh translation would be simpler and would turn out better stylistically as well as produce a much tidier result. So he asked me to translate these books, and I translated them all. This happened when we were in ar-Raqqah at the time of al-Maʾmūn's campaigns. He handed the translation to Zakarīyāʾ b. ʿAbdallāh, known as aṭ-Ṭaifūrī, when he was about to return to Baghdad, in order to have it copied there. However, fire broke out on board the ship on which Zakarīyāʾ was travelling. The book was burned. No copy of the translation survives.

A few years later I translated the work from the beginning for Bukhtīshūʿ b. Jibrīl. For the last eight books a number of Greek manuscripts were at my disposal. These I collated and produced a single correct copy from them which I then translated with the utmost accuracy and in the best style I was able to master. For the first six books only a single manuscript, and besides a very faulty one, was at my disposal at the time. I was therefore unable to produce these books in the manner required. Later I came across another manuscript and collated the text with it and corrected it as much as possible. It would be better if I could collate a third manuscript with it if only I were fortunate enough to find one. For Greek manuscripts of this work are rare, since it does not belong to the works that were read in the school of Alexandria.

From the Syriac manuscripts of my translation Ḥubaish b. al-Ḥasan translated this work for Muḥammad b. Mūsā. Then, after he had translated the work, he asked me to go through the last eight books critically for him and correct possible mistakes, and I did this for him successfully.

The translation of the Sophistic[*i Elenchi*]

9. Ibn an-Nadīm, *al-Fihrist*, ed. G. Flügel (Leipzig, 1871), p. 249; (Cairo, 1348), p. 349. An English translation of the *Fihrist* by B. Dodge has been published in New York and London, 1970.

The Sophistic—that is, 'the misleading philosophy'—was translated into Syriac by Ibn Nāʿimah and Abū Bishr Mattā and into Arabic by Yaḥyā b. ʿAdī [on the basis of the Syriac translation] of Theophilus.[2]

Authors of commentaries: Quwairī wrote a commentary on this work. Ibrāhīm b. Bakkūsh al-ʿAshshārī translated Ibn Nāʿimah's Syriac translation, with corrections, into Arabic. Al-Kindī wrote a commentary. A commentary on the Sophistic[i Elenchi] by Alexander is said to have been found in Mosul.

10. From the Parisian Aristotle manuscript, cf. ʿA. Badawī, *Manṭiq Arisṭū* (Cairo, 1952), III, pp. 1017 f., and the French translation in Kh. Georr, *Les Catégories* (Beirut, 1948), pp. 198 f.

I have copied this translation from a manuscript written by Shaikh Abū l-Khair al-Ḥasan b. Suwār. It ends with the following remarks:

I have copied this translation from a manuscript which appears to me to have been written by Abū Naṣr al-Fārābī. The first part of that manuscript was carefully written and correct, but the second was faulty.

Shaikh Abū l-Khair b. Suwār says: In order to understand the ideas expressed in the language from which he is translating, the translator must first grasp them in the sense of the original author and must be familiar with the usage of the language from which he is translating as well as that into which he is translating. However, the monk Athanasius was not familiar with Aristotle's ideas in this work. Hence it was inevitable that mistakes crept into his translation. Since the translators mentioned above, who rendered this book into Arabic on the basis of the Syriac translation of Athanasius, had no commentary at their disposal, they relied on their own insight in order to understand the ideas of the work. Everyone endeavoured to arrive at the truth and to understand the purpose intended by Aristotle. In the light of their understanding of the Syriac translation of Athanasius they translated it into Arabic, each in his own way. As we desire to become acquainted with the views of each one of them, we have here reproduced all the translations we were able to obtain, so that all of them may be studied and jointly used for the comprehension of Aristotle's meaning.

The excellent Yaḥyā b. ʿAdī composed a Syriac and Arabic commentary on the Sophistic[i Elenchi]. I have seen most of it and estimate that it comprises about two-thirds of the work. I presume that he completed it, but after his death it could not be found among his books. My opinions about this fluctuate. Sometimes I think that he may have destroyed it because he was dissatisfied with it, while at other times I suspect that it was stolen, which I consider more likely. He produced the said translation before compiling his commentary, hence it is a little obscure, for he did not always grasp the meaning correctly and based his translation on the Syriac text.

Nowadays there also exists a manuscript of the Greek commentary on the Sophistic by Alexander of Aphrodisias. At the beginning a quire is missing. Very little of it has so far been made accessible [through translation].

As I have heard, Abū Isḥāq Ibrāhīm b. Bakkūsh translated this work from Syriac into Arabic, and, in collaboration with the Greek priest and geometrician, Yuḥannā, who is known by the name of Ibn Fatīlah, worked on the correction of a number of passages on the basis of the Greek text, but I have not seen his work.

Abū Bishr is also said to have corrected the first translation or produced another translation, but I have not seen his work.

I have noted all this here in order that those who use this book should be fully informed about the situation and understand why I have reproduced here all translations in the manner described.

II

BIOGRAPHY AND CULTURAL HISTORY

When did the ancient Greek scholars live? What did they say, think and write? What kind of people were they? How did science and scholarship develop in Hellas? What was the Greek national character like? How did the Muslims come in contact with the Greek heritage? All these questions aroused great interest among the Arabs and were much discussed. The answers they found are not without interest even today.

Relatively much biographical information on ancient scholars was available in Islam. While the Muslims did not know Diogenes Laertius, they did have access, for example, to the *History of Philosophers* by Porphyry, which is lost to us and which dealt with philosophers from the legendary beginnings till the age of Plato. They also had a monograph biography of Aristotle. Ample information on the ancient physicians appears to have been available in an historical work by John Philoponus. Our own information on late Hellenistic physicians and physicists is worse rather than better than that of the Arabs. Autobiographical details to be found in certain works, especially those of Galen, were particularly valued. Despite this, there remained innumerable gaps, and misunderstandings were inevitable. The fact is that our own knowledge is based on the philological work of several centuries, and this, of course, was lacking in Islam. Chronology presented special difficulties. Not before the introduction of the era of the hijrah was there a consistent and continuous system of time reckoning over a large territory. In classical antiquity, no single era had been able to secure general acceptance, so that the sources rarely give unambiguous dates easily intelligible to later generations. Besides, Muslims (like Christian Europeans up to modern times) never completely grasped the principle of minus dates for the period preceding the epoch year of the era. When they were confronted with synchronistic dates, as was not infrequently the case, it was very difficult for them to interpret them. They also found it practically impossible to fit the information about scholars, meagre as it was, into the political history of antiquity, known to them in the most rudimentary fashion. We consider it self-evident that Galen could not have been in touch with Jesus and that Ptolemy could not have been a member of the dynasty of the Ptolemies. Arab biographers faced here problems which required careful discussion once they had been raised, and their correct solution was a considerable achievement. Generally speaking, they were able to report a surprising amount of good and correct biographical information, albeit mixed with false and quite absurd stories (for example, Socrates in the barrel, Nicomachus of Gerasa as the father of Aristotle).

Later Arabic biographers as a rule did not have any choice but to take over the material collected by their predecessors. Sometimes they abbreviated it, sometimes they elaborated a little on it. Sometimes, however, they endeavoured to uncover and use new sources. Additional titles found occasionally in bibliographies of Greek scholars compiled by later authors were derived from actual manuscripts of works of whose existence earlier writers had been unaware, or which had not been accessible in their age, since they had not yet been translated. This could easily give rise to errors. A title might be listed in the belief that it was new and had been hitherto overlooked while it referred, in fact, to a work known and already listed under a title that was differently worded.

Form as well as content of ancient scholarly biography were taken over. Thus we find two ways of presenting biographical information which are so closely related as to be barely kept apart: there are biographies composed of brief factual data and a bibliography, and there are those that combine biographical information slanted towards stories and anecdotes with a larger or smaller number of aphorisms. Minor philosophers were mostly known to the Arabs by name only, and here their source was late Hellenistic florilegia. It may be noted in passing that the forms of ancient biography exerted no influence on the later highly developed

Muslim biographical literature which grew out of conditions peculiar to Islamic civilization.

As it was considered necessary to learn about the life and achievements of individuals, so there was felt the need to know about the general history of ancient science and scholarship. Here the emphasis was on philosophy. However, scholars were aware that early philosophers, especially the 'pre-Socratic philosophers' (a term familiar to Muslim scholars), had as a rule also been scientists. Hence, mathematics and astronomy were included in the history of philosophy. The history of medicine, on the other hand, was known through special treatises. In its broadest outlines the Arabic view of the development of ancient science and scholarship agrees with our own, a result of the fact that both are based on views formed in antiquity.

The personality and character of individual scholars were portrayed by means of traditional clichés, derived in large part from theories developed in physiognomics. The supposed Greek national character was also found outlined in works on physiognomy, or it was deduced from what were generally considered to be the most typical achievements of the Greeks. Since the diverse people which had accepted Islam were engaged in constant competition with one another, it was of existential interest for all of them to make valid comparisons between the national characteristics thought to distinguish the great civilized nations, in order to have a kind of model for their own ambitions. In determining the Greek national character, it was not simple, nor was it really desirable, to make a distinction between contemporary Greeks—the Christian Byzantines—and their ancestors in ancient times. It was generally agreed that only the highest praise could do justice to the importance of the Greeks. Even excessive admiration is not infrequently expressed. However, there was another side to the story. Islamic orthodoxy felt compelled for religious reasons to fight Greek science and scholarship and therefore was naturally tempted to depict the Greek heritage as the arch enemy created by Satan. Yet hostile theologians directed their fury not so much against the Greek 'philosophers' themselves since they were, after all, pagans and hence not responsible for their own ignorance, as against their Islamic followers who, having been granted knowledge of the truth, should have seen through and condemned

Greek folly. The situation is vividly described in a humorous tale ridiculing the narrow-mindedness of an orthodox Hellenophobe at the turn of the ninth to the tenth century (cf. I. Goldziher, 'Stellung der alten islamischen Orthodoxie zu den antiken Wissenschaften', in *Abh. Preuss. Akad. d. Wiss.*, phil.-hist. Kl. 1915, no. 8; English trans. F. Rosenthal, *Aḥmad b. aṭ-Ṭayyib as-Sarḫasī* [New Haven, 1943] pp. 86 ff). However, the Christian Ḥunain in his treatise 'in defence of Galen' had already pointed out that one ought to accept only the scientific views of the ancients and not the religious opinions they occasionally expressed.

> If the reader finds a remark in classical works beginning with the words 'Galen (or Plato, Aristotle, etc.) says', and it turns out to be a strictly scientific discussion of the subject under investigation, he should study it carefully and try to understand it. If, on the other hand, it concerns questions of belief and opinion, he must take no further notice of it, since such remarks were made only in order to win people over to the ideas expressed in them or because they concern old, deeply rooted views.

(Ibn al-Maṭrān, Bustān al-aṭibbā', manuscript of the Army Medical Library, Cleveland, Ohio).

It was clear to the Arabs that they owed their knowledge of Greek civilization to individual patrons and, above all, during the first century of the ʿAbbāsids, to the ʿAbbāsid caliphs who sponsored and generously supported the translators and greatly encouraged their activities for personal as well as political motives. The Arabs were also not unaware that what was translated was primarily works used in the curriculum of the schools established before the coming of Islam (cf. chap. I, no. 10). Furthermore, they thought about the problem of the ways and means by which the school tradition was transmitted to them from the old centres of Greek scholarship and, as in many other cases, may have found the right answer. It is never easy to trace the course of cultural history, or to check on questionable generalizations regarding an alleged national character, or to sort out biographical data distorted by centuries of neglect. Wherever this is attempted, as it was in the world of Islam, there can be no doubt that the motivation behind it was a deep devotion to the subject and a strong historical consciousness.

Biographies of Greek scholars

1. Plato

From al-Mubashshir, *Mukhtār al-ḥikam*, ed. ʿAbd-ar-Raḥmān Badawī (Madrid, 1958), pp. 126–8, with slight changes based on manuscripts of the work. On the author, cf. F. Rosenthal, 'al-Mubashshir ibn Fātik', in *Oriens*, XIII–XIV (1961), pp. 132–58. Numerous aphorisms, which have not been translated here, conclude the biography.

Plato in Greek means extensive or wide. The name of Plato's father was Ariston. As descendants of Asclepius, both his parents belonged to the Greek aristocracy. His mother in particular was a descendant of Solon the law-giver.

At the outset of his career Plato began by studying the art of poetry and philology and made great progress. But one day he was with Socrates when he was excoriating poetry. Socrates's remarks appealed to him so much that he abandoned his attempts at poetry. He joined Socrates and studied with him for five years. Then Socrates died, and when Plato heard that some followers of Pythagoras lived in Egypt, he travelled to them in order to learn from them.

Before he became attached to Socrates, he had inclined in philosophy to the views of Heraclitus. Subsequently, however, he abandoned the school of Heraclitus. He retained his views concerning matters of sense perception, those of Pythagoras concerning intellectual matters, and those of Socrates concerning problems of ethical behaviour.

Then Plato returned from Egypt to Athens. There he established two schools of philosophy where he taught. Then he travelled to Sicily, where the well-known story with the local tyrant, Dionysius, took place, and he had to suffer much hardship at his hands. Later Plato succeeded in escaping from him. He returned to Athens where he led an exemplary life. He did much good and helped the weak. The Athenians wished to entrust him with the administration of their affairs, but he refused because he felt that they were not behaving as he thought right. As their evil customs were deeply rooted, he knew that he would not succeed in weaning them away from them. It was clear to him that he would perish like his teacher Socrates, if he dared to attempt it, though Socrates had not endeavoured to establish perfect mores.

Plato reached the age of eighty-one. He had good character qualities, was noble in action and did a great deal of good for all who were close to him as well as for strangers. He was gentle, thoughtful and patient.

He had many disciples. After his death two men took over his educational work: the first, Xenocrates, taught in Athens, in a place known as the Academy, and the second, Aristotle, in the Lyceum, also in the district of Athens.

Plato expressed his philosophy in obscure allusions and allegories, so that his aims are clear only to sages trained in philosophy.

He was a pupil of Timaeus and Socrates. From them he derived most of his views. He compiled many books. Fifty-six are known to us by title. Some of them are large and contain a number of books. His works are arranged together in groups of four, called tetrads. They have a common purpose, but each one of them also has a particular purpose, subordinate to the general purpose. Each tetrad connects with the preceding one.

Plato was of brownish complexion and medium height. He had a good figure and was perfectly proportioned. He had a handsome beard and little hair on his cheeks. He was silent and thoughtful. He had dark blue pupils which flashed in the white of the eyes. Low down on his chin he had a black birthmark. He was extremely capable. He spoke in a friendly manner. He loved to be alone in lonely rural places. One could usually detect his presence through hearing him weep. When he wept, he could be heard two miles away in deserted rural districts. He wept uninterruptedly.

2. Theophrastus

From Ibn an-Nadīm, *al-Fihrist*, ed. G. Flügel (Leipzig, 1871), p. 252; (Cairo, 1348), p. 353.

Theophrastus: a pupil of Aristotle and his sister's son. One of those mentioned by Aristotle in his will and appointed by him to head the school after his own death. He wrote the following works:

On the Soul, one book.
On the Heavenly Phenomena [meteorology], one book.
On Education, one book.
On Sense Perception and the Sensibilia, four books, translated by Ibrāhīm b. Bakkūsh.
On Metaphysics, one book, translated by Abū Zakarīyā' Yaḥyā b. 'Adī.
On Botany, translated by Ibrāhīm b. Bakkūsh, of which a commentary on part of the first book exists.
A commentary on the *Categories* is attributed to him.

Ibn Abī Uṣaibi'ah, *'Uyūn al-anbā'*, ed. A. Müller (Cairo-Königsberg, 1882–4), I, p. 69, mentions two further titles:

On the Oneness [of God] to Democritus.
On Physical Problems.

3. Ptolemy

From Ibn al-Qifṭī, *Ta'rīkh al-ḥukamā'*, ed. A. Müller and J. Lippert (Leipzig, 1903), pp. 95–8.

Ptolemy the Claudian[1] is the author of the *Almagest* and other works, an authority on the mathematical sciences and one of the most distinguished Greek scholars. He lived at the time of the Roman Emperors Hadrian and Antoninus, two hundred and eighty years after Hipparchus. Many people who claim to be well versed in the history of the [pre-Islamic] nations imagine that he was one of the Greek Ptolemaic kings who ruled in Alexandria and elsewhere after Alexander's death. However, that is an obvious mistake, since Ptolemy mentions in the *Almagest*, in the eighth chapter of the third book, which deals with all the motions of the sun and the observations of it and all the other circumstances related to it, that he had made astronomical observations in the seventeenth year[2] of Hadrian's reign. He mentions that from the first year of Nebuchadnezzar [Bukhtnaṣṣar] to the autumn equinox of that year there was a total of 879 years, 66 days and 6 hours,[3] which he divided as follows: from the first year of Nebuchadnezzar to the death of Alexander of Macedon, the ancestor of Alexander Dhū l-Qarnain, there was a total of 424 Egyptian years; from the death of Alexander to the reign of Augustus, the first Roman emperor, there were 294 years; and from the first year of the reign of Augustus to the time of the mentioned observation of the autumn equinox there were 161 years, 66 days and 2 hours. These figures show clearly when he actually lived, that is, 161 years after the Augustan age. Scholars well informed regarding the history and chronology of the ancient nations and races agree that this Augustus was a Roman ruler, that he conquered Cleopatra, the last of the Greek Ptolemies, who was a woman, and that Greek rule came to an end as a result of this victory. This shows clearly enough that those who believe that he was one of the Ptolemaic kings are mistaken.

Knowledge of the motions of the stars and acquaintance with the secrets of the firmament reached their zenith with this Ptolemy. In his hands was combined all the knowledge of this discipline that had been dispersed among Greeks, Romans and other inhabitants of the Western half of the earth. He brought order into it and clarified all the obscurities. As far as I know, nobody after him would have dared to compose a work like the *Almagest* or undertaken to imitate it. Some scientists like al-Faḍl b. Ḥātim an-Nairīzī, for example, wrote what were in effect comments and explanations to it. Others wrote what were in effect abridgments and approximations, for instance, Muḥammad b. Jābir al-Battānī and Abū r-Raiḥān al-Bīrūnī al-Khuwārizmī, the author of the *Qānūn al-Mas'ūdī*, written for Mas'ūd b. Maḥmūd b. Sebuktigin, where he followed Ptolemy's model; further, Kūshyār b. Labbān al-Jīlī in his *Zīj* [astronomical tables]. The intended and coveted aim and ambition of the scholars after Ptolemy were to understand his work as it was and to master thoroughly all its parts one after the other. No work on any ancient or modern science is known that exhausts its subject in its entirety and in all its details, with the exception of three books: this *Almagest* on astronomy, Aristotle's work on logic and the 'book' of Sībawaih of al-Baṣrah on Arabic grammar.

Muḥammad b. Isḥāq an-Nadīm[4] says in his work: Ptolemy, the author of the *Almagest*, lived at the time of Hadrian and Antoninus who reigned over the Greek Empire. In their time he observed the stars and composed the *Almagest* for one of them. He was the first to make spherical astrolabes, astronomical instruments, the planispheres, measuring apparatuses and instruments for astronomical observations. A number of scholars before him, among them Hipparchus, are said to have observed the stars. It is also said that Hipparchus was his teacher. That is nonsense, since there were nine hundred years between the two observations.[5] Ptolemy was the greatest astronomical observer and the most skilful maker of instruments for astronomical observations. Astronomical observations can only be carried out by means of instruments, and the first to carry out observations must make the necessary instruments as well.

The *Almagest* consists of thirteen books. The first to attempt to explain and translate it into Arabic was Yaḥyā b. Khālid b. Barmak. A number of scholars explained the work for him, but they did so incorrectly, and he was dissatisfied with their work. Therefore he entrusted Abū Ḥassān and Salm, the president of the academy [*bait al-ḥikmah*], with explaining the work, and they did so correctly. They brought in experienced translators and endeavoured to produce a correct text. After examination of the work produced by various translators, they retained what was expressed most lucidly and clearly. Al-Ḥajjāj b. Maṭar is also said to have translated the *Almagest*, but an-Nairīzī is not supposed to have translated it [?].[6] Thābit corrected the old, unsatisfactory translation of the entire work. Isḥāq translated it, and then Thābit corrected it again but not so well, his first correction having been better.

The following are Ptolemy's [other] well-known works that were translated into Arabic:

A book [*Tetrabiblos*] written for his pupil Syrus, translated by Ibrāhīm b. aṣ-Ṣalt and corrected by Ḥunain b. Isḥāq. Eutocius wrote a commentary on the first book. Thābit wrote a synopsis of the first book and exposed the ideas contained in it. Further commentaries were written by ʿUmar b. al-Farrukhān, Ibrāhīm b. aṣ-Ṣalt, an-Nairīzī and al-Battānī.

On Nativities.

On War and Fighting.

On the Determination of Portions.

On the Passage of the Years of the World.

On Illness and Taking Medicine.
On the Course of the Seven.
On Captives and Prisoners.
On Seizing and Subduing Fortunate Constellations.
Which of Two Opponents Will Be Successful.
On the Lot, in the form of tables.
Reporting on the Conditions of the Stars.
The Geography, about the inhabited part of the earth, well translated in Arabic by al-Kindī and also available in Syriac.

4. Galen

From al-Mubashshir, pp. 288–93, Badawī, with slight changes based on manuscripts of the work.

Galen was one of the eight leading ancient physicians, referred to as authorities in medicine, who are the heads of the medical schools and the teachers of the teachers. The first physician from whom the other ancient physicians descended was Asclepius I; the second was Ghūrus; the third was Mīnus;[7] the fourth Parmenides; the fifth Plato; the sixth Asclepius II; the seventh Hippocrates; and the eighth was Galen. He was the seal of the great physicians. After him there were only less important physicians, all of whom had learned from him.[8]

He was born almost 200 years after the time of Jesus. From his birth to the present year 440/1048 [1049] about 860 years have elapsed. He composed many books, both short and long, a total of approximately four hundred. His long works are very large, detailed and circumstantial. Sixteen of these works must be studied by all who wish to know medicine.

His father took the greatest trouble with his education. He spent a fortune on him, summoning teachers from distant cities and paying them high salaries.

Galen was born and grew up in Pergamon in Asia. He travelled to Athens, Rome, Alexandria and other places for study. He studied medicine with Herminus [?][9] and learned geometry, philology, grammar and other disciplines from a number of geometricians, grammarians and rhetoricians. He also studied medicine with a woman called Cleopatra and got many remedies from her, in particular those serving for the treatment of women. He travelled to Egypt and stayed there for some time in order to study the drugs in use there, especially opium in Assiut in Upper Egypt. Later he left Egypt in order to return home via Syria. He fell ill on the journey and died in al-Faramā, a city on the Green Sea,[10] on Egypt's furthest border.

From his youth Galen had felt attracted to exact knowledge.[11] He studied it and was extremely eager for knowledge, diligent and receptive. Since his thirst for knowledge was so great, he studied the material his teacher had just taught him as soon as he left the latter's house, even in the street, until he arrived home. The young men who attended school with him were ever appealing to him reproachfully to allow himself time to play and joke with them. Sometimes he did not reply to them at all because he was too engrossed in his studies. However, occasionally he asked them what it was that induced them to play and joke. When they replied that they felt a desire for it, he explained to them that he preferred knowledge to play and that their pleasures were therefore hateful to him while he loved what he was doing. People wondered at him and said: 'In addition to his great fortune and his respected position, your father also has a son who has a desire for knowledge.'

His father was a geometrician, but also a farmer. His grandfather was the head of the carpenters' guild and his great-grandfather a surveyor.

Galen came to Rome for the first time at the beginning of the reign of Antoninus, who ruled after Hadrian. He wrote a book on anatomy for the consularis Boethus, a Roman city prefect, when the latter wished to travel from Rome to his home town, Ptolemais, and asked him to procure for him a book on anatomy. He also wrote a work on anatomy in several volumes during his stay in Smyrna with Pelops, his second teacher after Satyrus, the pupil of Quintus. He proceeded to Corinth for the sake of another famous man, a pupil of Quintus, named Aephicianus [?],[12] and when he heard that some famous pupils of Quintus and Numisianus lived in Alexandria, he went there. Later he returned to his home town, Pergamon in Asia. Then he travelled to Rome and operated there in front of Boethus. His constant companions were the peripatetic philosopher, Eudemus, and the Damascene, Alexander of Aphrodisias, who had been appointed at that time to give the Athenians public lectures and instruct them in the philosophical sciences in the spirit of the peripatetic school. The city prefect of Rome, Sergius, the son of Paulus [Sergius Paullus], was their constant companion, since he was highly versed in philosophical problems in word and deed.

In one of his works Galen mentions that he went to Alexandria for the first time and had returned from there to Pergamon, his native city and that of his ancestors, when he was twenty-eight years old. In another place he mentions that he returned to his native country from Rome when he was thirty-seven years old.[13] He mentions that many of his books and valuable utensils [furniture] were burned in the city where the ruler's library was situated. Some of the manuscripts that were destroyed by fire had been written by Aristotle, Anaxagoras and Andromachus. He had corrected their texts upon instruction by his highly competent teachers and by scholars who had transmitted them from Plato. He had travelled to distant cities until he corrected most of these texts. He mentions that the work of Rufus on theriacs and poisons, the treatment of poisoned individuals and the composition of medicines as suited to the cause of the illness and the time [season of the year ?] was among the books destroyed by fire and that he had written it in black silk on white brocade and spent a great deal of money on it, since it was so precious to him.

Greek rulers were always building level roads through difficult territory, filling hollows, cutting through high mountains and banishing fear of them. They were always constructing various kinds of bridges, erecting strong walls, building aqueducts and diverting rivers. They were occupied with the subjection of enemies and conquest of countries. They cared for the administration of their empire, not for the satisfaction of the desires of the body. They were concerned with science and medicine. Each of them paid men to collect medicinal herbs everywhere and to send them to him under seal so that they would not be falsified in any way. When these drugs reached the ruler, and scholars had tried them out, he ordered them to be distributed in his country among his subjects, in order to benefit them. Stipends were always made available for this purpose.

Galen was of brown complexion. He was well proportioned, had broad shoulders, broad hands, long fingers and beautiful hair. He loved song, music and reading. He was of medium height and walked neither too fast nor too slowly. When he laughed, he showed his teeth. He chatted a great deal and was rarely silent. He frequently attacked his colleagues. He travelled a lot. He smelled agreeably and wore clean clothes. He loved to ride and to take walks. He mixed with rulers and leaders. He died at the age of eighty-seven years, seventeen of them spent as a child and student and seventy as scholar and teacher.

5. A list of pre-Islamic scholars and philosophers who have biographies in the *Ṣiwān al-ḥikmah* of Abū Sulaimān al-Manṭiqī as-Sijistānī, from the anonymous recension of the *Ṣiwān* in the Istanbul MS Murad Molla 1408.

The individual biographies follow upon an extremely important introduction dealing with the history of science and scholarship. Many of the names listed below still await identification. In some cases such identification may be possible with the help of the preserved Greek florilegia. Here only a few notes have been added and mere speculation has been avoided as much as possible. Al-Mubashshir's chapter on aphorisms translated below (chap. IV, B, no. 15, cf. further chap. XII, no. 7) may be compared for similar material.

Thales
Anaximenes
Anaxagoras
Archelaus
Pythagoras
Socrates
Plato
Aristotle
Alexander of Macedon
Diogenes, the Cynic
ash-Shaikh al-Yūnānī[14]
Theophrastus
Eudemus
ʾskhywlws[15]
Hermes
Solon
Homer
Democrates [Democritus]
Ṭymʾnʾws [Timaeus ?]
Melissus
Xenophon
Euclid
Hippocrates
Cebes[16]
Basilius
Ptolemy
Aristippus
Ṣwlyn
Dʾryws
ʾthrwdṭys [Herodotus ?]
Balīnās [Apollonius of Tyana]
Pericles [?]
Mwyrṭws[17]

Aristophanes
Fylsws
Euripides
Archimedes
Mhr'rys
Qndy's
Dym's
Plutarch [?][18]
Protagoras
Ghrghwrysws [Gregory ?][19]
Simonides
Thwthrdydhs [Thucydides ?]
Bnsl'lns [Psellos ?][20]
'jfs [= 'jys Agis]
Stratonicus
Kh'ws[21]
Epictetus[22]
B'rgh'fs[23]
Fndwrs [Phaedrus ?]
Fl'sṭs [Cleostratus]
Nyqwrs [Epicurus ?]
Telemachus
Bswmyws/n
'rws
Aeschines
'nksyws
'byryws ['sryws] [uncertain reading]
'wmnyws [Ammonius ?]
Sophocles
'swbws [Aesop]
Yn'fnwbṭs [uncertain reading]
M'swjs
Mwrwn the Sophist
'brmsds
Fwrs
Philistion[24]
Zeno [the elder and the younger]
Blwṭys [Plotinus][25]
'sqr'ṭys [Isocrates ?][26]
Mmslws
Antiochus [?]
Kh'r'frn [M'r'frn, Chairemon ?][27]
Fynws
Yq'ywn [Nicanor]
Br'ṭwls
Nyf'lws
'st'ns the orator [-sthenes]
Xenocrates [?]
Bnd'rs[28]
's'bs [Aesop]
B'nydws
Demosthenes
Deucalion
Dymyqws[29]
L'fn [*Lakōn* Lacedaemonian][30]
King 'rwn[31]
Mwswryws[32]
Polemo [Aflīmun]
S'frsṭs
Xenocrates
Antisthenes
Anacharsis
Ṭymṭrs
'n'khws ['nwkhws aṣ-Ṣaqlabī Anacharsis the Scythian]
Hesiod
Frsṭrkhs
Timon
Philo [?][33]
Fqr'ṭys

Qrsṭs [Theophrastus!] the Peripatetic
Socrates the poet
Blwn
Bnlsws [Mlsws]
Eumenes
ʾnʾkhwrs the judge
Kwrs
Zosimus [?][34]
ʾswys [Aesop ?]
Smʾnyds the musician [Simonides ?]
Thmʾnys
Wʾqbqyṭys
Yfṭws
Bʾrfds
Flʾsylʾws [Agesilaus]
Agis[35]
Mmws
ʾnkswm
Mʾnʾfyls
Fylmws the Pythagorean
ʾwfwrs
King Mauricius
ʾsʾbs
Fʾnydrws
Dymwsyʾs
Secundus[36]
Themistius
Porphyry
Alexander of Aphrodisias
ʾllynws[37]
Ammonius
ʾrmydnws
Galen
Yaḥyā an-Naḥwī [John Philoponus]

The history of scholarship among the Greeks

6. Ṣāʿid al-Andalusī, *Ṭabaqāt al-umam* (Cairo, n.d.) pp. 22–6; French trans. R. Blachère (Paris, 1935), pp. 57–62.

The fourth nation [after the Indians, Persians and Chaldaeans], that of the Greeks, possessed great importance among the peoples and was very famous in all regions. Their rulers enjoyed great respect among the inhabitants of every zone. One of these rulers was Alexander, the son of Philip the Macedonian, who is known by the name of Dhū l-Qarnain. He undertook an expedition against the Persian king, Darius, the son of Darius, which led him as far as the latter's palace. He upset his throne and destroyed his empire and his power. After that, he proceeded against the rulers of the East, the Indians, the Turks and the Chinese. He conquered some of them. Then all of them surrendered to him. They came to meet him with great gifts and sought to keep him at a distance by means of ample tributes. Incessantly did he march through the distant frontier regions of India and China and everywhere else in the Orient until all rulers on earth unanimously obeyed his rule, bowed to his might and agreed that he was prince of the earth and ruler of all zones.

After him there were a number of Greek rulers known as Ptolemies, singular Ptolemy. They exercised strict control over their subjects and their provinces. Their rule persisted until the Romans defeated them. This victory meant the end of Ptolemaic rule, and their empire was incorporated into the Roman Empire so that a single Roman Empire came into existence in the same way as the Persians had done with the Babylonian Empire, when they took it over and the two Empires were united into a single Persian Empire.

The land of the Greeks was situated in the northwest quarter of the earth. Its southern border was the Roman Sea [Mediterranean] and the Syrian and northern Mesopotamian border regions. Its northern border was the land of the Alans and the adjacent northern empires. Its western border was the border region of Romania, whose capital is Rome. Its eastern border was the capital of Armenia and Derbend. The straits between the Mediterranean and the Pontus [Black Sea] divided the Greek Empire into two parts, so that the greater part of it lay to the east and the smaller to the southwest.

The language of the Greeks [*Yūnānīyūn*] is called Greek [*ighrīqīyah*]. It is one of the richest and most important languages in the world.

As to religion, the Greeks were generally Ṣābians, that is, worshippers of the stars and idolaters.

Their scholars used to be called philosophers [*falāsifah*]. Philosopher [*failasūf*] means in Greek 'friend of wisdom'. The Greek philosophers belong to the highest class of human beings and to the greatest scholars, since they showed a genuine interest in all branches of wisdom, mathematics, logic, natural science and metaphysics, as well as economics and politics.

The Greeks considered five of their philosophers to be the most important. The earliest among them was Empedocles. After him there followed in order Pythagoras, Socrates, Plato and Aristotle, the son of Nicomachus.

As mentioned by the scholars familiar with the history of [pre-Islamic] nations, Empedocles lived at the time of the prophet David. He learned philosophy from Luqmān in Syria. Then he returned to the land of the Greeks. He propounded opinions regarding the creation of the world which on the surface give rise to the impression that the fact of the resurrection of the dead was being attacked. Hence some people refuse to have anything to do with him. A group of Bāṭinites[38] adopted his philosophy. They assume that he expressed himself in allegories that are rarely understood. Muḥammad b. ʿAbdallāh b. Masarrah al-Jabalī al-Bāṭinī of Cordoba occupied himself very intensively with the philosophy of Empedocles. He was the first to try to combine the divine attributes and claim that all of them amounted to one and the same thing and that if one attributes to God the attributes of knowledge, goodness and power, He does not therefore contain in Himself different concepts called by these names, but is in truth one, and in contrast to all other existing things, contains no plurality at all. What is one in the world is in danger of becoming manifold. This is caused by the parts, concepts or opposites contained in it. The essence of the Creator, however, is exalted above all this. It is Abū l-Hudhail Muḥammad b. al-Hudhail [b.] al-ʿAllāf al-Baṣrī who represented this view of the divine attributes.

Pythagoras lived some time after Empedocles. He learned philosophy in Egypt from the companions of Solomon, the son of David, who had gone from Syria to Egypt. He had previously learned geometry from the Egyptians. Afterwards he returned to the land of the Greeks where he introduced the study of geometry, natural science and religious knowledge. We owe to his acute mind the discovery of the science of melodies and composition, as well as the explanation of music as arithmetical proportions. He claimed to have learned that through prophetic illumination. From him we have wonderful allegories and far-reaching thoughts [?] concerning the order and composition of the world according to the properties and sequences of numbers. With regard to the resurrection he holds similar views to Empedocles. Above the world of nature there is a spiritual world of light, whose radiant beauty reason is unable to grasp. Pure souls yearn for it. Every man who trains his soul correctly and frees it from arrogance, pride, hypocrisy, envy and other desires of the body, acquires the right to enter the spiritual world and to gaze freely at the elements of divine wisdom to be found there. The things that delight the soul would then come to him of themselves, like melodies which force themselves on the sense of hearing of their own accord and need not be sought. Pythagoras compiled distinguished works on arithmetic, music and other subjects.

Socrates was a disciple of Pythagoras. He confined himself to the metaphysical disciplines of philosophy. He avoided worldly pleasures and openly declared that he did not agree with the Greeks with respect to their worship of idols. He opposed the leaders of the Greeks by means of arguments and proofs, and they incited the people against him and forced their ruler to kill him. The ruler imprisoned him in the hope that he would succeed in calming the people. Yet he was eventually forced to make him drink poison in order to save himself from the malice of the rabble. Earlier discussions had been held between Socrates and the ruler which have been preserved. Socrates is the author of noble admonitions, virtuous instructions and famous sayings. Regarding the divine attributes, his views resembled those of Pythagoras and Empedocles, but on the resurrection he held weak views, far removed from pure philosophy and true doctrines.

Like Socrates, Plato was a disciple of Pythagoras, but he only became known as a philosopher after Socrates's death. He was descended from a noble and learned family. He mastered all aspects of philosophy. He compiled many books and had a number of famous disciples. Since he used to teach philosophy walking to and fro, he and his pupils were given the name of Peripatetics [*mashshā'ūn*]. Near the end of his life, he entrusted his most outstanding disciples with the teaching and research, while he himself withdrew from people and devoted himself exclusively to the service of his Lord. Among his works are the following:

Phaedo on the soul.
Politics [the *Republic*].
The spiritual Timaeus on the order of the three worlds of the intellect, that is, the world of divinity, the world of reason and the world of the soul.
The physical Timaeus on the composition of the physical world. Plato composed these two books for one of his pupils who was called Timaeus.

Aristotle, the son of the Pythagorean, Nicomachus of Gerasa—Nicomachus means 'conqueror of opponents' and Aristotle means 'a possessor of perfect virtue'. Nicomachus belonged to the Pythagorean school. He is the author of famous works on arithmetic. His son Aristotle was a disciple of Plato. . . .

7. Ibn an-Nadīm, *al-Fihrist*, p. 245, Flügel; (Cairo, 1348), pp. 342 f.

Concerning the question as to who was the first philosopher: In reply to my enquiry as to who was the first philosopher, Abū l-Khair b. al-Khammār expressed himself to me in the presence of Abū l-Qāsim ʿĪsā b. ʿAlī as follows: In his *History*, Porphyry of Tyre expressed the opinion that Thales the Milesian, the son of Mʾls [=Milesian], was the first of the seven philosophers. The work is available in Syriac translation and two of its books have been translated into Arabic. Abū l-Qāsim has confirmed that he expressed himself thus and has not denied [the truth of the report].

Other scholars state that Pythagoras of Samos, the son of Mnesarchus, was the first philosopher. Plutarch says that Pythagoras was the first to call philosophy 'philosophy'.[39] He composed epistles [an epistle ?] which are [is?] known as 'the golden'. The name is derived from the fact that Galen used to copy them in gold because he valued them so highly.[40] Books by Pythagoras, which we have seen, are the following:

Epistle on intellectual leadership.
Epistle to the tyrant of Sicily.
Epistle to Syfʾns about the discovery of ideas.

These epistles are to be found together with Iamblichus's commentary.

Subsequently philosophy was further discussed by Socrates of Athens, the city of philosophers and scholars, who was the son of Suqrāṭīs [! leg. Sophroniscus] but in such a way that little became known about it. Books by Socrates that have been published [translated] include one 'On politics'. His epistle 'On the good way of life' is supposed to be really his own.

According to another report, Socrates means 'one who holds health'. He was an Athenian, an ascetic, rhetorician and philosopher. The Greeks killed him because he contradicted them; this story is well known. Artaxerxes was the ruler who had him killed. Plato was a disciple of Socrates. According to a handwritten note of Isḥāq b. Ḥunain, Socrates lived approximately as long as Plato. According to a handwritten note of Isḥāq, Plato lived to be eighty years.

The nature of the Greeks

8. From the *Physiognomy* of Polemo [Aflīmūn], ed. G. Hoffmann in R. Förster, *Scriptores Physiognomonici* (Leipzig, 1893), I, pp. 243–5. Cf. E. C. Evans, *Physiognomics in the Ancient World* (Philadelphia, 1969, *Transactions of the American Philosophical Society*, n.s., LIX, 5), pp. 14 f.

The Greeks and the pure Greek race

Here I would like to describe the appearance of the Greeks in their pure form, without any other racial admixture. They are people who share their land with many other people who find them and their country desirable, either on account of their luxurious life and moderate temperament and climate, or because of their scholarship, their good way of life and their good laws. They are the inhabitants of Argos, Corinth and other Greek regions.

The pure Greek is of medium height, neither too tall nor too small, neither too broad nor too slim. He possesses an erect figure, is handsome of countenance and appearance, of reddish-white complexion, and has neither too much nor too little flesh. He has well-proportioned hands and elbows, is alert and a quick learner. He possesses a head which is neither too large nor too small, a strong and powerful neck and soft red hair which is curly or wavy and smooth. His face is angular, his lips are soft, his nose is straight and regular. His eyes are moist, bluish-grey and very mobile and shining. Such is the appearance of the pure Greek.

The greatness of the Greek achievement

9. Moshe b. ʿEzrā, *al-Muḥāḍarah wa-l-mudhākarah*, from the third chapter. Arabic text in *Vostochnyya Zametki* (St Petersburg, 1895), p. 215; cf. B. Halper, p. 54, and A. Diez Macho, *Mošé Ibn ʿEzra* (Madrid–Barcelona, 1953), p. 120. The passage appears in connection with a statement of Galen that 'the Greek language is more melodious and expressive' and that all other tongues sound like 'the grunting of pigs and the croaking of frogs'. Ar-Rāzī had contested this statement in his work *On Doubts concerning Galen*. Cf. Ibn Ḥazm, *Iḥkām* (Cairo, 1345–8), I, p. 34.

It is quite clear that the Greek nation occupied itself most correctly with wisdom and philosophy as well as with the study of the propaedeutic sciences, logic, natural science and metaphysics [theology], the latter constituting the final and noblest goal on account of its great usefulness in connection with the hereafter. This people possessed political and economic knowledge and created clever speeches and notable philosophical sayings, so that 'philosophy' and 'Greek' became synonyms.

A characterization of the Byzantines

10. Al-Jāḥiẓ, *Kitāb al-Akhbār*, quoted by Nashwān al-Ḥimyarī, *Sharḥ Risālat al-Ḥūr al-ʿīn* (Cairo, 1367/1948), pp. 227 f., in a discussion of the problem of why people very clever in worldly affairs could be extremely obtuse in religious matters.

Then we turned to the Byzantines [Rūm]. We found that they were physicians, philosophers and astronomers. They are familiar with the principles of music, can manufacture [Roman] scales [*qarasṭūn*] and are informed about the world of books. They are excellent painters. If one of their painters paints a portrait of a person without omitting anything, he is still not satisfied and is willing to present him as a young man, a mature man or an old man, as required. Even that does not satisfy him, and he paints him weeping or laughing. That also is not enough for him, and he represents him as handsome, charming and distinguished looking. However, he is still discontented and distinguishes in his painting between a quiet and an embarrassed laugh, between a smile and a laugh strong enough to make tears flow from one's eyes, between joyous laughter and mocking or threatening laughter.[41] He can paint a picture within a picture and repeat the process two or three times.

The Byzantines possess an architecture different from that of others. They can produce carving and carpentry as nobody else can. Besides, they have a holy book and a religious community. It is unmistakable and undeniable that they possess beauty, are familiar with arithmetic, astrology and calligraphy, and have courage, insight and a variety of great skills. Negroes and similar peoples have little intelligence, since these qualities are remote from them.

PLATE I

Skepsis, Historia and Poiesis in the Umayyad castle of Quṣair ʿAmra (first half of the eighth century)

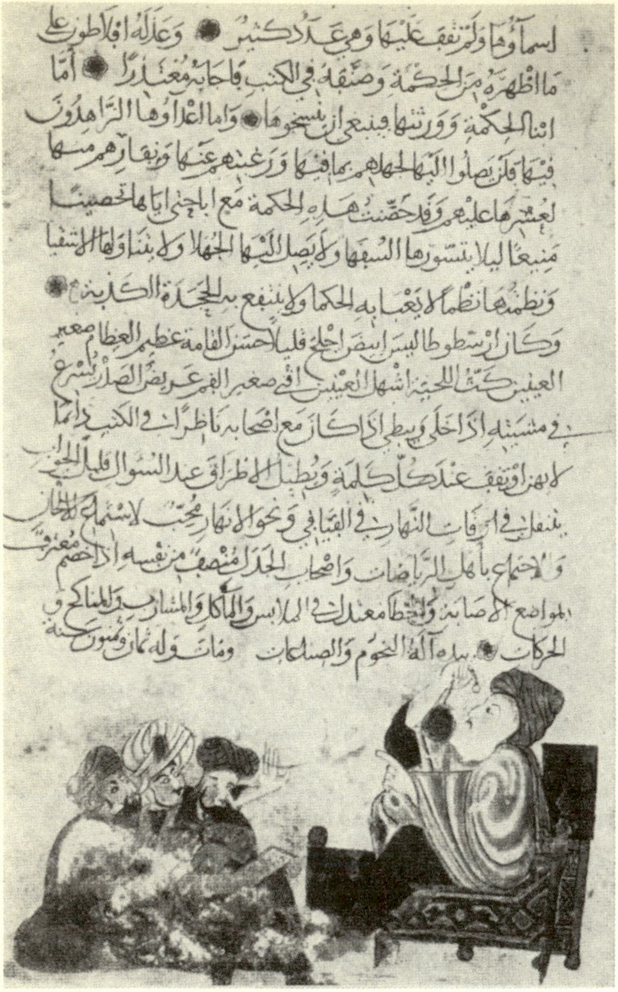

اسماؤها ولم نقف عليها وهي عدد كثير ● وعذله افلاطون على
ما اظهره من الحكمة وصنفه في الكتب فاجابه معتذرا ● اما
اننا الحكمة وورثتها فينبغي ان نسخو بها ● واما اعداؤها الزاهدون
فيها فلن يصلوا اليها لجهلهم بما فيها ورغبتهم عنها ونفارهم منها
لعسرها عليهم وقد حصنت هذه الحكمة مع اباحتي اياها تحصينا
منيعا لئلا يتسورها السفهاء ولا يصل اليها الجهلاء ولا يتناولها الاشقياء
ونظمتها نظما لا يعيا به الحكماء ولا ينتفع به الجهلة الكذبة ●
وكان ارسطوطاليس ابيض اجلح قليلا حسن القامة عظيم العظام صغير
العينين كث اللحية اشهل العينين اقنى صغير الفم عريض الصدر يسرع
في مشيته اذا خلا ويبطئ اذا كان مع اصحابه ناظرا في الكتب دائما
لا يهذر ويقف عند كل كلمة ويطيل الاطراق عند السؤال قليل الجواب
يتنقل في اوقات النهار في الفيافي ونحو الانهار محب لاستماع الالحان
والاجتماع باهل الرياضات واصحاب الجدل منصف من نفسه اذا خصم معترف
بمواضع الاصابة والخطا معتدل في الملابس والمآكل والمشارب والمناكح و
الحركات ● بيده آلة النجوم والساعات ومات وله ثمان وستون سنة

PLATE II

Aristotle and his disciples

Despite all this, they believe that there are three gods, two secret and one visible, just as a lamp requires oil, a wick and a container. The same applies [in their opinion] to the substance of the gods. They assume that a creature became creator, a slave became master, a newly created being became an originally uncreated being, but was then with a crown of thorns on the head crucified and killed,[42] and then disappeared, only to bring himself back to life after death. He is believed to have enabled his very slaves to seize and imprison him and give them power to crucify and kill him. In this way he is said to have intended to set a comforting example to his prophets and to make himself popular with them by putting himself on their level. Then they would consider all that happened to them as insignificant and would not feel proud of their own deeds but value them only for their Lord's sake.—Their excuse is worse than their crime! . . .

If we had not seen it with our own eyes and heard it with our own ears, we would not consider it true. We would not believe that a people of religious philosophers [*mutakallimūn*], physicians, astronomers, diplomats, arithmeticians, secretaries and masters of every discipline could say that a man who, as they themselves have seen, ate, drank, urinated, excreted, suffered hunger and thirst, dressed and undressed, gained and lost [weight], who later, as they assume, was crucified and killed, is Lord and Creator and providential God, eternal and not newly created, who lets the living die and brings the dead back to life and can create at will a great deal more for the world, and that they still take pride in his crucifixion and slaying, as do the Jews.

How the Arabs became acquainted with the Greek heritage

11. Ibn an-Nadīm, *al-Fihrist*, pp. 241–3, Flügel; (Cairo, 1348), pp. 336–40.

According to another report, philosophy was prohibited in olden days, and only sages and those known to be receptive to it by nature were permitted to occupy themselves with it. Philosophers used to study the horoscopes of those who wished to become philosophers. If someone's horoscope indicated that he was destined for philosophy, they accepted him as an attendant and instructed him in philosophy. Otherwise, they did not do so. Philosophy was known among the Greeks and the Romans before Christianity. When the Romans became Christians, it was forbidden to them. They burnt part of the philosophical literature and part of it they preserved in libraries. They were not allowed to discuss anything philosophical that contradicted the prophetic laws. Later the Romans [Byzantines] lapsed from Christianity and turned again to the views of the philosophers. The reason was this: The Roman Emperor Julian, whose minister was Themistius, the commentator of Aristotle's works, was staying in Antioch when Sābūr Dhū l-Aktāf attacked him. Julian defeated him, either in battle or, as is related, because Sābūr had marched to the land of the Byzantines in order to seize control of it. However, his intentions became known and he was seized—reports differ on this point. Julian penetrated into Persian territory as far as Jundīsābūr. To this day there is a breach [in the wall] there called 'the Byzantine breach'. The Persian leaders, their knights and other guardians of the Empire appeared there. The siege lasted a long time, and Julian had difficulty in capturing the city. Meanwhile, Sābūr was kept prisoner in Julian's castle in Byzantine territory. His daughter fell in love with him and let him escape. He succeeded in passing through the country unrecognized reaching Jundīsābūr and entering it. This gave his friends there fresh courage. Soon they made a sally and attacked the Byzantines since they regarded the escape of Sābūr as a favourable omen. Julian was taken prisoner and Sābūr had him killed. The Byzantines were left without a ruler. Now Constantine the elder was in the army, and as the Byzantines could not agree whom they should appoint as ruler and, besides, were too weak to resist him, since Sābūr was interested in him, Sābūr appointed him ruler. Later he also showed himself favourably inclined to the Byzantines for his sake and allowed them to leave his territory after imposing on Constantine the condition that he would plant an olive-tree for every date palm that had been felled in southern Iraq and Persia, and would send him from Byzantine territory first implements and then people in order to rebuild what Julian had destroyed. This he did. So the country became Christian again, as it had been. Philosophical works were again prohibited, as before, and stored in libraries to the present day. In olden times the Persians had translated some works on logic and medicine into Persian, and these were later translated further by ᶜAbdallāh b. al-Muqaffaᶜ and others into Arabic.

According to another report, Khālid b. Yazīd b. Muᶜāwiyah used to be called the sage [philosopher] of the Marwānids [Umayyads]. He was a distinguished man who had great interest in and love for the sciences. He was interested in alchemy. By his command a group of Greek philosophers who resided in the capital of Egypt and mastered the Arabic language well were brought to him. He commanded them to translate books about alchemy from Greek and Coptic into Arabic. This was the first translation from a foreign language in Islam.

Under al-Ḥajjāj Arabic was introduced through Ṣāliḥ b. ᶜAbd-ar-Raḥmān, a client of the Tamīm and son of a prisoner of war from Sijistān, as the language of the financial administration, instead of Persian, which had been used till then. Ṣāliḥ wrote documents in Persian and Arabic for Zādānfarrūkh b. Bīrī,[43] the secretary of al-Ḥajjāj. Since Ṣāliḥ noticed that al-Ḥajjāj found him pleasant company, he warned Zādānfarrūkh, telling him: 'You brought me in touch with the Amīr. Now I have noticed that he finds me pleasant company and I am not sure whether he will not prefer me to you, and you would then lose your respected position.' However, Zādānfarrūkh replied: 'Do not imagine anything of the kind! He needs me more than I need him, since he could not find anybody else to keep his accounts in order.' Whereupon Ṣāliḥ proposed to him to introduce the Arabic language for bookkeeping, if it so pleased him. Zādānfarrūkh challenged him to produce for him a few lines of Arabic as a test, and he did so. Thereupon Zādānfarrūkh ordered him to feign illness which he accordingly did. Al-Ḥajjāj sent him his personal physician Theodore, who, however, could not discover any illness in him and reported to Zādānfarrūkh to that effect. Then Zādānfarrūkh commanded him to tell [the truth]. During the insurrection of Ibn al-Ashᶜath Zādānfarrūkh was killed on his way home, and al-Ḥajjāj appointed Ṣāliḥ secretary in place of Zādānfarrūkh. Ṣāliḥ reported to him about his negotiations with Zādānfarrūkh concerning the change in the financial administration. Thereupon al-Ḥajjāj decided to implement this reform and entrusted Ṣāliḥ with it. Mardānshāh, the son of Zādānfarrūkh, asked him what he would do about

Persian *dahōye* and *shashōye*, and he replied that he would write instead the Arabic *ʿushr* 'a tenth' and *niṣf ʿushr* 'half a tenth'. Then he asked him what he would do about *wīd*, and he replied that he would write 'and further' in its place. He said that *wīd* meant a plus sign for addition. Then Mardānshān cursed him: 'May God exterminate you as you have exterminated the Persian language!' The Persians offered 100,000 dirhams to Ṣāliḥ should he declare himself incapable of introducing Arabic as the language of the financial administration. However, he insisted on the reform and carried it out. ʿAbd-al-Ḥamīd b. Yaḥyā used to say: 'Ṣāliḥ is a remarkable fellow! What an immense favour he has done the secretaries!' Al-Ḥajjāj allowed him time for the change in the financial administration.

The language of the financial administration in Syria was Greek [*rūmī*]. At the head of the financial administration in the service of Muʿāwiyah b. Abī Sufyān stood Sarjūn b. Manṣūr. His successor was Manṣūr b. Sarjūn. The change in the financial administration took place at the time of Hishām b. ʿAbd-al-Malik through Abū Thābit Sulaimān b. Saʿd, a client of Ḥusain. He had been chief of the department for the composition of documents under ʿAbd-al-Malik. According to another view, the change had already taken place under ʿAbd-al-Malik. He had given an order to this effect to Sarjūn, but he took too long over it, which annoyed ʿAbd-al-Malik. Hence he consulted Sulaimān and said: 'I shall introduce Arabic as the language of administration and leave him behind [that is, Sarjūn, whose services would no longer be required].'

Why there are so many books to be found in these parts on philosophy and the other ancient sciences.

One reason for this is al-Maʾmūn's dream. He dreamed that he saw a man of reddish-white complexion with a high forehead, bushy eyebrows, bald head, dark blue eyes and handsome features sitting on his chair. Al-Maʾmūn gave the following account of his dream: I had the impression that I was standing respectfully in front of him. I asked him who he was. He replied: 'I am Aristotle.' I was happy to be with him and asked if I might address a question to him. He granted me permission, and I said: 'What is good?' He replied: 'Whatever is good according to reason.' I asked:

'What else?' He replied: 'Whatever is good according to religious law.' I asked: 'And what else?' He replied: 'Whatever society considers good.' I asked: 'What else?' And he replied: 'Nothing else.' According to another tradition, al-Ma'mūn said: 'Give me further instructions.' And Aristotle replied: 'He who is loyal to you for gold, consider him to be like gold. It is your duty to believe in the oneness of God.'[44]

This dream was of the most far-reaching significance for the translation activity. A repeated exchange of letters took place between al-Ma'mūn and the Byzantine emperor, whom he had just defeated, and he asked in writing for permission to send people to select books on the ancient sciences from those preserved in the libraries of Byzantine territory.

First he would not allow it, but later gave his consent. Thereupon al-Ma'mūn sent scholars, among them al-Ḥajjāj b. Maṭar, Ibn al-Biṭrīq and Salm, the president of the academy [*bait al-ḥikmah*], and they made their choice among the material which they found there and took it along to al-Ma'mūn. He ordered them to translate it, and this was done. Yuḥannā b. Māsawaih is also supposed to have been one of those sent at that time to Byzantine territory.

Muḥammad b. Isḥāq [Ibn an-Nadīm] says: The three sons of the astronomer Shākir [Banū Shākir al-Munajjim], Muḥammad, Aḥmad and al-Ḥasan, of whom more will be said later, were also interested in the export of scholarly books from Byzantine territory. They spent large sums on it. Ḥunain b. Isḥāq and other scholars, whom they sent into Byzantine territory, brought them back precious and rare works on philosophy, geometry, music, arithmetic and medicine. Qusṭā b. Lūqā al-Ba'labakkī also brought a few and translated them himself or had them translated for him.

Abū Sulaimān al-Manṭiqī as-Sijistānī says that the Banū l-Munajjim paid salaries to a number of translators, among them Ḥunain b. Isḥāq, Ḥubaish b. al-Ḥasan and Thābit b. Qurrah. These salaries amounted to about 500 dinars a month, for which they had to translate and to be available.

Muḥammad b. Isḥāq says: I myself have heard how Abū Isḥāq b. Shahrām said in a public lecture that there is an old temple in Byzantine territory with a door greater than any that has ever been seen, with two iron leaves. In olden times, when the

Greeks still worshipped stars and idols, they greatly revered this temple, prayed and offered sacrifices in it. He said: 'I begged the Byzantine emperor to open it for me. At first he did not wish to allow this because it had remained locked since the introduction of Christianity. However, I did not cease to entreat him, write to him and beg him orally when I had an audience with him. . . . So he finally proceeded to have it opened. It turned out then that the interior was so beautiful and so generously equipped with marble and multicoloured stones, with inscriptions and sculptures, that I have never seen or heard about the like of it. Furthermore, several camel-loads of old books were found in this temple.' He went on exaggerating until eventually he spoke of a thousand camel-loads. 'Some of these books were quite worn, others were as they had been originally, while others again were worm-eaten. . . . There I have also seen exquisite golden and other sacrificial implements. . . . After I had left, the door was again locked. It had been a special favour shown me by the Byzantine emperor that I was permitted to enter'. . . . This occurred in the time of Saif-ad-daulah. The building is thought to be a three days' journey from Constantinople. The inhabitants are Chaldean Ṣābians, whom the Byzantines allowed to keep their faith in return for payment of a poll-tax.

12. Ibn Abī Uṣaibi'ah, II, pp. 134 f., Müller, trans. M. Meyerhof, 'Von Alexandrien nach Bagdad', in *Sitz. Ber. Preuss. Akad. d. Wiss.*, phil.-hist. Kl. 1930, pp. 394 and 405.

Abū Naṣr al-Fārābī has given the following account of the appearance of philosophy [in Islam]. Philosophy was popular in Alexandria in the time of the Greek rulers and after the death of Aristotle until the end of the woman's rule. The teaching of it continued unchanged after the death of Aristotle during the reign of thirteen rulers. During their reign twelve teachers, one of them named Andronicus, taught philosophy in succession. The last of these rulers was the woman whom the Roman Emperor Augustus defeated and had killed. He took over the rule and, when he had secured it, he inspected the libraries and found there manuscripts of Aristotle's works, written in his lifetime and in that of Theophrastus. He also found that scholars and philosophers had written books on the same ideas as Aristotle. He ordered the books written in the lifetime of Aristotle and his pupils to be copied and used as textbooks and all other books to be excluded. Andronicus was appointed by him to supervise this task. He ordered him to copy manuscripts and take them to Rome and to leave further copies at the school in Alexandria. He also commanded him to leave a teacher as his deputy in Alexandria and to travel to Rome with him. In this way it happened that philosophy was taught in both places. Thus it continued until the coming of Christianity. Then the teaching of philosophy came to an end in Rome, while it continued in Alexandria until the Christian ruler looked into the matter. The bishops assembled and took counsel together on which parts of the teaching of philosophy should be kept and which should be abolished. They decided that the books on logic could be taught up to the assertoric figures [in the first half of the first book of *Analytica Priora*[45]], but no further, since they believed that everything beyond that would harm Christianity, whereas the permitted material could be used for the promotion of their religion. This then could be taught publicly while all the remaining studies were kept secret until, much later, Islam came. The teaching of philosophy was transferred from Alexandria to Antioch. There it remained for a long time, but in the end only a single teacher survived. He had two disciples who left and took the [text]books with them. One of them was from Ḥarrān, the other from Marw. The one from Marw had two disciples, Ibrāhīm al-Marwazī and Yuḥannā b. Ḥailān. Bishop Isrā'īl and Quwairī were the disciples of the Ḥarrānians. They travelled to Baghdad. Isrā'īl occupied himself with religious matters and Quwairī began to teach. Yuḥannā b. Ḥailān also occupied himself with religious matters. Ibrāhīm al-Marwazī returned to Baghdad and settled there. Mattā b. Yūnān was a disciple of al-Marwazī. What they studied at that time went up to the end of the assertoric figures.

Concerning himself, al-Fārābī reports that he had studied logic with Yūḥannā b. Ḥailān to the end of the *Analytica Posteriora*. What comes after the assertoric figures used to be called the part which is not studied. Eventually it was studied. Then it became customary among Muslim teachers to continue beyond the assertoric figures as far as it was humanly possible for the students. Hence al-Fārābī said that he had studied logic to the end of the *Analytica Posteriora*.

III

THE CLASSIFICATION OF THE SCIENCES AND METHODS OF RESEARCH AND TEACHING

A predilection for systematic classification of the sciences is very noticeable in Muslim civilization. It is due to the classical heritage, which through it exercised perhaps its most pervasive influence upon intellectual life in Islam. It originated in Greek logic. In a way, it proved detrimental to intellectual progress, since it created the illusion, to which scholars often succumbed, that what was classified, was known and understood. It provided, however, a method indispensable to genuine scholarship and proved extremely fertile in the history of Muslim intellectual endeavours.

Muslim scholars are agreed as to the fundamental division of the sciences into Arabic sciences and foreign (that is, predominantly Greek) sciences, and there is a core of truth to it. As far as the 'Greek' sciences were concerned, they took over from late Hellenistic times an established canon of individual disciplines, classified by and large in the same manner we find dominant also in medieval Christendom. This canon is known to be derived from a division of the sciences, most familiar to the Arabs, into theoretical (mathematics, natural sciences, metaphysics) and practical (ethics, economics, politics), the definition of the former group going back to Aristotle himself, and that of the latter to his school (cf. F. Rosenthal, in *Journal of the American Oriental Society*, LXXVI [1956], pp. 27–9). The trend in Islam was towards subdividing the individual disciplines into more and more specialized fields, and eventually, the supposedly independent disciplines were counted in the hundreds. Philosophers regarded it as desirable and essential to establish a logical connection between the individual disciplines and thus demonstrate their position in the structure of the world. The burning problem, however, was how to establish an acceptable relationship between the sciences other than originally Islamic religious sciences and Islam as a religion claiming to have all worthwhile knowledge contained in its religious writings. This was in a sense a skirmish in the titanic struggle between religion and philosophy. It was bound to end in the same way, namely, undecided in theory but with the victory in fact going to the theologians. The significance of this skirmish for the development of Muslim civilization cannot be overestimated. It determined which disciplines were allowed to be pursued and to what extent. It also provided the basis for the often very necessary justification of the right of certain disciplines to exist and be cultivated.

Aristotelian logic and, in particular, the formal introductions to it composed by the commentators, also deeply influenced other aspects of Muslim scholarly methodology. The traditional Ancient Oriental concept that knowledge was based upon the concatenation of transmitted facts loosely associated with one another continued, it must be admitted, to hold sway over much of the outward manifestations of Muslim intellectual life and deprived it of what we would consider a proper methodical approach. Yet, Muslim scholars, including, in the end, most of the representatives of Muslim religious scholarship, were conditioned by the Aristotelian commentaries and their methodology to view the construction of a scholarly work and the meaning and purpose of scholarly writing in the light of Aristotelian logic. From the standpoint of cultural history, it was by no means wrong to ascribe to Aristotle an exhaustive, if brief, list of reasons for which works with a claim to scholarly value deserve to be written (cf. Ibn Khaldūn, *Muqaddimah*, trans. F. Rosenthal [New York, 1958], III, pp. 284 ff.).

The specific contribution of antiquity to individual features of the educational system highly developed in Islam seems to have been comparatively small. General superficial similarities are naturally numerous. The ethos of the teacher–pupil relationship, as described, for example, not only in the special works on education but also in philosophical and alchemical literature, had its roots in classical antiquity. But the fact that Muslim education was directed towards religious subjects required for a different content different external forms. The translation literature gave the

Arabs some inkling of a curriculum that was not determined exclusively by religion, but the idea found an echo only once, in later Islamic Spain, and never exerted any practical effect.

The classification of the sciences

1. From the introduction to al-Khuwārizmī's brief encyclopaedia of the sciences (*Mafātīḥ al-ʿulūm* [Cairo, 1349/1930], pp. 4 f.). The work is mainly concerned with scientific terminology. Cf. C. E. Bosworth, in *Isis*, LIV (1963), pp. 97–111, and the Persian trans. by Ḥusain Khadīv-jam (Teheran, 1347/1969).

I have divided my work into two books. One of them is devoted to the sciences of the Islamic religious law and the Arabic sciences connected with it, and the second to the sciences originating from foreigners such as the Greeks and other nations.

Division of chapters in the first book (6 chapters with 52 paragraphs): (1) jurisprudence (11 paragraphs), (2) speculative theology (7 paragraphs), (3) grammar (12 paragraphs), (4) secretaryship (8 paragraphs), (5) poetry and prosody (5 paragraphs) and (6) history (9 paragraphs).

Second book (9 chapters with 41 paragraphs): (1) philosophy (3 paragraphs), (2) logic (9 paragraphs), (3) medicine (8 paragraphs), (4) arithmetic (5 paragraphs), (5) geometry (4 paragraphs), (6) astronomy–astrology (4 paragraphs), (7) music (3 paragraphs), (8) mechanics (2 paragraphs) and (9) alchemy (3 paragraphs).

2. From the introduction of al-Fārābī, *Iḥṣāʾ al-ʿulūm*, ed. ʿUthmān M. Amīn (Cairo, 1350/1931), pp. 2 f.; ed. Á. González Palencia (Madrid, 1953), pp. 7–9, trans. pp. 3 f.

In this book we intend to enumerate the generally known sciences one by one and to give a general survey of each individual science, also to point out possible subdivisions and to give a general survey of each subdivision. The sciences can be classified in five groups, that is:

(1) Linguistics, with subdivisions
(2) Logic, with subdivisions

(3) The mathematical sciences, that is, arithmetic, geometry, optics, mathematical astronomy,[1] music, technology[2] and mechanics

(4) The natural sciences and metaphysics, both with subdivisions

(5) Politics, with subdivisions, jurisprudence and speculative theology

Anyone desirous of studying one of these sciences will find the content of this book useful, as he will learn from it which science he should pursue, what he ought to study and what he can learn through his study, what use it has and what advantage he may derive from it. Thus he need not choose the science he wishes to pursue, blindly and at his own risk, but can approach it with insight and understanding.

Furthermore, this book will enable him to compare the different sciences and to find out which science is better or more useful or more accurate, more reliable and effective, or less significant and effective.

Furthermore, it is useful in order to expose someone who claims to master a science, when this is not, in fact, the case. Should he be asked to give a general survey of it and all its subdivisions when he is not well-informed, he would then show that his claim is false, and his deceit would be exposed.

The book, furthermore, makes it possible to ascertain whether a person, who is well versed in a science, has truly mastered it or some of its subdivisions, and how far his mastery goes.

The book can be of use to the educated layman who wants to gain an overall impression of all the sciences, as well as for people who wish to be taken for scholars.

3. From the *Rasā'il Ikhwān aṣ-ṣafā'* (Cairo, 1347/1928), I, pp. 202–4, an encyclopaedia compiled in the tenth century by a group of scholars who called themselves the 'faithful friends'.

Thus we have concluded our discussion about the quiddity of the sciences as well as the diverse problems and the answers required by them. Now we wish to mention their genera and kinds in order to guide those who strive for knowledge towards the attainment of their aims and objects. The soul's longing for the various sciences and fields of learning corresponds to the body's desire for food of different taste, preparation and smell.

Know then, my brother, that the sciences to which mankind devotes itself include three genera. These are the propaedeutic sciences, the conventional sciences of the religious law and the real philosophical sciences.

The propaedeutic sciences consist of those disciplines which were mainly created in order to assure a livelihood and to promote worldly prosperity. There are nine kinds of them: (1) writing and reading, (2) lexicography and grammar, (3) arithmetic as required for bookkeeping and commerce, (4) poetry and prosody, (5) augury, omens and the like, (6) magic, talismans, alchemy, mechanics and the like, (7) trades and crafts, (8) retail and wholesale trade, agriculture and animal husbandry and (9) biography and history.

The sciences of the religious law that were created for the healing of souls and for the quest for future life consist of six kinds: (1) the science of the Revelation, (2) the allegorical interpretation of the Qur'ān, (3) reports and traditions (of the Prophet and other recognized early Islamic authorities), (4) jurisprudence, ordinances and laws, (5) prayers, sermons, asceticism and mysticism and (6) the interpretation of dreams. The scholars who occupy themselves with the science of the Revelation are the Qur'ān readers and experts. The scholars who occupy themselves with the allegorical interpretation of the Qur'ān are the imāms and successors of the prophets. The scholars who occupy themselves with the traditions are the *ḥadīth* scholars. The scholars who occupy themselves with the ordinances and laws are the jurists. The scholars who occupy themselves with prayers and sermons are pious worshippers, ascetics, monks and the like. And the scholars who occupy themselves with the interpretation of dreams are the dream interpreters.

The philosophical sciences consist of four kinds: (*a*) the propaedeutic-mathematical, (*b*) the logical, (*c*) the natural and (*d*) the metaphysical sciences.

The propaedeutic-mathematical sciences consist of four kinds:

(1) arithmetic [*arithmāṭīqī*], that is, knowledge of the quiddity of numbers, how many different kinds of numbers there are,

what their properties are, how they originate from the number one, which precedes two, and what results when one combines one kind of number with another.

(2) Geometry [*jūmaṭriyā* or, in Arabic, with a word derived from the Persian, *handasah*], that is, knowledge of the quiddity of planes [and bodies], how many different kinds of them there are, what properties they possess, what results when one combines one [plane] with another and how they begin with the point, the basic feature of the line, which is for geometry what the number one is for arithmetic.

(3) Astronomy [*asṭurnūmiyā*] or [knowledge of] the stars, that is, knowledge of the spheres, stars and signs of the zodiac, how many there are, how distant they are [from the earth and from one another], how large they are, how they are composed, how quickly they move, how long their revolutions take, what the quiddity of their natures is and how they indicate things that come into being before they do so.

(4) Music [*mūsīqī*] or the science of composition, that is, knowledge of the quiddity of proportions, the way in which things of different substances, distinct forms, opposite powers and antagonistic natures can be united and composed so that they are no longer averse to one another but are composed harmoniously, become united and one and produce one effect or more.

For each of these arts[3] we have compiled a special treatise to serve as a kind of introduction.

The logical sciences consist of five kinds:

(1) Poetics, that is, knowledge of the art of poesy.

(2) Rhetoric, that is, knowledge of the art of oratory.

(3) Topic, that is, knowledge of the art of discussion.

(4) Analytic [*Analytica Posteriora*], that is, knowledge of the art of demonstration.

(5) Sophistic, that is, knowledge of the art and manner in which opponents dispute with one another.

Ancient as well as later philosophers have discussed these arts and sciences and composed many books about them, which have been preserved and are still available. Aristotle composed three further books as introductions to the *Book of Demonstration* [*Analytica*

Posteriora], that is, *Categories*, *Peri Hermeneias* and the *First Analytic* [*Analytica Priora*]. . . . Porphyry of Tyre composed a book entitled *Eisagoge*, which is an introduction to logic. . . .

[On pages 205–9 the authors deal with the seven kinds of natural sciences, namely (1) the material principles of matter, form, time, space and motion, (2) heaven and earth, (3) generation and decay, (4) atmospheric phenomena, (5) mineralogy, (6) botany and (7) zoology, and the five kinds of metaphysical sciences, namely (1) recognition of the Creator, (2) spiritual beings, (3) matters concerning the universal and individual soul, (4) prophetical guidance, guidance as exercised by caliphs and imāms, politics as it affects the subjects, economics and ethics and (5) the Resurrection.]

4. Ibn Ḥazm, *Marātib al-ʿulūm*, ed. I. R. ʿAbbās, *Rasāʾil Ibn Ḥazm al-Andalusī* (Cairo, n.y. [1954]), pp. 78–80.

At all times and in all nations everywhere the sciences have been divided into seven parts. The first three are (1) the science of the religious law as possessed by every nation, since every nation has some belief, which can be positive or negative, (2) the history of the nation concerned and (3) the science of the language it speaks. The various nations all differ from one another in respect of these three sciences. The remaining four sciences, however, are the same everywhere, namely (4) astronomy, (5) arithmetic, (6) medicine, that is, concern with the human body, and (7) philosophy. Philosophy includes knowledge of all matters as they are according to their definition, from the highest genera to individual particulars, as well as knowledge of divine matters [metaphysics].

As we have explained earlier, all religious laws, with the exception of the religious law of Islam, are invalid. Hence it is necessary to concentrate on the true religious law and on everything that can deepen knowledge of it. The science of the Muslim religious law is divided into four parts: (1) the science of the Qurʾān, (2) the science of the *ḥadīth*, (3) jurisprudence and (4) speculative theology [*kalām*].

The science of the Qurʾān deals with the reading and the meaning of the Qurʾān. The science of the *ḥadīth* deals with the texts and transmitters of traditions. Jurisprudence deals with the laws derived from the Qurʾān and those derived from the *ḥadīth*, as well as with matters about which Muslims in their entirety agree or disagree, and various correct or incorrect ways of [legal] deduction. Finally, speculative theology deals with doctrinal views and the demonstrable or undemonstrable arguments used by the speculative theologians.

Grammar deals with an original fund of information based on tradition and explanatory rules, newly invented. Lexicography is based exclusively on tradition.

The science of history possesses a number of principles for the arrangement of historical material, namely dynasties, annals, topography and classes [of scholars belonging to one particular generation], or else it does not use a method of arrangement of any kind. The most reliable historical information we possess is on Islamic history, the history of the beginnings of Islam, the Muslim conquests, the caliphs and sultans, their rivals, their scholars, as well as all that belongs to it. Israelite historical information generally is reliable, but it has been partly interpolated. It is only reliable from the time of the immigration of the Israelites to Syria down to their second exile, but not for earlier periods. Greek [*Rūm*] historical information is reliable from Alexander onwards but not for earlier periods. One cannot expect to have any historical information on the Turks, Khazars and other northern peoples, or of the Negroes in Africa, since these peoples possess neither any kind of science nor books and histories. Furthermore, we lack all information, which we would dearly like to have, on the history of the Indians and the Chinese, though we know that both these peoples possess exact knowledge and a large literature. The historical information on extinct nations such as the Copts, Southern Arabs, Syrians [Assyrians], Hasmoneans [? *ʾshmʾnīyūn*],[4] Ammonites, Moabites and other peoples, is completely lost. Only some false and grotesque stories have survived. Persian historical information is only reliable from Darius, the son of Darius, onwards; it is very reliable from the time of Ardashīr b. Bābak [the Sassanians] onwards. The student of history may only occupy himself with the material which we have described as reliable, but not with unhistorical material, since he should not waste his time with useless things. He knows now what is unreliable historical material and can save himself the trouble of occupying himself with it. He can use his efforts better by devoting himself to the material recommended by us.

Genealogy is a subdivision of the science of history.

Knowledge of the stars deals with astronomic conditions and their scientific basis, as well as with astrology, which is to be mentioned later.

The science of numbers deals with the establishment of rules concerning numbers, their scientific basis, their practical application for measuring, etc.

Logic is divided into an intellectual and a sensual part. The first is concerned with metaphysical and physical data, the second exclusively with physical.

Medicine falls into two parts, namely, medicine of the soul and medicine of the body. The medicine of the soul is prepared by logic to remove excess and deficiency in ethical matters and to observe the right means, thereby leading to moral improvement. The medicine of the body deals with the natures [humours] of the body and the composition of the limbs as well as with illnesses, their causes, the medicines with which they can be fought and the selection of effective medicines and foods. The medicine of the body again falls into two parts, namely, (1) operations to be carried out manually [*cheirourgia*, surgery], for example, setting limbs, lancing boils, cauterizing and amputation, and (2) control of illness through the powers inherent in medicines. It is further divided into the following two parts: (1) the preservation of health, so that one does not become ill, and (2) in the event of illness, its treatment.

Poetics deals with the transmission of poems, their meanings, beauties and defects and the parts of which they consist as well as with metre and form.

Furthermore, there are two sciences which result from the combination of all the sciences mentioned above, or two or more of them, namely, rhetoric and dream interpretation.

When applied in the service of God and for clarifying the realities as well as for the instruction of the ignorant, rhetoric is a virtue. But when applied for opposite purposes, it is a useless business, an expenditure of effort and a waste of life on something harmful—may God protect us from such a calamity.

Dream interpretation is a natural gift, supported by knowledge.

Only after the interpreter shows that he is both naturally gifted and knowledgeable can this science be considered reliable, not before.

5. Ibn Sīnā, *Kitāb an-Najāh* (Cairo, 1357/1938), pp. 72–4.

The sciences are either different from one another or related to one another. The sciences that are different from one another are those whose objects have nothing to do with one another in respect of either their essence or their genus, for example, arithmetic and natural science. The sciences related to one another are either of equal rank, or some are contained in others, or some are subordinate to others. Sciences of equal rank are, for instance, geometry and arithmetic which have objects of related genus, since both spatial extension and numbers are a kind of quantity; or natural science and astronomy, since they have one and the same object, namely, the world, but regard it from different points of view, since astronomy regards it from the point of view of its movement and rest, combination and separation, etc., which has generally somehow to do with quality, whereas natural science regards it [the world] from the point of view of the quantification of its essence and accidents. Hence, natural science and astronomy have most problems in common, but the reasoning of astronomy produces causal relationships, while that of natural science establishes the facts of existence. Furthermore, astronomical reasoning starts from an active cause, while that of natural science starts from a formal cause.

An example of sciences of different ranks, where some are contained in others, are the conic sections in geometry, since conic sections deal with one kind of geometry's objects.

In sciences of different ranks, where some are subordinate to others, the object of the higher science may not in fact be a genus of the lower one's object, but corresponds to a genus in its general validity, even though it has not the general validity of a genus; since, if it had the general validity of a genus, it would not be impossible for the lower science to be a kind of it, like the conic sections in geometry, and as is the case with the partial sciences in their subordinate relation to the first philosophy [metaphysics] whose object is the absolutely existent as absolutely existent. Or else the higher science may be a genus for the lower one's object.

In that case, however, the lower science is not directly considered as a kind of the higher one, but is connected with some sort of accident and has taken on an object in conjunction with this accident. One studies its essential accidents under this aspect. This applies if one considers [the science of the] moving spheres as subordinate to geometry or if one regards optics as subordinate, since its objects are lines that have the accidental quality of being assumed to be linked with the glance of an eye which penetrates a transparent medium and then reaches the sides of a material body. Sometimes the object belongs to one science and the accident to another, in which case one should study the matter from the point of view of the science to which that accident belongs, which is strange to it but essential to another object. Thus it is with music, for example. Its object is tones, which belong to the accidents of natural science. Thus one studies the tones in music from the point of view of something which in music is accidental but which is essential to another object, namely the proportion of numbers. Therefore [music] is subordinate to arithmetic, and not to natural science.

On the collaboration of sciences

Collaboration of sciences takes place in such a manner that what constitutes a problem for one science is used as a premise in another. Thus the science with the problem assists the one with the premise. This can occur in three different ways:

1. The one science may be subordinate to the other. Then the lower science receives its principles from the higher one, for example, music from arithmetic, medicine from natural science and all the sciences from the first philosophy.

2. Or both sciences may share the same object like natural science and astronomy, both of them concerned with the universe. Natural science studies the substance of the object, and astronomy its accidents. Whoever studies the substance of an object thereby supplies the student of another science with its principles. Thus the astronomer, for example, learns from the natural scientist that the movement of spheres is bound to be circular.

3. Or both sciences may share the same genus, one of them studying a simple kind, such as arithmetic, for example, and the other a more complex kind, like geometry, for example. Whoever

studies the simpler one thereby supplies the principles for anyone studying another science. Thus, for example, arithmetic helps geometry, as the tenth book of Euclid shows.

Islam and the sciences

6. Abū l-Ḥasan al-ʿĀmirī, *al-Iʿlām bi-manāqib al-Islām*, according to the Istanbul MS Ragib 1463, 3a–6a; ed. A. ʿA. Ghurâb (Cairo, 1387/1967), pp. 84–97.

Knowledge means that one grasps something as it is, without mistake and error. There is the knowledge which belongs to the religious community, and there is philosophical knowledge. The masters of the religious sciences are the recognized philosophers. Every prophet is a philosopher but not every philosopher is a prophet.

The religious sciences consist of three branches. One of them relies on sensual perceptions, namely, the science of the *ḥadīth* scholars. The second rests on the intellect, namely the science of the religious philosophers. The third involves both sensual and intellectual perception, namely, the science of the jurists. Linguistics is an instrument serving all three branches.

The philosophical sciences also consist of three branches. One of them rests on sensual perception, namely, natural science. The second rests on the intellect, namely, metaphysics. The third involves both sensual and intellectual perception, namely, mathematics. Logic is an instrument serving all three branches.

The common people sometimes use the word 'science' for any trade whatsoever. Empiricists sometimes use it for ideas empirically acquired, for example, fortune-telling based on augury through observation of the flight of birds or based on shoulder blades and footprints.

There are sciences which philosophers consider reprehensible, and which, in their opinion, should not be taught to the masses, since they are convinced that their application is more harmful than useful. Such sciences are, for example, magic, conjuring, amulets and alchemy.

Once this is clear, we must go a little further and state that it is one of God's greatest gifts that He created man with a spiritual love for the sciences. However, man's natural capacity does not permit him to master all branches of knowledge exactly, and an essential link has therefore been created between human nature and the various subjects of science by some mysterious mark. I mean, one man feels drawn to one branch of knowledge, another to another. Personal choice or the will of the one who has the power of decision over him determines this matter. The person concerned appears increasingly enthusiastic about his special branch of knowledge and familiar with it, so that he eventually assigns it a special place in his heart, since he loves it so dearly and prefers it to any other knowledge, even if it is less valuable. Hence, the proverb: 'One is hostile to what one does not know.'

Since this is admitted, and we have no further doubt that acquaintance with the value of every branch of knowledge is of great help for a correct choice between the sciences, we can now direct our attention to this problem.

Some scholars of the *ḥadīth* [*Ḥashwīyah*] have attacked the philosophical sciences on the assumption that they contradict the religious sciences and that all those interested in the philosophical sciences and occupied with their study forfeit this world and the next. In their view, they contain only impressive words and empty phrases, varnished over with deceptive ideas, so as to deceive poor blockheads and lead astray conceited fools. That is not right. Like the religious sciences, the foundations and branches of the philosophical sciences rest on dogmas in harmony with pure reason and confirmed through fully valid proofs. One knows very well that there should be no contradiction between the demands of the true religion and what proofs confirm and reason demands. Hence, he who masters the philosophical sciences is blessed with three advantages. In the first place, he is extremely close to perfect human virtue in that he is familiar with the true reality of things and has the possibility of controlling them. Secondly, he has insight into all that reveals the wisdom with which the Creator has created the various things in the world, and he understands their causes and results and the wonderful order and splendid arrangement they have. Thirdly, he is well versed in the arguments against traditional claims and is in no danger of soiling himself with vain dogmas through a blind belief in authority.

As we remarked, the philosophical sciences consist of three

branches, namely, mathematics, natural science and metaphysics, while logic serves all of them as an instrument. Now we must mention briefly the good points of each of these four branches and then devote ourselves to the various kinds of religious sciences.

Mathematics has five branches, namely, arithmetic, geometry, astronomy, music and mechanics.

Exercise and skill in arithmetic are a source of the profoundest joy to human reason. An intelligent person who studies the peculiarities of its parts by themselves and in conjunction with one another can never enjoy them enough and is convinced that the value and importance of arithmetic constitute an inexhaustible wonder. Besides, it is free from contradictions and doubts. Furthermore, one appeals to it as an arbitrator in matters of commerce. God has said [Qur'ān 19. 94/94]: 'We have counted and calculated them', and [Qur'ān 72. 28/28]: 'He has counted everything.'

Geometry follows arithmetic in value and importance. It is easier to understand because it is concerned with sensual prototypes, and it is more far-reaching, for without its aid the arithmetician cannot extract irrational roots, nor the surveyor determine the shapes of sites, nor human reason calculate the extent of the seas and the height of mountains. Besides, it is useful to all gifted architects, carpenters, sculptors and goldsmiths and is used for the manufacture of astronomical instruments as, for example, spheres [spherical astrolabes ?], astrolabes, armillary spheres and sun-clocks.

Astronomy, as everyone knows, is a noble science. It examines the form of the upper world according to quantity and quality as well as the movement of every heavenly body. It seeks to discover the causes of eclipses and studies various phenomena, such as retrograde and rectilinear motions, movement and rest as found among 'the receding, the running' [Qur'ān 81.15f./15f.] stars [planets] as well as the visibility and invisibility, the rising and setting of the fixed stars. An intelligent man whose knowledge extends to heavenly phenomena, undoubtedly possesses a considerable share of bliss. Hence God has rebuked all who refrain from occupying themselves with this noble science and said [Qur'ān 30.8/7, cited not quite literally]: 'Did they not think about the creation of the heaven and the earth? God has created these only for truth.' On the other hand He has praised those blessed with an interest in noble astronomy and said [Qur'ān 3.191/188]: 'Those who mention God when standing and sitting and on their sides and reflect on the creation of the heavens and the earth, etc.'

Music, as everyone knows, is a noble science. On it depends the reasoning conceiving the possible and impossible combinations of powers and quantities in the heavenly and earthly worlds and, indeed, in the spiritual and corporeal worlds. Without its active aid, astronomers would be unable to verify their claims regarding the conjunctions [?] and the mixture of the rays of the stars, nor could the prosodists establish the causes for the restriction of the metres to fifteen in five circles.[5] The Messenger of God has said: 'Adorn the Qur'ān with your voices.'[6]

Mechanics is a discipline that shares in both mathematics and natural science. It enables one to bring forth hidden water from the interior of the earth and also to conduct water through water-wheels or fountains, to transport heavy objects with the application of little energy, to construct arched bridges over chasms, to erect other wonderful bridges over deep streams and to accomplish many other things, whose mention here would take up too much room.

From this survey of the utility of the mathematical sciences one can gather that there is no contradiction at all between them and the religious sciences.

Natural science deals with sensually perceptible physical objects. All substances in this world can undoubtedly be divided into two parts. Firstly, there are those that were originally created through the perfection of divine omnipotence, for example, the heavenly spheres, the stars and the four elements and, secondly, those that have been brought into existence from them secondarily through divine subjugation.[7] The latter fall into three parts, namely (1) things that develop in the atmosphere as, for example, snow, rain, thunder, lightning, strokes of lightning and meteors, (2) things that develop in mines [in the interior of the earth] as, for example, gold, silver, iron, copper, quicksilver and lead, and (3) things that develop between the interior of the earth and the atmosphere, which are classified as plants and animate beings. From natural science some noble crafts have developed, such as, for example, medicine, the culinary art[8] and the use of dyes and varnishes.

Its abundant results and great utility are well attested. According to tradition, the great Imām ʿAlī b. Abī Ṭālib said: 'Science consists of two sciences, namely, the science of religions and the science of bodies.' And God has said [Qurʾān 2.164/159]:

> In the creation of the heavens and the earth and in the difference between night and day and in the ships that carry across the sea what is useful to man, and in the water which God sends down from heaven to revive the dead earth, and in all the animals which He has dispersed on earth and in the change of the winds and in the clouds, which are pressed into forced labour between heaven and earth, there are indeed signs for intelligent people.

From this survey of the utility of natural science one can gather that there is no contradiction at all between it and the religious sciences.

The purposes of metaphysics can only be grasped through the power of pure reason. This power is called *lubb* in Arabic, *lubb* meaning the 'quintessence' of each thing. Metaphysics is a science which is exclusively designed for the investigation of the first causes of the emergence of existing things in the world, and furthermore, for the awesome and incontestable knowledge about the nature of the One, the Unique, the Being, which is the aim of all endeavour. The gain of such a blessing is undoubtedly identical with the attainment of eternal bliss. It is difficult to reach unless we draw on all other objects of knowledge to assist us for this purpose, as we have mentioned in our book *al-ʿInāyah wa-d-dirāyah*. Only he who has gained this knowledge has been called a sage [philosopher] by the ancients. It is absurd to assume that there could be any contradiction between a science leading to such a result and the religious sciences.

Logic is despised by the *ḥadīth* scholars [*Ḥashwīyah*] and this has influenced the attitude of a group of religious philosophers [*Mutakallimūn*]. They have advanced two arguments. Firstly they say:

> As outstanding religious philosophers, we have studied the works on logic and found nothing but obscure words and strange phrases in them. Had the authors of those works been blessed with any ideas that correspond to the truth,

> they would surely have taken great pains to clarify them, and among the works on logic, there would surely be at least one whose study would spare us the search for someone able to explain to us the ideas contained in it.

This argument has no validity. That the mind of the religious philosophers did not suffice to understand the meaning of works on logic does not prove that these are useless, especially since someone who admits that his mind does not suffice to grasp all the ideas contained in logic proves thereby that his judgment as to whether [logic] corresponds to the truth or is contrary to it is definitely to be rejected and it is therefore necessary for him to examine once again what he has blamed or praised in order to understand the content of logic and adjudge its value.

The second argument of the religious philosophers is of the following kind:

> As the logicians claim unanimously, the greatest benefit to be derived from the acquisition of logic is that it teaches skill in the use of the rules of inference from the known to the unknown. The relationship of logic to the speculative sciences can be compared to that of prosody to the various kinds of poetry. Surely we do not doubt that man's natural talent is adequate for producing poems, and in that case one does not need prosody. Similarly, whoever is able to draw logical conclusions through his own insight can also manage without [the formal study of] logic. Every intelligent religious philosopher has, thanks to his own insight, understanding for [logical deductions]. Hence it appears quite self-evident that [the formal study of] logic would be a misfortune for him.

This argument, too, has no validity. Even if an intelligent man happens to be able to draw correct logical conclusions, he would only be able to prove to his opponent, who disputed their validity in his presence and claimed that another rule of logic contradicting the one applied by him was correct, that the disputed rule is correct if he can appeal to the consistent and reliable system [of logic]. The situation is about the same as one in which one disputes the metrical correctness of a verse and claims that it is a case of the irregularity[9] [permitted by prosodists] called *ziḥāf*. I mean, one can only decide the contradictory claims on the strength of prosody.

Hence, both arguments against the study of logic have proved worthless. We must thus describe the primary use of this craft, which we can do as follows: Logic is an intellectual instrument, which alone properly enables the rational soul to distinguish between truth and untruth in speculative problems and between good and evil in practical problems. One can roughly compare the use of this instrument with that of a gauge with which one measures objects of knowledge. Logic controls question and answer as well as contradiction, contrast and fallacy. It helps to resolve doubts, expose misleading statements and support other ideas which may serve to verify claims that have been raised. Besides, it also confers an intellectual pleasure, which provides a cheerful calm in matters of cognition to such an extent that the soul by itself becomes a propagandist for the acquisition of philosophy, not in order to earn the praise of friends thereby, but in order to be blessed with the realization of truth and the joy of certainty.

As we know, there is a group of pious men who consider every kind of literary culture reprehensible and claim that those who devote themselves to the acquisition of such a culture must be of two kinds, namely, those who wish to be praised for their fluency of tongue and fine mode of expression and those who wish to impress the great and noble men of this world with literary brilliance and thus eventually to attain benefit and rank. Both types are thereby cheated out of devoting themselves to the service of God or of pursuing the search for wisdom [philosophy]. The pious men who make such claims are making a great mistake. Here we are dealing with a craft that is concerned with a clear and eloquent mode of expression [*bayān*][10]—which is to cultivated souls what bridle and harness are to horses, since an eloquent man can change the souls of others from one condition to another through his eloquence, especially since words have exactly the same relationship to ideas as bodies to souls. The praiseworthy deeds of noble souls can only appear in bodies which are distinguished by an outstanding temperament. Similarly, true ideas can only attain their form through pleasant words. The Messenger of God has said [in a very frequently quoted *ḥadīth*]: 'Magic belongs to a clear and eloquent mode of expression.' And God has said [Qur'ān 55.3f./2f.]: 'He has created man and taught him a clear and eloquent mode of expression.' Hence extensive knowledge of the language is not so much the gift of being able to express oneself well, but to express oneself tersely, as is the case, for example, in poetry, sermons, letters and proverbs. In each of these four groups, one finds eloquent aphorisms and wonderful parables which are useful and serve to sharpen the mind. Hence, they have been immortalized in books only when it was possible to say, in view of their great capacity for survival, that they are living speech. If it is observed how they serve to settle quarrels in company and to remove animosity and antagonism, how they help to gain influence over kings and dignitaries and to adorn one's own observations with the account of their noble deeds and good remarks, it must surely be admitted that anyone who declares them false dares to despise something which is really very significant. Exalted spirits who master such subjects and hand them on to others are thus inspired to higher things. Anyone interested in listening to them is induced to secure some portion of them for himself, since it might provide a good subject for conversation one day.

The utility of the philosophical and metaphysical sciences is thus proved clearly enough. However, the primary purpose of our work is the appropriate demonstration of the religious sciences, and we have had to discuss in detail the points mentioned above only in order to show that the religious sciences are more useful than all the others. Therefore we must turn now to the religious sciences.

The scientific method of research

7. From the introduction of the Commentary on Aristotle's *Categories* by Abū l-Faraj ʿAbdallāh b. aṭ-Ṭayyib, according to the MS *ḥikmah* 1m of the Egyptian Library in Cairo.

The blessed Hippocrates held the view that the crafts arose and developed because an original creator transmits to a successor what he had created earlier. This successor examines it critically and adds to it as far as is possible for him. This process continues until the craft achieves perfection.

Hence, Aristotle, the physician, considered it better for original creators to live in warm countries, since they require a very acute mind. The perfecters should, on the contrary, rather live in cold countries, since they must be calm and steady.

In our studies we have followed in the footsteps of our predecessors and taken pains to understand their works well. We have also discovered, in connection with obscure statements and explanations of them, a number of ideas going beyond what they had said. Therefore, we would like to add our few statements to their numerous ones and gather all the material in one single commentary, which would save the user the great trouble of having to consult the earlier commentaries.

Since we love truth and prefer to use the method of the ancients, we must begin to do everything as they did. Before the study of Aristotle's *Categories* all commentators have occupied themselves regularly with the ten main principles which are of no little use to philosophy and necessarily belong to it. While philosophy itself is studied by them at the beginning of *Eisagoge*, they are here occupied with something that necessarily belongs to it. This is done in order to underline the great importance of philosophy, so that we should not regard the instrument [that is, the categories and the rest of logic] with whose help we study, as something irksome.

The ten main principles are the following:

(1) The number of philosophical schools and the etymology of the name of each school.

(2) The division and enumeration of Aristotle's works and the mention of their various purposes and the final aim that each of them serves.

(3) Discussion of the starting-point for the study of [Aristotelian] philosophy.

(4) Discussion of the method to be followed from beginning to end.

(5) Discussion of the final aim to which [Aristotelian] philosophy brings us.

(6) Discussion of the qualities of scholarship and character which a teacher of Aristotle's works should possess.

(7) Discussion of the qualities of receptivity and character which a student of Aristotle's works should possess.

(8) Discussion of the form of Aristotelian linguistic expression.
(9) Statement of the reason why he expressed himself obscurely in some of his arguments.
(10) The number of the principles which one must bear in mind before [the compilation of a commentary on] every book.

Before we consider each of these points more closely, we must explain why the number is ten, neither more nor less. It can be explained as follows: philosophy is a subject as well as something which has its special designation.[11] Whoever studies it does so either for its own sake or with a view to its designation. In the latter case, this leads to a discussion of the different schools. If, on the other hand, one studies philosophy for its own sake, one can do so either by comparing it with something else or by not comparing it with something else.[12] In the former case one is obliged to consider two main factors, the teacher and the pupil. This is necessary because philosophy is something to be perceived through the intellect, and one must either learn or teach the intelligibilia. If, on the other hand, one does not consider philosophy in comparison with something else, one can begin to study it either as a whole or in sections. In the former case, it is necessary to occupy oneself with the division of Aristotle's works, since a division is no more than making many out of a single item. If, on the other hand, one occupies oneself with philosophy in sections, one must consider six factors, namely (1) the point of departure of Aristotelian philosophy, (2) the method followed by Aristotle, (3) his final goal, (4) the study of his form of linguistic expression, (5) the study of the reason why he expressed himself obscurely in some of his arguments and (6) the study of the principles which one must bear in mind before [the compilation of a commentary on] every book. Hence there are ten principles, neither more nor less.

The Greek educational system

8. From the *Nawādir al-falāsifah* attributed to Ḥunain b. Isḥāq, according to the Munich MS Aumer 651, 8b–10a, 16b–17a; German translation, based on the medieval Hebrew translation, by A. Loewenthal (Berlin, 1896), pp. 61 f. and 68 f.

These philosophical gatherings originated from the fact that the rulers of the Greeks and of other nations used to teach their children philosophy and instruct them in various kinds of literary culture. They erected for them houses of gold, decorated with a variety of pictures, which were to serve to refresh hearts and attract eyes. The children stayed in these picture houses in order to be educated with the aid of the pictures found in them. For the refreshment of souls and the engagement of hearts the Jews, too, equipped their temples with sculptures, the Christians painted their churches and the Muslims decorated their mosques [with mosaics[13]].

When a princely pupil had completely mastered a science or acquired some wisdom or literary culture, he would, on the festival when the inhabitants of the kingdom gathered in such a house, ascend, after prayer and benediction, with a crown on his head and in jewelled robes, the steps to a seat fashioned of marble and decorated with pictures and sculptures, and discuss before witnesses the wisdom he had acquired, and recite the piece of literary culture he had made his own. His teacher was greatly honoured and given presents; the youth himself was also honoured and considered a sage because of his wit and intelligence. The temples, too, were honoured and provided with curtains. Wax candles were lit and fragrant incense was offered up. The people themselves were dressed up in many diverse ways. This is customary till today among the Ṣābians and Magians. Jews and Christians have altars [?][14] in their temples, and the Muslims have pulpits in their mosques.

[As an illustration there follows the legend of an alleged pupil of Plato, named Niṭāfūrus, a son of King Rūfisṭānus, who failed and in whose place Aristotle then passed the examination with distinction.]

The [above mentioned] kind of wise sayings together with the Greek script is the first thing that the philosopher teaches his pupil during the first year of instruction.[15] After that he lets him go on to grammar and poetry and then gradually to law, arithmetic, geometry, astronomy, medicine and music. After that he studies logic and finally philosophy, namely, the sciences of the heavenly phenomena.[16] These are ten sciences which the pupil learns in ten years.

IV

PHILOSOPHY

'*Falsafah* is a Greek word which means "love of wisdom". The original form of *failasūf* is *fīlāsūf*, which means "friend of wisdom". *Fīlā* means "friend" and *sūf* "wisdom".' This modest philological note still interested al-ʿĀmilī in the sixteenth century. He took it from the history of religions and philosophy of ash-Shahrastānī, who preceded him by five centuries (al-ʿĀmilī, *Kashkūl* [Cairo, 1380/1961], II, pp. 40, 360; ash-Shahrastānī, *Milal*, Cureton, p. 251). He could have found it another three centuries earlier in the Graeco-Arabic translation literature. In fact, in the Islamic Orient, as with us, philosophy is a discipline which is Greek both in name and content. Despite the intensive development which it underwent among the Islamic peoples in the course of time, a Westerner in search of 'Oriental' philosophies is unlikely to discover a specifically 'Islamic philosophy' at all comparable to Buddhist or Confucian philosophy as self-contained entities.

On the classical model, the expression *falsafah* usually refers to all the scholarly and scientific disciplines within the purview of Aristotelianism and thus to what Arabic literature, as we have seen, described as foreign or Greek sciences. In the present chapter we confine ourselves to philosophy in the narrower sense, that is, logic, ethics and metaphysics. Incidentally, it is noteworthy that among the Muslims logic is frequently not included under philosophy; instead they speak of logic *and* philosophy, assigning to logic the role of an 'instrument' (organon) for the attainment of philosophy. Further, metaphysics is sometimes viewed as being apart from and above philosophy, which is not surprising considering its intimate relationship to the dominant theological concerns of Islam. On the other hand, as in classical antiquity, economics and politics can scarcely be separated from ethics, since as a rule they continued to be treated in an ethical-pragmatic rather than in an empirical way. In a certain sense something similar also applied to natural science, which was essentially based not on an empirical but on a logical foundation; yet since it possesses a somewhat greater degree of independence, a special chapter (chap. V) has been devoted to it.

A. LOGIC

Of all the Greek sciences, logic was the one that always found defenders and courageous, though often not very numerous, representatives among the Muslims. The orthodox usually regarded it with particular suspicion, because they saw in it the root of all evil, the starting-point for every attack on the true religion and the dangerous weapon which could help the enemies of the faith win at least a temporary victory. It exercised a powerful appeal upon thinking minds, however, and it was obviously and undeniably useful for all kinds of scholarly research. It was not possible, nor was it considered desirable, to dispense with compiling and studying introductory works on logic. It was indeed the auxiliary science which enabled Muslim scholars to give all their intellectual activities the necessary theoretical foundations. It provided a generally valid method of research (cf. chap. III) and the only approach available in the Middle Ages to dealing with such basic problems of physics as, for example, the problem of the nature of time, space, vacuum and motion. More than that, it constituted the principal point of contact between the 'Greek' and the 'Arabic' sciences, as can be observed in connection with grammar and, at a later date, in connection with the science of the principles of jurisprudence (*uṣūl al-fiqh*).

Considering the importance of logic, the space devoted to it here is most inadequate. The few passages presented here may be supplemented slightly from the previous or the following chapter. Insufficient as it all is, it gives a certain impression of the nature of traditional logic. A history of logic illuminating its peculiar aspects and importance in Islam is another desideratum. A start at filling this gap has been made by N. Rescher's useful *Development of Arabic Logic* (Pittsburgh, 1964). We also have only a few scattered aids, none of them really exhaustive, for gaining an insight into the crucial subject of logical terminology, the most useful among them still being the *Lexique de la langue philosophique d'Ibn Sīnā* and the *Vocabulaires comparés d'Aristote et d'Ibn Sīnā* by A.-M. Goichon (Paris, 1938–9).

1. From the Arabic translation of *Analytica Priora* 24a–b, ed. 'Abd-ar-Raḥmān Badawī, *Manṭiq Arisṭū* (Cairo, 1948), I, pp. 103–8. Badawī's text which has been used here must be regarded as highly provisional (cf. R. Walzer, 'New Light on the Arabic Translations of Aristotle', in *Oriens*, VI [1953], pp. 120 ff., reprinted in R. Walzer, *Greek into Arabic* [Oxford, 1962], pp. 60 ff.). The translation attempts to render the Arabic text without excessive regard for any modern understanding of the meaning of the Greek text.

First we must mention the thing which we are here examining and the aim towards which we strive. The thing we are examining is demonstration, our aim demonstrative science. Afterwards we wish to explain what is a premise, a term, a syllogism, which syllogism is perfect and which imperfect and, then, what is predicated of the whole thing or not predicated of anything of it.

A premise is a positive or negative statement about one thing concerning another. It is either universal or particular or indefinite. By universal I mean that which can be stated about the whole thing or about one of its details. Particular is what can be stated about part of a thing or not about part of it, or not about the whole thing. Indefinite is what can or cannot be stated about a thing when the whole or part is not mentioned, for instance, the statement that 'knowledge of opposites is one and the same' and that 'pleasure is not good'.

The difference between the apodictic, that is, the demonstrative, premise and the dialectical, that is, the polemical, premise is that the demonstrative premise constitutes one of the two parts of a contradiction, since the demonstrator is not bent on polemics but strives for the establishment of truth, while the dialectical premise constitutes a question as to [the correctness of one of] the two parts of a contradiction. There is no difference between the demon-

بسم الله الرحمن الرحيم

PLATE III

The 'Blue Iris' and the 'White Iris'

PLATE IV

The Peloponnese and Crete in Idrīsī's world map

strative and the polemic premises in respect of the resulting of a syllogism in both cases, since the demonstrator as well as the questioner draws a [syllogistic] conclusion when he accepts something stated or not stated about a thing.

According to what we have said, the syllogistic premise is thus generally either a positive or negative statement of a thing about a thing. The demonstrative premise, which is true, is derived from first principles. The dialectical premise belongs either to the questioner, and then it is a question about [the correctness of one of] the two parts of a contradiction, or to the person who draws a [syllogistic] conclusion, and then it is the acceptance of a praised view, as has been explained in the Topics, the work about dialectics. In the discussion which we shall soon resume, we shall explain at length the premise and the difference between syllogistic, demonstrative and dialectical premises. What we have said is sufficient for our present purposes.

What we call a term is that into which the premise can be dissolved, like that which is stated and that of which it is stated, whether with the addition of 'it exists' or 'it does not exist', or without 'it exists' or 'it does not exist'.

The [syllogistic] conclusion is a statement from which, when more things than one are assumed in it, something else necessarily follows from the existence of those assumed things as such. I mean by 'as such' that they require no other thing for that which follows from the premises from which the [syllogistic] conclusion was drawn except those premises.

A perfect [syllogistic] conclusion is one which requires nothing further for the explanation of what follows of necessity from its premises. An imperfect [syllogistic] conclusion is one which requires for the explanation of what follows of necessity from its premises one or more things which follow of necessity from the premises from which it was drawn but which have not been used in the premise.

Something is said to be stated of the whole, if there is nothing in the whole assembly of given facts of which that statement cannot be made. The same applies to what is not stated of anything of it.

The use of logic

2. Ibn Sīnā, *ash-Shifā'* (*Manṭiq*, *Madkhal*), ed. I. Madkour, M. el-Khodeiri, G. Anawati and F. el-Ahwani (Cairo, 1371/1952), pp. 16–20.

Since the perfection of man as a human and rational being, as will be explained in the appropriate place, lies in his recognizing truth for its own sake and goodness in order to practise and utilize it, and since man's first and original nature can contribute little to that end on its own and most of what he attains of it depends on acquisition and since such acquisition is the acquisition of something unknown and the acquisition of the unknown comes about through something which is known, man must first begin to learn how he can acquire something unknown through something known, and in what condition the known things are, how they are arranged in themselves so that they can transmit knowledge of the unknown, that is to say, so that if they are properly arranged in the mind and their form is fixed in the mind in the proper arrangement, the mind can advance from them to the unknown which one seeks and know it.

One can know something in two kinds of ways. Firstly, one may simply perceive it[1] so that, if it has a designation and one pronounces it, its meaning appears to the mind, but without any relationship to truth or untruth. Thus one can say, for example, 'man' or 'do that'. If the meaning of the words in such an expression are familiar to a person, he has perceived it. Secondly, apperception may take place together with perception, so that, for example, the statement that 'everything white is an accident' arouses not only a perception of the meaning of these words but also apperception that it is so. If one doubts whether a statement is true or not, it is a matter of perception, since there can be no doubt concerning something that one has not perceived or understood. However, one has not yet apperceived it. Every apperception is linked with perception, but not vice versa. Such perception causes an understanding of the form and composition of a combination like the above-mentioned one of white and accident. Apperception, on the other hand, lies in understanding the relationship of such a form to the things themselves as congruous. Denial stands in contrast to this.

Not knowing also rests on both these processes, perception and apperception. Both require acquisition so that something can become known, and the acquisition takes place on the basis of something previously known and in a form and manner that accord with that known thing, whereby the mind can proceed from knowledge of such a known thing to knowledge of the unknown. Now there is something whose perception can cause knowledge of the unknown as well as something whose apperception can cause knowledge of the unknown. It is not customary to give a comprehensive name to the comprehensive idea whose knowledge causes the perception of something, or it is not known to us; to this belong, as will become apparent, definition, description, example, mark and designation, and there is no comprehensive general name for all together. On the other hand, we have the name 'reasoning' for that which is first properly known and then leads through apperception to the knowledge of something else. [Syllogistic] conclusion, induction, comparison and other things also belong to it.

The aim of logic is to acquaint the mind with a knowledge of these two things. Man should be able to recognize how a statement which produces perception must be constituted if it is to define the true nature of a thing, and how it must be constituted if it is to refer to it without transmitting recognition of the true nature of the thing, furthermore by what means it becomes incorrect and simulates a false effect and why that is so and what intermediate steps there are. Then he should also be able to recognize how a statement which produces apperception must be constituted if it is to produce an irrefutably certain apperception, and how it must be constituted if it is to produce an approximately certain apperception and how it must be constituted if it is to evoke the impression that it is one of these two, although this is not the case, but it is invalid and incorrect; furthermore, how it must be constituted if, without being decisive, it should appear probable, appealing or satisfactory, also how a statement must be constituted if it is to move the soul to progress or to hold back, to joy or to sadness, as apperception and denial do, without producing appreciation but merely simulating it—many such simulations act like genuine apperception; for example, if one says that honey is bitter and causes vomiting, one is naturally reluctant to eat it, even if one knows that such a statement is to be denied, just as one would be reluctant to eat it if that claim had really been confirmed through apperception or something fairly similar—what intermediary steps there are and why they are so. Whoever wishes to study perception and apperception in this sense needs premises which can help him to know both, and the craft in question is logic.

It may happen to someone that in his natural disposition there appear both definition producing perception and reasoning producing apperception. We are dealing here, however, with an unscientific process, and one cannot be certain that he will not make mistakes under different circumstances. For if man's natural disposition and talent in this respect could make scientific treatment superfluous, as is the case in many matters, one would not encounter those contradictions in scholarly views which do, in fact, exist, and individuals would not always contradict themselves when they rely on their natural talent. As in most other human actions, human nature does not suffice for this without the acquisition of a scientific system even though they may sometimes hit the target like a shot without a marksman. Of course, even the best knowledge of logic cannot save a person from occasional mistakes, not because logic itself is unreliable and does not protect from mistakes, but because he frequently forgets it and refrains from using it. In this respect, one can distinguish different cases. Firstly, the logician may not master his science completely. Secondly, he may master it completely but occasionally make no use of it and be satisfied with his natural talent. Thirdly, it may happen frequently that he is incapable of applying it or forgets it. In spite of all this, anybody who possesses knowledge and masters logic and applies it does not make as many mistakes as somebody who does not master logic. Furthermore, if he repeats one and the same action connected with logic many times, he can avoid any possible negligence, since the logician who blunders several times in succession is capable of correcting his manner of action, unless he is extremely stupid. Hence, frequent repetition guards him against negligence in important logical decisions, even though he may make mistakes in unimportant points. After all, human views cover extremely important and less important things. The logician's zeal can succeed in establishing with certainty the important things among them by examining his mode of action according to the rules of logic. Here reference to logic protects from mistakes, just as, for example, a person may add up the different parts of a calculation several times as a check so that he need have no doubt as to the result.

Man needs logic for his perfection, unless he possesses an inspired special quality which can spare him the acquisition of logic. Logic is to inward insight, which is called 'inward speech [*logos*]', what grammar is to verbal expression, which is called 'external speech', or what prosody is to poetry. Prosody, it is true, is of little help in writing poetry, and a healthy natural talent renders it superfluous, just as the natural literary talent of the Bedouins renders a knowledge of Arabic grammar superfluous for them. Logic, on the other hand, is not superfluous for people who must acquire knowledge of the sciences through study and reflection, except where we are dealing with an individual who possesses divine inspiration. Such a man is in comparison with all those who depend on reflection as is a Bedouin in comparison with those who are not Arabs by birth.

3. A *fatwā* of the fourteenth-century religious scholar Taqī-ad-dīn as-Subkī (*Fatāwī as-Subkī* [Cairo, 1355–6], II, pp. 644 f.). Cf. R. Brunschvig, 'Pour ou contre la logique grecque', in *Convegno Internazionale 9–15 Aprile 1969* (Rome, 1971, *Acc. Naz. Lincei, Fondazione A. Volta, Atti dei Convegni*, XIII), p. 185–209.

Question: If somebody wants to occupy himself with the Islamic sciences, would it be useful and rewarding for him to occupy himself with the study of logic, and is a person who disapproves of it a fool?

Answer: He must first occupy himself with the Qur'ān, the Prophetic traditions and jurisprudence until he is thoroughly familiar with them and has fully mastered the correct dogmas and is clearly convinced that Islamic religious law and the scholars proficient in it are to be revered and that philosophy and the scholars proficient in it are to be rated lower than the Islamic dogmas. If he is firmly grounded in that, and he knows that he possesses sound reason, so that no doubts of any kind can beset him with regard to proved arguments, and if he can find a religious, well-intentioned teacher firm in his beliefs—or, should his teacher not possess these qualities, at least he does not adhere to his statements on questions of faith—then he may occupy himself with logic and he will profit from it and find it useful in the study of the Islamic and other sciences. It is one of the best and most useful sciences for any kind of research. In itself logic has no value at all.

Anybody who claims that logic is unbelief or something prohibited is a fool ignorant of the actual meaning of unbelief and of what is allowed and forbidden. Logic is a purely intellectual science just like arithmetic, only the latter cannot lead to corruption, since it is used only in connection with the determination of the legal shares of inheritance, surveying or financial affairs, and the man who knows it feels no sort of contempt for others, nor is it an introduction to any other, possibly harmful, science. Logic, on the other hand, it is true, is not corrupt in itself, but the man who knows it is arrogant, considers other people contemptible and always believes that people who do not master logic deserve no attention whatever. In addition, logic opens to him the path to the study of all other philosophical sciences, both that of natural science, in which there is no error, and that of metaphysics, where most of the philosophers' claims are erroneous and contrary to Islam and the religious law of Islam. If anybody confines himself to it, without the safeguard of a previous correct foundation, one must fear that consciously or unconsciously he will succumb to heresy or to some philosophical doctrine.

So much can be said briefly and concisely about logic. It is like a sword which can be used either for the holy war or for highway robbery.

B. ETHICS

Ethics deals with the proper behaviour of the individual, the management of family and household (economy) and the administration of larger human associations (politics). *ʿIlm al-akhlāq*, 'the science of character qualities', is the commonly used term in Muslim civilization, at any rate for individual ethics (cf. R. Walzer and H. A. R. Gibb in the second edition of the *Encyclopaedia of Islam*, *s.v.* Akhlāq).

Economics deals with the character qualities which the various members of a household, father, mother, children and slaves, must possess in order to ensure harmonious living together; it includes also business ethics as dependent on the moral qualities of merchants and tradesmen. Politics may be treated with a view to its practical aspects, as in the *Secretum secretorum* ascribed to Aristotle, whose sources still remain obscure, or in the late Hellenistic exchange of ideas between Alexander and Aristotle. Here, stark realism hides behind an ethical enquiry. On the other hand, political theory developed as it was in Islam on a Platonic basis (cf. E. I. J. Rosenthal, *Political Thought in Medieval Islam* [Cambridge, 1958], pp. 113 ff.) is frankly ethical, transferring the classical doctrine of human virtues and vices, the intellectual hopes and aspirations of the individual, to the larger community. This doctrine could enter Islamic life without great difficulties, since its general human validity appeared obvious, even in such controversial matters as the relationship of the sexes or the relationship of the individual to authority, and conflicts with Muslim religious concepts were comparatively easy to avoid. Hence ideas from classical ethics could penetrate even the science of tradition and mysticism.

Greek aphoristic wisdom made another important contribution to Muslim ethics. It found its way into Arabic literature through the translation of anthologies of wise sayings of which there were many in late Hellenism, and of popular works like the Alexander legend, a very few of Plutarch's works, the sentences of Secundus, or the allegory of Cebes, and even of moral poems like the Pythagorean 'Chrysā Epē' ('Golden Words'), the *Monostichoi* (gnomic verses) of Pseudo-Menander, or the *Carmen Morale* of Gregory of Nazianzus. Pregnant aphorisms had been a highly esteemed form of literary expression in the ancient Orient since times immemorial. They were also known and widespread among pre-Islamic Arabs, as shown by the predilection of Arabic poetry for sententious formulation. Greek gnomic wisdom thus found the soil prepared for ready acceptance in the Islamic world. The wealth of ideas it contained was inexhaustible. Collections of Greek sayings were continually copied, and individual sayings were widely quoted, either literally or with a certain freedom. Arabic authors contended that Greek wisdom literature already influenced the Arabic poetry of the ʿAbbāsid period (cf. also chap. XII, no. 5). Where Greek origin is neither directly attested nor indirectly suggested by linguistic and stylistic criteria, the commonness of the ideas expressed in the sayings sometimes makes it difficult to prove. However, there is sufficient evidence for Greek influence upon Muslim literature through this channel.

Eudaimonia as the goal of ethics

1. Abū l-Ḥasan b. Abī Dharr, *Kitāb as-Sa'ādah wa-l-is'ād*, ed. M. Minovi (Wiesbaden, 1957–8), pp. 10 f. According to Minovi, Abū l-Ḥasan b. Abī Dharr is Abū l-Ḥasan al-'Āmirī. This is possible in view of the time of the composition and the contents of the work. The agreement in name is, however, limited to Abū l-Ḥasan. We might assume that al-'Āmirī wrote the work when he was still young, especially if al-Fārābī was still alive at the time of its composition (A. J. Arberry, 'An Arabic Treatise on Politics', in the *Islamic Quarterly*, II [1955], pp. 9–22). This could also explain why the Ibn Abī Dharr part of the name appears only here (and never later in connection with al-'Āmirī).

Aristotle says: Happiness is an activity of the soul through perfect virtue [*Nicomachean Ethics* 1102a 5–6, cf. also 1177a 12, 1099b 26). We exist through life and activity, and activity is more enduring than life.

My use of the word 'through virtue' means that activity takes place with a *logos*.

My use of the word 'perfect' means that all his activities are virtuous, not just at certain times and under certain circumstances, but during his whole life, at all times and under all circumstances.

An activity is virtuous only if its beginning and goal are right and if one proceeds from the beginning to the goal in the right manner.

The beginning is the free choice which causes movement, and the goal is that to which the movement leads, that for whose sake the activity takes place, that which moves to activity. Hence we say that the goal is really the beginning.

The beginning is right when the passive potentiality is available, and the goal is right when the formative figurations are right.

The procedure is right when patience and perseverance are applied to it in the way the *logos* demands.

The formations may be virtuous or base. They divide into those of the body and those of the soul.

The virtuous formations of the body are the corporeal goods, namely, health, strength and beauty.

The virtuous formations of the soul are the psychological goods. Some of them belong to the animal concupiscent soul, namely, moderation [*sōphrosynē*], courage and justice. Some belong to the rational soul which has the knowledge for action, namely, the intellective [*mutaʿaqqilah*] formation. . . . The animal soul can obtain the virtuous formations only through the rational soul if it obeys it and submits to its commands. [This quotation as found in the preserved manuscript appears to be incomplete.]

From Galen's Ethics

2. The first book of Galen's *Ethics*, which is preserved only in Arabic, according to the edition of P. Kraus, 'Kitāb al-Akhlāq li-Jālīnūs', in *Bulletin of the Faculty of Arts of the Egyptian University*, V (1939), pp. 25–34. Cf. R. Walzer, *Greek into Arabic* (Oxford, 1962), pp. 142 ff.; J. N. Mattock, in S. M. Stern, A. Hourani, and V. Brown, eds, *Islamic Philosophy . . . To Richard Walzer* (Oxford, 1972), pp. 235–60.

Character is a condition of the soul which induces man to carry out psychologically conditioned actions without reflection and free choice. This is shown by the fact that there are people who are greatly terrified if they unexpectedly hear a terrible noise, or those who laugh involuntarily when they see or hear something amusing. Sometimes they wish to avoid doing so but cannot. Therefore, philosophers have investigated whether character belongs exclusively to the irrational soul or whether it is partly linked to the rational soul.

We are convinced that the movement of the soul induced by the character, which takes place without reflection, whereby it feels a longing for or disgust with something or a liking or dislike and similar things shows that the character qualities belong to the irrational soul. Observations which we can make as to the character qualities of children and irrational beings point in the same direction. Thus we can observe that some animals, like hares and deer, for example, are cowardly, that others, for example, lions and dogs, are brave, and that others again, for example, foxes and monkeys, are cunning. Some, dogs, for instance, are trusting towards men, while others are wild and scared of them, for example, wolves. Some animals, lions, for example, like to live alone; others, like horses, love to join together in herds, while others again, storks, for example, like to live in pairs. Some animals gather food and store it, for example, bees and ants, while others such as pigeons seek their food from day to day. Some steal useless things, for example, magpies which steal and hide the stones of rings, signet rings and silver and gold coins. Hence the ancient philosophers said that irrational animals possess character qualities.

Aristotle and other scholars hold the view that character qualities are to some extent connected with the rational soul, but belong in the main to the irrational soul. Some later scholars have said that all character qualities belong to the rational soul and, not content with that, even included emotions of the soul, such as anger, desire, fear, love, pleasure and grief. This is obviously wrong.

I have clarified this in the work which I have compiled about the views of Hippocrates and Plato (ed. Kühn, V, p. 363). There I have proved that man possesses, firstly, something with which he can think, secondly, something else which rouses anger in him and, thirdly, something which rouses desire in him. In the present book I am not interested to know whether these three things are, as is claimed, different souls, parts of the human soul or three different powers of one and the same substance. Here I shall call that with which one thinks the rational and thinking soul, no matter whether it is a separate soul, a part [of one soul], or a power. That which rouses anger I call the irascible or animal soul and that which rouses desire, the concupiscent or vegetative soul.

Now let us consider every kind of character quality and of accidents and see to which of the three we should allocate them. However, let us first determine the general difference between action and accident and say: As long as the human soul remains in the condition in which it is, it is in a way quiet and inert. When its condition changes, it appears to us as if it moves. A movement can originate either from the moving object itself or it can be caused by something else. The first kind of movement we call action and the other accident. For example, if somebody moves an object from one place to another, then the movement of the hand is an action of the man and of the hand, while the movement of the object is an accident which happens to it. Thus it is with regard to local movement. As an example of [qualitative] change, we can take a person who walks in the sun and becomes tanned. The dark colouring is an accident of the body and the tanning an action of the sun.

Such is the meaning of accident, if one uses it in contrast to action. Accident has a different meaning if one uses it in contrast to the natural. The natural is like the health of something, and the unnatural like its illness and symptoms. One and the same thing can be natural for something and unnatural for something else.

Excessive movements of the two animal souls of man are not natural for him, simply because they are excessive. All excess is incompatible with good health. Furthermore, the movements of those two souls harm the powers of the rational soul. The concupiscent soul differs from the rational. The Creator has only given it to man because it is necessary for life and procreation. Anyone who no longer feels any desire at all would rather die than take nourishment. Similarly, if no pleasure were connected with copulation, nobody would practise it. The sexual impulse is a tyrant which does not permit the rational soul to attain understanding and clarification of anything. When pleasure exceeds the proper measure, it is harmful. It is one of the rational soul's activities to regulate its measure and the times appropriate to it. In general, the rational soul can function alone, without any kind of aid, if dealing, for example, with the recognition of truth or agreement and difference between things. However, it can only restrain the concupiscent soul from excessive movement with the aid of the irascible soul. Man can only restrain his concupiscent soul from untimely and excessive movement if his irascible animal soul is powerful and strong.

In my opinion, natural warmth is the substance underlying the power that lends patience and stability to human actions. The stronger the movement of a man's natural warmth, the more he can move, and just as cold produces laziness, inertia and weakness, thus warmth produces energy, movement and the power to act. Hence youth and wine stimulate movement and aggressiveness, while old age and cold medicines produce laziness and weakness and, in the course of time, finally cause all activity and movement to stop.

The irascible soul is to the rational soul as the dog to the huntsman or the horse to the rider. Though they help him to do what he wants, they sometimes move at the wrong time and to the wrong extent. Sometimes they even harm him. The dog may injure him [hamstring the horse ?]. The horse may run away with him, and together they fall into a deep hollow and perish there. His activity is to determine the right time and the right measure for their movements, and virtue consists, for them, in allowing themselves to be guided by his will and, for him, in his skill in hunting and riding. How easy it is to guide them and how useful they are depends on the length of their training by him. Neither every dog nor every horse is equally easy to train. There are headstrong and obstinate ones whose training requires much time and a long period of practice, and the huntsman and the horseman are also themselves inexperienced at times.

The rational soul must, therefore, necessarily love beauty, yearn for truth and know the agreements and differences of things. The irascible soul must let itself be guided easily and the concupiscent soul must be weak. Everything which performs its movements and does its own actions is strong. If it refrains from them, it is weak. Whoever has been used to moderation from youth has moderate desires, while a person who has not always curbed or suppressed his desires from youth is greedy. Education slows down the irascible soul and weakens the concupiscent soul. The power of the irascible soul cannot be broken through education, but it is slowed down and made amenable to guidance by it. In my opinion anyone who is by nature very cowardly and greedy cannot be made really brave and moderate through education.

We call the praiseworthy states of the human soul 'virtues' and the reprehensible ones 'vices'. These states of the soul fall into two parts, namely, (1) what develops in the soul after reflection and contemplation and with the aid of the power of discernment, and that is called 'knowledge', 'assumption' or 'opinion', and (2) what happens to the soul without reflection, and that is called 'character qualities'.

Some character qualities are already noticeable among children from birth, before they can think, namely, [the feeling for] pain in the body and anxiety in the soul. That is why they cry, for every child possesses within its power of imagination the capacity to perceive what agrees with him and what disagrees with him, just as he possesses an [innate] liking for what agrees with him and an aversion for what disagrees with him. Hence, he strives for all that agrees with him and avoids what disagrees with him. Similar qualities can be found by nature in all irrational beings, which means that they feel what affects their bodies and imagine that it partly agrees and partly disagrees with them, and they have a longing for that which agrees with them and avoid what does not agree with them. There are children who, when they have reached the second year of life, attack, with their hands and feet, those whom they suspect of having harmed them. This shows that in addition to the capacity of realizing what does and what does not agree with them, they now also possess the capacity to realize the causes effecting this. In addition, they now possess the desire to revenge themselves on those who have harmed them, and they feel love for those who remove that which harms them. For now they have a happy smile for their nurses and wish to hit and bite those who injure them. This accident is called 'anger'. It makes the eyes fiery red, and the whole face appears red and hot and full. Hence the desire to want revenge on that which harms one, as well as to avoid what causes pain and to pursue what causes pleasure, is natural to man and need not be learned. The conduct of children mentioned above did not rest on thought and on the the insight gained from it to the effect that it was right to wish to take revenge on that which harms, but they acted naturally, just as people naturally pursue what causes pleasure and avoid what is harmful.

When children reach the third year of life, expressions of shame or shamelessness can be perceived in them. One notices that some children who have done something forbidden to them are ashamed and avoid looking at the person who reproves them for it, or that they rejoice in praise. On the other hand, the exact opposite applies to other children. This appears in children who have not yet been intimidated by blows and threats. If they are ambitious and expect to receive praise, they can take a lot of trouble. A child ambitious by nature, not from fear of a sensual object or desire for it, will succeed. Otherwise, he will not succeed. He will learn nothing, and he will not accept character training or book learning.

The unthinking and unintentional inclination of children towards virtue or vice is further demonstrated by the observation that if a child is harmed by his playmates, some of them have pity for him and come to his aid, while others laugh at him and sometimes collaborate in harming him. Some children can be observed to help others out of difficulties, while there are some who bring others into mortal danger, scratch their eyes out and strangle them. Some of them do not wish to give away anything they own. Some are envious while others are not. All this is already apparent before education starts. Generally speaking, no action, accident or character quality can be found in adults which cannot already be observed in them when they are children. The claim that all accidents occur through insight and thinking is thus incorrect; for everything that develops from insight and thinking is definitely not an accident but a correct or false assumption or knowledge. An accident, on the other hand, is an unthinking, unconsidered and unintentional animal movement.

Strictly speaking, discussion of these things is out of place here. The only reason why, in my investigation of the subject of the present book, I have started with observations that can be made on children is the desire to facilitate differentiation between pure animal movements and all that contains an admixture of assumptions and opinions derived from the rational soul. This is extremely useful for the person who wishes to acquire praiseworthy character qualities and to get rid of reprehensible ones. For there are people who, without reflection, live with whatever naturally agrees with them and refrain from what disagrees with them. There are others who after pondering and reflecting about the nature of things have attained the insight that it is fitting to pursue what naturally agrees with them and to refrain from what disagrees with them, or vice versa. From that moment onwards, and for the rest of their lives, all these people have allowed their way of life and their actions to be determined by their natural inclination and acquired insight. Somebody who assumes that the enjoyment of food and drink and all sensual experience is a good feels a many times greater natural inclination to pleasure in his concupiscent soul. Anyone who assumes that [political] leadership is a good feels a many times greater natural inclination to tyranny and dominance over others in his irascible soul. Such a growth of the natural inclination leads from humanity to bestiality. Those, on the other hand, who realize that knowledge of the nature of every thing in the world is a good strengthen thereby the inclination of their rational soul to demonstrative knowledge and the truth. This results in their renouncing ambition, desires, leadership and political power and abandoning the pleasures of copulation, eating, drinking, property and all other things enjoyed by those mentioned earlier.

It is necessary to study the actions and motives of men who have passed the age of childhood. It will be found that they are partly due to character and partly to insight [*doxa*]. Natural and habitual actions rest on character; actions which come about through thought and reflection rest on insight. By exposing and explaining the erroneousness of bad insights one can remove them from the soul, but when it is a matter of natural or habitual actions, such a procedure may damage them but never remove them completely. A character is developed through being constantly accustomed to things that man sets up in his soul and to things that he does regularly every day, as I shall describe later. Yet, as regards the possibility of improving [bad] character qualities, the child is to the old man like a tree in its first growth to the same tree when fully grown. The young tree bends easily in every possible direction, whereas it is difficult, and sometimes quite impossible, to transplant a fully grown tree. Hence we can notice that in old age men are in the same condition as in their young manhood, sometimes even more pronouncedly so.

It is necessary to determine the external signs of the character qualities. I begin with men whose character is marked by rage and anger. Anger and rage have been said to differ in degrees of intensity. It has also been said that a man's 'rage' is directed against friends who make a mistake or are negligent, while his 'anger' extends to other people. Accordingly, 'anger' against friends is not pure anger, since it is inevitably distressing to hurt somebody one likes, and anger is, therefore, mingled with distress in this case.

He who thinks when he is angry appears dignified; he who does not think when he is angry appears foolhardy. An angry person has the special characteristic of shouting and making threats. A brave man does not do that; for his reason does not desert him in a similar situation. Hence, he is not foolhardy and does not proceed unarmed like a wild beast against an armed enemy, but he does what is required. If he intends to fight, he makes use of the art of war and the weapons of war. If he takes part in a wrestling bout, he makes use of the art of wrestling. The same applies to all the other arts for which one requires strength and aggressiveness. The man who thinks and assesses his position when he is angry will always apply the art suited to his purpose. Should he, however, be overcome by anger to such an extent that he can no longer think, then he would not be able to apply correctly the art he requires in order to be able to resist what angers him. Intense anger is not far removed from madness. How, then, could it be an accident of the rational soul? Under the influence of such accidents, especially when they are strong, one ceases to think.

The brave man and the foolhardy man, either of whom may be greatly moved by anger, differ in that the anger which animates the foolhardy is immoderate and uncontrolled by thought, while the anger of the brave is moderate and controlled by thought. Bravery is accompanied by seriousness and shame, and foolhardiness by levity and shamelessness. A foolhardy man who goes to war either does not do so in a good cause or, in the event of his doing so, his good intentions will be frustrated as soon as he gives free rein to his foolhardiness. Therefore, such people lose their shame, and under the influence of foolhardiness do not even listen to their superior or understand what he says or obey him.

Bravery springs from the rational soul's pursuit of beauty and from the irascible soul's obedience to the rational, provided it is by nature in the right condition for resistance to frightening things. Foolhardiness occurs in wartime when the rational soul does not pursue beauty and the irascible soul is conditioned in such a way as to remain untouched by things which frighten other people. One can pursue beauty thoughtlessly and haphazardly in two ways. Firstly, on the basis of correct assumptions and, secondly, on the basis of false assumptions. With thinking one can pursue beauty in three ways, firstly, on the basis of correct assumptions, secondly, on the basis of false assumptions and, thirdly, on the basis of knowledge. Hence, audacity appears as a character quality in six [!] forms which share a natural condition of the irascible soul—namely, the one which makes a man bold. The rational soul causes the differentiation. He who is bold without knowledge and design is not called brave. If anybody haphazardly undertakes something dangerous which he imagines to be beautiful, he is said to possess fanaticism [*muḥāmāh*].

If somebody is no longer ignorant of the [nature of a] thing which he assumes to be evil, then he is no longer afraid of it. This happens in the case of people who deal with harmless snakes, or irrational animals which fear other animals when they see them for the first time, for example, when horses see camels or elephants; only when experience teaches them that they do them no harm are they no longer afraid of them. It does not require audacity to proceed against things which do not arouse fear in the person who sees them; one can only speak of bravery when a person fears what he attacks because he imagines that this is more beautiful. It is natural to detest and avoid two kinds of things, namely, what one considers evil and what one considers ugly. Bravery in resistance of ugliness is more significant than bravery in resistance of evil. The opposite applies to cowardice. An example of bravery in resistance of ugliness is the man who in battle prefers death to flight, or one who prefers to be tortured rather than give false testimony against his friend. Even slaves have behaved in this manner towards their masters though they had not been trained [for it].[2] This proves that the love of beauty exists naturally in some people and that the love of beautiful deeds in those who love beauty belongs to the love of God in those who prefer that [love]. It invalidates the claim of those who say that beauty is no more than a conventional term coined by man.

Beautiful actions are said to be partly that which serves the achievement of a desired goal that is a good. Thus people who desire pleasure and prosperity, for example, always prefer what leads to those, even if it should be harmful. He who is of the opinion that good is virtue and virtuous actions, and evil the opposite, and hence is not of the opinion that death and pain are evil must avoid greed, foolhardiness, injustice and cowardice, and cling to moderation, bravery, justice and sense. Whoever is afraid of cowardice must then be called courageous. That is idle talk.

The nature of ugliness differs from that of evil both in imagination and in fact. Similarly, the nature of beauty differs from that of good. Just as symmetry of limbs produces beauty of the body, symmetry of [the parts of] the soul produces in man beauty of the soul. One can speak of symmetry of [the parts of] the soul and of bodies in two ways. Firstly, it can be a condition of both, without their also practising the activity of that condition. Secondly, it can lie in the actions produced when they act. Beauty and ugliness in the soul correspond to beauty and ugliness in the body. In the soul good and evil take the place which health and sickness take in the body. Just as we detest ugliness in the body, we also detest it in the soul. Ugliness of the soul [as a whole] consists of injustice since injustice is the ugliness of all three [parts of] the soul. On the other hand, ugliness of the single parts of the soul lies in the corruption not of justice but of one of the other virtues.

He who chooses pleasure and not beauty as his goal prefers to be a pig instead of an angel. For the angels consume no food and do not procreate, since their substance remains unchanged. On the other hand, because the bodies of living beings change and decay, the Creator has given them for their preservation the desire for food and procreation, and with the desire He has mingled pleasure in order to spur them on to pursue those needs. Whoever, in accord with his nature and by his actions, makes this pleasure his goal behaves like a pig, and whoever by nature has a love of beauty and beautiful deeds follows the example of the angels. Hence he deserves to be called 'divine', while those who surrender themselves to pleasures must be called 'beast'. Goodness and beauty are desirable things, and evil and ugliness are things to be avoided. Therefore, an action that is good and beautiful must be chosen by all men. This is generally agreed.

The pairing of these four can occur in different ways, hence men differ in this respect. Some prefer what they consider beautiful to what they consider good. These are brave men; those who do the opposite are cowards. Man must accustom his rational soul to love beauty and make his irascible soul subservient to it. If it is bold by nature and education, he must teach it tractability, and if it has no boldness, it then becomes better than it was. It cannot, however, attain the condition of bravery, since unlike the strong, the weak cannot acquire power through exercise. Bodies with a tendency to sickness cannot become healthy and strong through treatment and exercise. The same is the case with the soul.

Excerpts from a general survey of ethics

3. From Miskawaih, *Tahdhīb al-akhlāq* (Cairo, 1322), pp. 3_{4-16}, 6_{25}–7_{6}, 26_{6-10}, 29_{10}–30_{29}, 42_{13}–43_{1}, 44_{32-36}, 47_{28-32}, 70_{32}–71_{10}; ed. C. K. Zurayk (Beirut, 1966–7), pp. 4_{10}–5_{9}, 15_{10}–16_{19}, 76_{17}–77_{2}, 86_{8}–91_{6},

127_{14}–129_{12}, 135_{9}–136_{2}, 144_{14-20}, 217_{10}–218_{12}. Cf. Zurayk's English trans. (Beirut, 1968), pp. 6, 14–16, 70, 77–81, 113 f., 123, 130 f., 192 f., and M. Arkoun's French trans. (Damascus, 1969), pp. 8 f., 23–5, 125, 138–44, 198–201, 211 f., 223, 323 f. See also R. Walzer, *Greek into Arabic* (Oxford, 1962), pp. 220 ff.

Character formation. Each body has a form. It can accept another form of the same kind as the first form only after having abandoned completely the first form. For example, if a body has accepted a triangular form or shape, it must first abandon the triangular shape before it can accept a quadrilateral or circular shape. The same applies to any kind of form, impressions [of signet rings], writing, etc., which a body can accept. A body can accept a different form of the same kind only after the first form has completely and utterly disappeared. Even if only some of the outlines of the first form remain, it cannot accept the second form completely. Rather do the two forms mingle, and the body does not have either of them completely. If, for instance, wax has accepted the impression of a signet ring, it can accept another impression only after the outlines of the first impression have disappeared. The same applies to silver when it has accepted the form of a signet ring. This is a perpetually valid law for all bodies.

But now we are able to observe how our souls are able to accept completely and perfectly the forms of the various sensually and intellectually perceptible things without abandoning the first form, without any exchange and without the disappearance of any [earlier] outline. On the contrary, the first outlines can be preserved completely and perfectly and the second can also be accepted completely and perfectly. The souls can continue to accept one form after another, without becoming at any time too weak or unable to accept any new form that comes to them. On the contrary, the appearance of further forms is strengthened by the first form. This particular quality of the soul is contrary to those of the body and enables man to become ever more intelligent the more he practises the sciences and literature. Hence the soul is not a body.

The three powers of the soul. Thus the student of the soul and its powers knows that there are three parts, namely, (1) the power which produces thinking, discernment and insight into the true nature of things, (2) the power which produces anger, bravery, the readiness to face dangers and the longing for [political] power, high rank and all kinds of honours, and (3) the power which produces desire, the craving for nourishment and the longing for the pleasures of eating, drinking, copulation and all other sensual pleasures.

These three differ from one another. This is known from the fact that the stronger power can harm the others, or that one of them can sometimes invalidate the activity of another. One regards the powers either as [independent] souls or as powers of a single soul. This is not the place for discussion of this problem. For the study of the character qualities it is enough to know that there are three different powers of which each may be stronger or weaker, according to temperament, habit or education.

The rational power is also called the angelic one. Its organ in the body is the brain.

The concupiscent power is also called the animal one. Its organ in the body is the liver.

The irascible power is also called the bestial one. Its organ in the body is the heart.

The number of the virtues and their opposite vices must therefore correspond to the number of these powers. A temperate and appropriate movement of the rational soul linked with yearning for the true sciences, not the alleged ones which are in reality stupidities, produces the virtue of knowledge from which wisdom derives. A temperate movement of the animal soul under the guidance of the rational soul, whereby the animal soul neither haughtily rejects the instructions of the rational soul nor greedily insists on following its own impulses, produces the virtue of moderation [*sōphrosynē*] from which the virtue of generosity derives. And should the irascible soul be temperate and willingly implement the instructions of the rational soul and neither get excited at the wrong time nor more heated than necessary, this produces the virtue of gentility, from which the virtue of courage derives. A balanced combination of these three virtues produces yet another virtue, which represents their perfection, namely, the virtue of justice. Hence philosophers unanimously agree that there are four virtues: wisdom, moderation, courage and justice.

Human goods. According to Porphyry and other scholars, Aristotle divided the good as follows: Goods are either noble, praiseworthy, potential or useful.[3] Noble goods are those that are noble in themselves and ennoble those who acquire them, namely, wisdom and reason. Praiseworthy goods are, for example, the virtues and beautiful voluntary actions. Potential goods are, for example, readiness to absorb the goods mentioned above. Useful goods are all those which one seeks not for their own sake but in order to attain [true] goods through them.

The degrees of the virtues.[4] Here I quote the words of the philosopher [Aristotle] from his work entitled *The Virtues of the Soul*, which have been literally translated into Arabic: The first degree of virtue which is called 'bliss' consists in man directing his will and his efforts to his welfare in the sensual world, the matters of the soul and the body that can be perceived by the senses and the psychological matters linked with or shared by both of them. His occupation with sensually perceptible conditions, however, must not exceed the proper moderation with respect to his conditions of sense perception. This is a condition in which man is confused by impulses and desires, but in a moderate and not an excessive manner, since he is closer to what is necessary than what is not necessary, for he endeavours to maintain the correct, moderate conduct concerning every virtue and not to exceed the measure determined by thinking even when it affects the sensually perceptible matters with which he is occupied.

The second degree is one where man directs his will and his efforts to the supreme welfare of the soul and the body, without allowing himself to be disturbed by any impulses and desires and without concerning himself more than necessary with sensually perceptible habits. He then has progressively more intensive degrees in this kind of virtue, since their places and degrees are numerous, one on top of the other. The reason for it is, firstly, the variety of human nature. Secondly, it depends on customs. Thirdly, it depends on the stations and positions that men occupy with regard to virtue, knowledge and understanding. Fourthly, it depends on their ambitions; fifthly, on their wishes and efforts, and also, furthermore, as they say, on luck.

From the end of this degree, that means from this kind of virtue, one passes on to the pure, divine virtue, where there is no longing for the future, no looking back to the past and no farewell to what is immanent, no glance at what is distant and no parsimony with what is near, no anxiety or fear of anything, no passion for any condition, no search for a share of human or psychological happiness or bodily needs or physical or psychological power. Rather, the intellectual part is active at the highest degrees of the virtues; this means that one looks for and occupies oneself seriously with divine matters, without looking for a reward, that is to say that the active and serious occupation with them is undertaken for their own sake. This degree, too, has always more intensive degrees for man according to his ambitions, his wishes, the amount of his serious endeavours, his natural strength, the extent of his reliability and his station within the conditions of virtue which we have enumerated. Finally, he becomes similar to the First Cause and emulates it and its actions.

The ultimate degree of virtue is the one where all man's actions are divine. Such actions are pure good. One does not undertake an activity which is pure good for anything else, but only for its own sake; for pure good is a goal for which one strives for its own sake, which means that it is something which one seeks for its own sake; and something which is a goal and above all a goal of supreme value cannot exist for the sake of something else.

When all man's actions become divine, all of them originate in his essence and his true being, namely, his divine intellect which is his true being. All other motivating instincts of his physical nature and other accidents of the two animal souls as well as the accidents of his imagination, whose origin lies in the two animal souls and the motivating instincts of his sensual soul, cease, disappear and die out. Then there remains for him neither will nor ambition apart from his activity for whose sake he does whatever he does. Rather does he do whatever he does without wanting or pursuing anything other than the activity itself; this means that he pursues no other purpose in his activity than the activity itself, and that is the way of the divine activity.

This condition is the ultimate degree of the virtues. In it man adopts the actions of the First Principle, the Creator of the Universe; this means he seeks no share, no payment, no recompense, no advantage in all he does. Rather, his activity itself is his purpose; this means he acts only for the sake of the being of the activity and not for his own being, that is, whatever he does, he does not do for the sake of anything except his activity itself and his being itself. 'His being itself' is identical with divine activity itself. The

Creator thus acts for the sake of His own being, not for the sake of anything else outside Him. For in this condition man's activity is pure good and pure wisdom, as we have stated. Hence he undertakes activity only in order to effect it and pursues no other goal thereby. Such is also the case with the special activity of God. God is not primarily active because of something else outside His being; this means that He is not active in order to direct the things of which we form part. Otherwise, His actions in the past, present and future would take place with regard to outside matters and for the purpose of their administration and the administration of their conditions and His concern with them. Consequently, outside matters would cause His actions. That is a shameful, ugly assumption, above which God is far exalted. God's concern for outside matters and His activity in administrating and supporting them are secondary. Whatever He does, He does not do for the sake of the things themselves but, again, for the sake of His being. He does it since His being in itself is better, not because of something less good or anything else.

Thus it is with man when he has reached the ultimate capability of imitating the Creator. Then he is primarily active because of his own being, which is identical with the divine intellect, and because of the activity itself. If he does anything through which he helps and is useful to someone else, it is undertaken by him secondarily and not primarily because of this other person. He is primarily active because of his own being and because of the activity itself, that means that he is active for the sake of virtue in itself and good in itself, since his activity is virtue and good. He is active not in order to derive any benefit or to avoid damage, not in order to boast and gain [political] power or to serve his ambition, but he is active for the sake of the activity itself.

This is the aim of philosophy and supreme bliss. Yet man can achieve this condition only when his will, which depends on outside matters, together with all accidents of the soul is annihilated, when his thoughts which originate from the accidents perish and when he is filled with divine consciousness[5] and divine ambition. He can only be filled by these, however, when he has wholly and completely liberated and cleansed himself from nature. Then he is filled with divine gnosis and divine longing, and acquires through what is established in his soul, that is, his being which is identical with the intellect, certainty of the divine matters, just as he also possesses the primary premises, which are called the first intellectual sciences. Yet the way in which the intellect perceives, grasps and achieves certainty of the divine matters in this state is more noble, subtle, evident and clear than in the case of perception by means of the primary premises, which are called the first intellectual sciences.

These are the words of this philosopher, which I have quoted here in the translation of Abū ʿUthmān ad-Dimashqī. Abū ʿUthmān is able to express himself well in both languages, Greek as well as Arabic, and his translations find approval by all who read these two languages. In them he proceeds to render Greek words and their meanings into Arabic very carefully. Words and meaning agree perfectly. Whoever wishes to refer to this book, *The Virtues of the Soul*, can study the words of the philosopher, just as I have quoted them.

Justice and free will. The philosophers have here posed a difficult problem, and answered convincingly, although it can perhaps be answered more convincingly in a different manner. We should like to present it in its entirety.

A sceptic could say that if justice is a voluntary action which the just man undertakes and through which he intends to acquire virtue and praise from his fellow men, then injustice, too, must be a voluntary action which the unjust man undertakes and through which he intends to acquire for himself viciousness and blame from his fellow men. It is ugly and shameful, however, to assume that a reasonable human being should intend to harm himself deliberately and voluntarily.

The reply of the philosophers for solving this problem is as follows: One who undertakes an action which incurs damage and punishment for him wrongs and harms himself, while supposing that he benefits himself. He behaves like that because he neglects to consult the intellect and makes a bad choice. An envious man, for example, sometimes harms himself, not because he prefers to harm himself, but because he assumes that in this world he benefits himself by liberating himself from the damage which his envy causes him. Such is the reply of the scholars.

The other reply is the following: Since man has many powers, which together make him a unique human being, one cannot deny that different actions corresponding to these powers can originate from him. But it is indeed a shameful and despicable assumption, which must be denied, that a single, simple thing having a single power could produce different actions by means of that power, not by means of the diversity of organs or capacities but just through that single power. It is, however, quite clear that man has many powers. Therefore he can, with each one of those powers, undertake an action opposed to the action of another power. This means when a hot-tempered man flies into a violent rage, he performs voluntarily actions which he would not perform when he is calm. The same applies to [sexually] excited people and emotional drunkards. In such instances people are in the habit of regarding the noble intellect as a mere servant and not consulting it. When the situation changes, anger is calmed and drunkenness has given way to sobriety [one can observe how] a reasonable man is surprised at himself, feels repentant and says: 'How could I ever have voluntarily performed such ugly actions!' The power which stirred in him incited him to perform an action which appeared good and beautiful to him in that situation, in order that the movement of that power could have its full effect. Then, when he calms down and consults his intellect, he realizes how ugly and pernicious that action was.

Man's powers which arouse various desires in him and cause him to seek honours even when he does not deserve them are very numerous, and his actions are correspondingly numerous. Yet when he accustoms himself to lead a virtuous life and to act only after he has paid heed to the unequivocal intellect and observed the firmly established religious law, then all his actions are orderly, not full of contradictions or standing outside the rules of justice, that is, equity, which we have previously discussed. For this reason we have stated that he is indeed happy who in his youth was privileged to familiarize himself with the religious law, to subordinate himself to it and to accustom himself to all its commands and who, when he has gone far enough to be able to understand causes and reasons, then studies philosophy. He will find it to be in agreement with the principles to which he has become accustomed earlier, and thus he will be confirmed in his views and strengthened in his insight and successful in all his plans.

Kinds of love and friendship. There are different kinds of love [or friendship] and just as many causes of it. One kind grows quickly and dissolves quickly. A second grows quickly and dissolves slowly. A third grows slowly and dissolves quickly. A fourth grows slowly and dissolves slowly. There are only these four kinds of love and no more, because men in their striving and conduct of life seek three things and a fourth composed of these three, namely, pleasure, the good, the useful and what is composed of these three.

The nature of friendship and love. The love [or friendship] which good people feel for one another is not caused by external pleasure or utility, but rather by the substantial harmony existing between two good people through their common striving after good and virtue. When they love each other on the basis of such a harmony, there can be no contradiction and quarrel between them. They admonish each other for the good and cultivate together justice and equality in the desire for the good. It is such equality in their mutual admonition for the good and in their desire for the good that makes them from more than one into one. Hence one defines a friend as 'another identical with you, yet different from you as an individual'.

The nature of sadness. Sadness is a pain of the soul caused by the loss of something loved or by missing something sought.[6] It is caused by the craving for material possessions and the quest for physical enjoyment and regret for what one has lost or missed of it. Sadness and grief because he loses loved things and misses things sought are only experienced by the person who assumes that the desirable things of this world which he acquires will last and always be with him and that all the missing things which he seeks must inevitably reach him and become his property. If he is honest with himself and realizes that nothing lasts permanently in this world of generation and decay, as this is possible only in the world of the intellect, then he will not desire and seek the impossible. If he does not desire that, he will not feel sad when he loses something he loves very much, or when he misses something he desires in this world. He will direct his efforts to pure objects and in all his ambition confine himself to the quest for desirable things that are lasting. He will turn away from what cannot because of its nature last permanently. When he acquires such transient things, he will put them into their proper place. He will only use them as much as he requires in order to avoid the pains caused by hunger, nakedness and similar necessities. He will abstain from all kinds of hoarding and accumulating, of ostentation and seeking glory, and not imagine that he would gladly wish for more of it. When he no longer owns such worldly possessions, this does not grieve him and he does not care about it. Whoever acts in this way will be secure and never feel grief. He will rejoice and never be sad. He will be happy and never unhappy. Whoever, on the other hand, does not take this warning to heart nor acts accordingly will constantly be grieved and incessantly sad; for there is always the loss of something loved and missing something sought. That is how things are in the world of generation and decay in which we live. He who wishes that what becomes and decays should not become and decay wishes for the impossible, and he who wishes for the impossible will never be successful and he who is not successful is always sad and he who is sad is unhappy.

The nature of pleasure

4. Excerpts in Persian from ar-Rāzī's treatise on pleasure, ed. and trans. into Arabic by P. Kraus, *Abi Bakr Mohammadi filii Zachariae Raghensis* (*Razis*) *Opera philosophica* (Cairo, 1939), I, pp. 148–55.

Pleasure is nothing more than a respite from pain, and pleasure exists only in the wake of pain. . . .

When pleasure lasts, it becomes pain. . . .

A condition that is neither pleasure nor pain is something natural, but not sensually perceptible. . . .

Pleasure is a liberating perception of the senses, and pain a painful one. Sensual perception is the influence of something sensually perceptible upon one who possesses sensual perception. Influence is an activity of what exerts influence within what bears influence, and bearing influence is a change in the condition of what bears influence. A condition is either natural or outside nature. . . .

When what exerts influence removes what bears influence from its natural condition, pain results, and when it restores what bears influence to its natural condition, pleasure results. . . .

What bears influence feels the influence at both extremes, until it returns again to its natural condition. In the intermediate condition it no longer feels the influence which it had previously felt. . . .

What bears influence feels, furthermore, pain in so far as it forsakes its nature, and pleasure in so far as it returns again from forsaking its nature to its nature. Ar-Rāzī comments on this that the return to the nature whereby a person feels pleasure can only occur after forsaking the nature through which he felt pain. He adds that it has thereby become clear that pleasure is nothing more than a respite from pain. . . .

The natural condition is not something sensually perceptible; for sensual perception occurs through an influence, and the influence of what exerts influence turns what bears influence into a condition different from that in which it is. On the other hand, no kind of change or influence from another condition can reach the natural condition. Since the natural condition cannot be reached from another condition, there is no sensual perception until such is felt by what bears influence, because sensual perception of a change of condition in man occurs either through forsaking nature or return to nature. The natural condition, however, is neither forsaking nature nor return to nature. . . .

The natural condition is, then, not sensually perceptible and what is not sensually perceptible is neither pleasure nor affliction. . . .

An influence which follows another influence can, in the case of two opposing influences, produce pleasure in what bears influence, as long as the earlier influence does not entirely cease to act upon what bears influence and as long as what bears influence has not returned to its condition. Yet when the earlier influence has ceased and what bears influence has returned to its natural condition, then the same influence that had produced pleasure in what bears influence now causes it pain. Therefore ar-Rāzī says that when that earlier influence has ceased and what bears influence has been restored to its natural condition and then what bears influence is removed from its natural condition to the other extreme, it suffers pain through forsaking its nature. And when what bears influence is restored to its natural condition through that influence, this provides him pleasure. Yet when it returns to its natural condition, it is thereby again deprived of pleasure.

When that influence continues, however, and he undertakes to remove it from its natural condition towards the other extreme, it begins to cause him pain again. Ar-Rāzī says further that it is now clear that the natural condition is a kind of intermediate condition for what bears influence, between forsaking nature which causes pain, and returning to nature which provides pleasure and rest. The natural condition is neither pain nor pleasure.

Here ar-Rāzī quotes the following example for explanation: A man enters a house which is neither so cold that he shivers from cold nor so hot that he breaks out in a sweat. His body has become accustomed to this house and feels neither heat nor cold. Now the house suddenly becomes so warm that the heat causes him immense pain, and he becomes quite weak. Then, again, a cool wind begins to blow gradually into the house and to cause pleasure through his return to nature to the man, to whom the heat had caused pain, since it had forced him to forsake his nature. It continues until the coolness restores him to the earlier condition which was neither cold nor warm. If the coolness persists, it begins to cause him pain instead of pleasure, since he now forsakes his nature for the other extreme. If, after the cold, the house begins to get hot again, he again experiences pleasure from the heat, since it restores him to his nature, and until he has returned to his natural condition, he feels pleasure. . . .

Sensual pleasure is nothing more than a respite from pain, and pain nothing more than forsaking nature. Nature is neither pain nor pleasure. . . .

When forsaking nature takes place gradually and return to nature takes place suddenly, no pain but only pleasure appears. But when forsaking nature takes place suddenly and return to nature takes place gradually, pain appears and no pleasure. . . .

Such sudden return to nature is called pleasure, since it constitutes a respite from pain. . . .

A man may, for example, feel pain gradually from hunger and thirst, and this constitutes for him forsaking nature. Finally, when he is very hungry and thirsty, he suddenly eats and drinks until he has returned to his natural condition in which he found himself earlier. This gives him pleasure. Pleasure appears in him because he has suddenly returned to his natural condition, and pain appeared in him through the hunger and thirst which had gradually induced him to forsake his natural condition. That return to the painless condition is called pleasure. It is nothing more than a rest from a piecemeal pain which suddenly disappears. . . .

When a healthy person suddenly receives a wound which suddenly causes him to forsake his natural condition, he feels pain thereby, and when the wound gradually heals in the course of time, he feels no pleasure. Sudden forsaking of nature is called pain, because pain appears, but return to the previous condition is not called pleasure because no pleasure appears.

Ar-Rāzī says that the pleasure of copulation is caused by the accumulation of a certain substance in a particularly alert and sensitive place. When that substance is long accumulated there and then suddenly leaves that place, this produces pleasure. . . . It is comparable to the pleasure derived from scratching when it itches. . . .

The pleasure felt at the sight of beautiful faces is explained by ar-Rāzī in the sense that people tire of unattractive and ugly companions and thus forsake their natural condition. The pleasure felt on hearing beautiful sounds he explains similarly in the sense that everyone who hears soft sounds after harsh ones feels pleasure. . . . Everybody feels pleasure when he sees light, but when he sees a great deal of light, closing of the eye and darkness also give him pleasure.

About Eros

5. From a work by Aḥmad b. aṭ-Ṭayyib as-Sarakhsī, quoted in the Istanbul MS Topkapusarai, Ahmet III, 3483, 240a–b. Cf. F. Rosenthal, in *Journal of the American Oriental Society*, LXXXI (1961), pp. 223 f.

As-Sarakhsī was asked why the lover on meeting his beloved presses his mouth on that of his beloved and tries to put his tongue into his mouth and kisses him continually and draws him close to himself. He gave the following reply: I say that Eros [*ʿishq*] is the excess of love [*maḥabbah*]. Love is the cause of the joining of things, and in the excess of joining there is nothing stronger than the union through which two become one. The soul of a living being achieves what the soul wants from the body, which is an instrument of the soul for all actions, only when the human soul finds Eros, which is the excess of love, which is the cause of the joining of things. Thus, with the aid of the excess of love, the soul strives to realize the strongest kind of absolute joining, since the excess of love is a cause of the excess of joining, which is its strongest realization. It desires union with the beloved as a living being, but it can find entry from the exterior to the interior only through the body, which draws from [the soul] breath, which sustains life and the substance of the animal power, which is a soul [breath ?], and keeps away from it all that might harm [the soul]. There is no better entry of this kind than the mouth and the nostrils which conduct air into the windpipe, since the only entries besides remain the tender pores at the roots of the hair. Hence the soul of the lover feels drawn to the mouth and kisses it and inhales through the nostrils the outgoing breath of the beloved which was only recently in contact with his nature and the powers of his soul, so that the two substances unite and the two powers join. By the insertion of tongues into mouths, it attempts to penetrate him and to reach his interior. Through drawing him close and hugging him, it attempts to unite its own body with that of the beloved, to absorb him by means of the pores so that nothing comes between the two bodies that might separate them, disrupt their joining or terminate their union. Yet when the soul lacks the true exchange [?], which is mingling, it strives for union of souls. It follows the desires and preferences of the beloved and agrees with him in his striving and assists him therein, so that the soul of the beloved joins in its love which becomes possible through its will. Then, when the soul of the lover wishes to find the love of the beloved and, under the influence of the will of the lover's soul, the soul of the beloved is prepared to love his soul, the two souls become like one, since they are united through harmony. For this reason the philosopher [Aristotle] has said: 'Your friend is another who is identical with you.' 'Another' refers to the difference of the two bodies. 'Identical with you' refers to the agreement of wills. The influence extends to all bodies, though it originates from a single soul. Briefly, we can say that friendship is the union of two friends' souls through harmony of the will.

The kinds of slaves

6. From a Hellenistic economic treatise edited by M. Plessner, *Der Oikonomikos des Neupythagoreers 'Bryson'* (Heidelberg, 1928), p. 164. Cf. Stob., *Flor.*, V, 681, Wachsmuth-Hense.

There are three kinds of slaves, namely slaves by law, slaves of desire and slaves by nature.

A slave by law is one for whom the [religious] law makes slavery obligatory.

A slave of desire is one despotically ruled by his desires and ideas so that he does not know how to master himself. That is a bad slave and a bad man, who is no good for anything.

A slave by nature is a person who possesses a strong body and is able to endure a great deal of work, but possesses only as much discernment and intelligence in his soul as are sufficient to allow him to be guided by somebody else, but are insufficient for him to manage himself. By his nature he is close to animals which human beings direct as they please. Such a man is a slave, even if he is a free man. It is best for him to have a master to manage him.

Professional ethics

7. From Plessner's edition of *Bryson*, pp. 152–4.

In earning a livelihood, one must avoid three things, namely, injustice, disgraceful conduct and a base character.

Injustice consists, for example, in giving short weight or false measure, in trickery in preparing bills, in denying a justified claim or making an unjustified claim, or committing similar serious crimes which, according to general opinion, ruin a person's livelihood, destroy his substance and cause frustration, because such things give a man a widespread bad reputation which deters people from dealing with him and induces whoever has to suffer from his unjust conduct to tell others about it. In the end all who had previously dealt with him as well as those who had not dealt with him keep away from him, and even if he should give up his evil ways, it would not help him, since his bad reputation has already spread far and wide.

Disgraceful behaviour consists of swearing, slapping and similar things which some people accept because they want something from somebody.

Base character consists in abandoning the calling of one's ancestors and one's family, though one is capable of practising it, and adopting a less respected calling. For example, a man whose ancestors and family were generals and governors, but who does not devote himself to that, though he is capable of it, but instead confines himself to song and music and the like. We do not say here that by continuing the despised calling of his ancestors a man acts like a person of base character or does something deserving blame. On the contrary, we claim that he deserves praise, if he is content with his lot and does not aim above his situation. If it were obligatory for everybody to seek a calling more respected than that inherited from his father, all men would be obliged to pursue a single calling, which would be the most respected of all callings. This would lead to the abolition of all other callings, and that calling at which everybody aims would also not be able to exist any longer, for it can only exist with the aid of the other callings, since all parts of the whole depend on one another, as we have explained earlier.

Plato on politics

8. The beginning of the first book of al-Fārābī, *Compendium Legum Platonis*, ed. F. Gabrieli (London, 1952), pp. 5 f.; cf. M. Mahdi, in *Journal of Near Eastern Studies*, XX (1961), pp. 1–24.

Someone enquired as to the cause of legislation—'cause' here means 'maker', and the 'maker' of laws is the law-giver—and received the following answer: The law-giver was Zeus. Among the Greeks Zeus is the father of man, the ultimate cause.

Then he proceeded to mention another legislation in order to show that laws are numerous, but their great number does not make them invalid. As proof, he quoted poems and the familiar stories known everywhere in praise of some ancient law-givers.

Then he hinted that it is right to examine the laws, since there are men who consider them invalid and wish to state that they are foolish. He showed that they stand on the highest level and above all matters of wisdom. And he examined the particulars of the law well known in his time.

Then Plato mentioned the cypresses and described the stations on the way used by both respondent and questioner. Most people assume that subtle ideas are hidden here, and that by the trees he meant men as well as additional difficult, complicated, offensive ideas which would take too long to enumerate. Their assumption, however, is incorrect. Rather was he intent on extending his exposition and linking explicit remarks with ones similar but not expressive of his goal, so that his true intention would remain hidden.

Then he turned to some statutes of that law that was well known among them and examined them. He attempted to determine what is right in them and accords with the demands of a healthy mind. This concerns company at meals and the use of easily carried weapons. He showed that the like of them is useful in many respects since it leads to harmony and aids one to master rough roads. Most of them travel on foot and do not ride.

Then he showed that the possession and use of suitable weapons, company [at meals] and harmony [among citizens] are all necessary since natures in general are always bellicose and those people particularly so. Furthermore, he showed the advantages of war and enumerated in all detail the various ways of waging war, clarifying the special as well as the general cases. He then turned to discussion of warfare and finally mentioned many of the advantages of the law, such as individual self-control, striving for the strength to subdue the evils of the soul and such as arise from outside, as well as striving for justice in every respect.

Furthermore, he showed in this chapter which city is the virtuous city [the ideal state] and which man is the virtuous man, namely, the city and the man who truly and rightly gain the upper hand. He further showed that it is true that men require a judge [*ḥākim*] and must obey him, and he showed the benefits resulting from that. He described the nature and the proper conduct of the acceptable judge. He must subdue all evil [evil doers ?], skilfully keep war away from mankind, and be a good administrator. He must begin with what is most appropriate, that is, the nearest thing, and advance gradually.

He showed that it is true that wars between men must be abolished and that that is what they greatly desire because it is to their own benefit. He established that this is only possible through obeying the law and observing its statutes. When the law demands warfare, it is for the sake of peace, and not for the sake of war, as, for example, somebody might be commanded to do something disliked because it will result in something commendable.

He further mentioned that prosperity without security does not suffice for man's livelihood. As proof, he quoted a poem by Tyrtaeus, a poet well known among them. He showed that praiseworthy courage does not consist in a man's bravely going forth to war but in that he masters himself and maintains peace and security as far as possible. As proof for this he quoted poems well known among them.

Then he showed that with such correct decisions the law-giver pursues the goal of drawing near to the divine countenance, receiving reward in the hereafter and acquiring the highest virtue that stands above the four ethical virtues.

He showed that there are men who act as if they were law-givers. These people pursue various goals. They hasten to enact laws in order to achieve their evil designs thereby. He mentioned them only in order to warn men so that they should not be deceived by such people.

9. From Abū l-Ḥasan b. Abī Dharr, *Kitāb as-Sa'ādah wa-l-is'ād*, pp. 179, 189 f., Minovi.

Plato says in the Laws: Partnership exists in social life, and each individual is bound to arrange his way of life in such a way that, firstly, he has in mind his own welfare, secondly, he can control his family [that is, his women] and his children and, thirdly, he regulates his relations with his countrymen properly. Furthermore the ways of life of people necessarily differ since the conditions in which they find themselves differ either by nature or owing to their ambitions and their understanding. Diversity, however, as he says, forms the basis for every kind of corruption. All this makes it essential for them to agree on a single law [*sunnah*] which will serve and benefit all together and each individual. . . . A law is that which brings disparate views together and makes them a single view and uniformly arranges the public welfare, which goes in different directions. . . . The ruler is the law's guardian and shepherd. He administers it and applies it to himself and to the inhabitants of his realm.

Plato says in the Laws: Since a cowherd is not allowed to be a cow nor a shepherd a sheep, and since the teacher of ignorant people is not allowed to be ignorant himself, the ruler and leader of people must ⟨not⟩ be a man [like them] but must be divine. The divine man is the philosopher, and a philosopher is one who has knowledge of divine and human things. It is not sufficient that he possesses knowledge, but he must be firmly grounded in philosophy; for if he is not firmly grounded in philosophy, he must either hesitate until he eventually knows what he must do, and postponement and delay can cause harm, or else he acts at random, and that results in arbitrariness, which is even more harmful. . . . He must be acquainted with the laws of his predecessors and the events of the past and know why they happened and what caused them. . . .

There is an assumption that a man of good natural ability and outstanding character qualities is fit to rule, especially if he knows what is beautiful and what is ugly. This assumption, however, is not correct. Only the man who has a proper understanding of philosophy is fit for rule; this means that he must master arithmetic, geometry and music. For only if he understands how to deal with numbers is he in a position to value everything correctly and rule effectively.

Aristotle on the forms of government

10. From the Arabic translation of the *Nicomachean Ethics* 1160a 31–1161a 4, A. J. Arberry in *Islamic Quarterly*, II (1955), p. 18 f.

There are three kinds of political groupings, and their excesses, that is to say, their corruptions, are also three. The three political forms are kingdom [monarchy], rule of the best [aristocracy] and a third that is formed of honours, which apparently could be aptly called the rule of honour [timocracy], but which most people are accustomed to call *politeia*, meaning conduct of life. The best is kingdom and the worst rule by the common people [democracy].

The excess of kingdom, tyranny, is, like the former, individual rule, but there is a great difference between the two, since the tyrant aims at his own advantage while the king aims at the advantage of his subjects. For nobody can attain rule who is not adequately provided and outstanding in all good things, so that he requires nought and, consequently, aims ⟨not⟩ at his own advantage but at that of his subjects. He who is not such a man is fit to become King by lot.

The tyrant is just the opposite since he seeks the good for himself. It is quite clear that he must be very evil, since the opposite of good is evil. He proceeds from kingdom to tyranny, because tyranny represents a deterioration of individual rule. The king who ⟨is evil⟩ becomes a tyrant.

From rule by the best [aristocracy] one proceeds to rule by the few [oligarchy] who are the worst rulers. They distribute the city's wealth in an improper manner and let all or most of the good things come to themselves. They endeavour always to entrust the same people with rule, so that the rulers are few and evil men, instead of all the most outstanding men who would be fit [rulers].

From rule of honour [timocracy] one proceeds to rule by the common people [democracy]; the two border on each other, since rule of honour also wishes to be mass rule and insists that all who are honourable are equal. Rule by the common people is not very bad, since it only slightly transgresses the [correct] ways of [political] conduct. In this manner the [political] ways of conduct change most, since the transition is so simple and insignificant. One can draw an analogy with what happens in the home. The relationship of a father to his children corresponds to that of a king to his subjects, since the father cares for his children. Hence, Homer called ⟨Zeus⟩ 'father', since a king's rule must be paternal. Among the Persians, however, the father's rule is tyrannical; for they treat their children like slaves, and the master's rule over his slaves is tyrannical, since he uses them only for his own advantage. The first [attitude] appears to be correct and that of the Persians false; for rule belongs to that which is different. Rule by the best [aristocracy] among men and women appears to be different. For it is proper for man to rule woman, who must be ruled by him, and he gives her all to which she is entitled. If a man possesses power over everything and rules it, he gets to oligarchy, and he does so because it is proper, not because it is better. Sometimes women exercise rule, should this occur by lot. Their rule does not rest on virtue, but comes about through wealth and power, just as in the case of government by the few [oligarchy]. Rule of brothers resembles rule of honour.

The Islamic ideal state

11. A brief summary of the contents of al-Fārābī, *Ārā' ahl al-madīnah al-fāḍilah* (*The Ideal State*), as included in the manuscripts of that work, from the edition of F. Dieterici (Leiden, 1895), pp. 1–4, trans. (Leiden, 1900), pp. 1–5; ed. A. N. Nader (Beirut, 1959), pp. 19–22. These editions will soon be replaced by a new edition by R. Walzer. Cf. the Spanish translation of M. Alonso Alonso, in *Al-Andalus*, XXVI (1961), pp. 337 ff.

I. About the thing which must be believed to be God, what it is, how it is constituted, how it must be described, in what way it is the cause of all other existing things, how they originate from it, how it creates them, how they are linked with it, how it recognizes and understands, what terms should be used for it and what should be understood by those terms.

II. About the existing things which must be believed to be angels, what each one of them is, how he is constituted, how he has been created [by God], what rank he occupies in relation to Him, what their ranks in relation to each other are, what originates from each one of them, how he is the cause of all that originates from him, what he administers and how he does so, and that each one of them is the cause of one of the heavenly bodies and administers it.

III. About the heavenly bodies in general, that each one of them is linked with one of the secondary beings and that each single one of the secondary beings administers the heavenly body linked with it.

IV. About the bodies which are to be found beneath the heavens, namely, the material bodies, how they are constituted, how many of them there are altogether, in what manner each one of them assumes a substance and in what manner it differs from the existing things mentioned above.

V. About matter and form, what they are, namely that through which bodies take on substance, their ranks in relationship to one another, what those bodies are which take on substance through them, which kind of existence each body assumes through matter and which through form.

VI. About the quality of the attributes of existing things that must be called 'angels'.

VII. Concerning the attributes of the heavenly bodies in general.

VIII. How the material bodies as a whole were created, which body was created first, which second, third and so forth in order until the last created, that the last created is man, as well as a summary account of the creation of each kind of them.

IX. How the persistence of each kind and of the individuals of each kind is regulated, how this occurs in a just manner, everything about it exceedingly just, well arranged and perfect, without any injustice, corruption and blemish, that this is necessary and that the nature of the existing things cannot possibly be otherwise.

X. About man, the powers of the human soul and its creation, which was created first, which second and which third, their ranks in relation to each other, which rules exclusively, which serves, which both rules and serves and which rules over which.

XI. About the creation of man's limbs, their ranks and their ranks in relationship to each other, which limb is ruler and which servant, how the ruling limb exercises its rule and how the serving limb performs its service.

XII. About male and female, what their power is, what they do, how children originate from them, in what way they differ and what they have in common, what is the cause of the creation of male and female, how it happens that a child sometimes resembles both parents, sometimes only one of his parents, sometimes his more distant ancestors and sometimes neither his paternal nor his maternal ancestors.

XIII. How the intelligibilia become impressed on the rational part of the soul, whence they arrive there, how many kinds of intelligibilia there are, what the potential intellect is and what the actual intellect. What the hylic intellect, what the passive intellect and what the active intellect, which rank it occupies, why it is called active intellect and what its activity is, how the intelligibilia must impress themselves on the potential intellect so that it becomes actual intellect, what will is and what choice, to which part of the soul these two belong, what supreme happiness is, what the virtues are and what the vices, what good deeds and what evil deeds are, and what beautiful and what ugly deeds are.

XIV. About the imaginative part of the soul, how many kinds of action proceed from it, how dreams occur, how many kinds of dreams there are, to which part of the soul they belong, what is the cause of true dreams, how revelation takes place, which man is fit to receive revelations, through which part of the soul such a man receives revelation, and the reason why many madmen predict the future accurately.

XV. About man's need for a social group and collaboration, how many kinds of human social groups there are, which are virtuous social groups and which is the virtuous city [the ideal state], of what they are constituted, how its parts are arranged, how different kinds of virtuous government arise in the virtuous cities, how the first virtuous ruler must be formed. What conditions a child or youth must be assumed to satisfy and what signs must be found in him in order that he might acquire the attributes required of a virtuous ruler and what conditions he must fulfil as an adult in order to be able to become a virtuous ruler; how many kinds of cities there are which represent the opposite of the virtuous city, what the ignorant city is, what the erring city is, and how many kinds of ignorant cities and governments there are.

XVI. Then he mentioned the different kinds of supreme happiness which await the souls of the inhabitants of virtuous cities in this world and in the next, as well as the kinds of misfortune which befall the souls of the inhabitants of cities which are the opposite of virtuous cities after death.

XVII. How rules must be constituted in the virtuous cities. Then he mentioned the things which give rise to corrupt and false principles in the souls of many people and form the basis of the views of ignorant [cities].

XVIII. A list of the various views which prevail in ignorant [cities] and determine the actions and various kinds of social groupings in ignorant cities.

XIX. A list of the corrupt principles which give rise to the views that cause the spread of misguided religious groups.

Practical politics: warfare and fame

12. From the exchange of political views between Aristotle and Alexander, as preserved in the Istanbul MS Fatih 5323. For the manuscript, cf. R. Walzer, *Greek into Arabic* (Oxford, 1962), pp. 139 f.; another manuscript which could not be consulted, is mentioned by M. Grignaschi (pp. 4 and 267, n.4). Though the text shows a lacuna,

the first excerpt appears to originate from the letter of congratulation which Aristotle allegedly sent to Alexander on the occasion of the conquest of Scythia. The third excerpt belongs to a discourse on popular politics [*as-siyāsah al-'āmmīyah*].

There are three things with whose help difficulties in war can be overcome, namely, the cleverness of the general, the strength of the troops and courage displayed in dangerous situations. These three are interconnected. Their collaboration holds out hope for victory.

Establish seven ranks for your army: the highest rank consists of the *aṣḥāb al-liqā'* [7] of whom you may have two in one and the same city only for exceptional reasons. The second rank consists of the *patrikioi*, who are below the *aṣḥāb al-liqā'*. The third rank consists of the *amīrs*, the fourth of the *quwwād*, the fifth of the *mubārizūn*, the sixth of the *'urafā'* and the seventh of the soldiers. Pay them, and pay every rank twice as much as the one immediately below it. Pay the soldiers liberally so that they can keep themselves and their families! Do not lay down a fixed limit for rewards! Pay when prices rise! Give presents on festivals! In this way you will gain more for yourself than just a small advantage. When you have offered pay, take care that it is paid them in full and ensure that it is not reduced in any way! Be friendly to them when you show yourself to them, and talk to them frequently and affably. When you go on a journey, make them a speech so that they are afraid and remain well disposed towards you. In case you are suspicious of a *ṣāḥib al-liqā'* or a *patrikios* or a soldier, or any officer—if he occupies a special position, abolish it; if he is a common soldier, and this is his first offence, pardon him!

Know that fame can be gained in three ways, namely, in the first place by promulgating laws, whereby Solon and Lycurgus attained repute; secondly, through experience of war and battles, whereby Themistocles and Brasidas gained fame; and, thirdly, through the foundation of cities, since many founders of cities have become very famous.

Some of the ancients became renowned in one region or another through one of these qualifications. You have gathered fine experience of war in several countries. You should, therefore, endeavour to acquire the other two qualifications and be concerned for laws and the welfare of cities, so that you may combine all three claims to fame in your own person.

Wise sayings

13. The Arabic version of the Pythagorean '*Chrysā Epē*' as quoted in Miskawaih's *Jāwīdhān khiradh*, ed. 'Abd-ar-Raḥmān Badawī, *al-Ḥikmah al-khālidah* (Cairo, 1952), pp. 225–8. The original Arabic translation of this very popular and frequently copied and quoted text was a literal rendering of the Greek original in the form available to the translator. Its text has not been reconstructed here, because it is more interesting to see which (mostly minor) changes the text underwent at the hands of the Arabs who used it. A study of the Arabic '*Chrysā Epē*' is expected from M. Ullmann. Cf. also M. Plessner, in *Eshkoloth*, IV (5722/1961), p. 68.

The Exhortation of Pythagoras,
known as 'The Golden', which Galen says
he recites every morning and evening.

After the fear of God the first thing which I exhort you to do is that you revere God and His saints, who are not overtaken by death, and honour them as demanded by the religious law and respect the oath. Thereafter I exhort you to do this in the service of those who are helpful in all their conduct. I exhort you further to revere the inhabitants of the earth by honouring them as the religious law demands and I exhort you to honour your ancestors and relatives.

I exhort you to take the best of all men as a friend, so that he might be a friend to you in virtue, and to be forbearing towards him in what you do, as long as that is useful to him, and as far as possible not to treat a friend badly because of some fault since possibility is close to necessity. This is the first that you must do.

Then you must accustom your soul to keep away from the things which I am about to mention. Firstly, as regards your stomach and your sex organs as well as anger and sleep.

Beware of doing anything ugly at any time, either when you are alone or when you are together with anyone else. You should be more ashamed of yourself than of anyone else.

Further, you must always endeavour to be fair in what you say and do.

Let it not happen that you act without previous reflection, but know that death overtakes every man without fail. Be moderate in the acquisition of property on the one hand and in expenditure on the other.

About damages through heavenly causes which men suffer, bear patiently those that happen to you, without complaining. Rather should you strive to allay them as far as you can. You must know that not a little of it happens to the best of men.

If you hear men talk much that is good and bad, do not be angry about it, and let it not happen that you avoid listening to it. If you hear a lie, bear it patiently.

Follow what I say in all you undertake.

Let nobody move you by word or deed to do or say something that is not good. Reflect before you act, so that you may not be blamed for something you do. Beware of saying or doing anything that might be considered foolish of you. Rather must you restrict yourself in all you do to what does you no harm. You should do nothing that you do not understand. Ascertain rather in every situation and with regard to every single action what you must do. Then you will enjoy your life.

You must not neglect the health of your body, but concern yourself about eating and drinking, and moderation with respect to both, as well as the various kinds of exercise. I consider as 'moderation' that which does no harm. Accustom yourself to lead a clean and undisturbed way of life. Beware of doing what could expose you to envy. Do not be extravagant, like a man who does not understand what he possesses. On the other hand, do not be miserly, which would make you ungenerous. In all matters moderation is best.

What you do should always be that which will cause you no harm. Think before you act. Let your eyes find no sleep before you have examined every single action which you have done in the course of the entire day. Before falling asleep you should study where you have exceeded the necessary, should you have done so, as well as what you have done of what you should have done and what you should have done but have not done. Start with your first action and continue the examination until you reach the last action. If you have done anything detestable, take it to heart, and if you have done anything decent, rejoice over it. That must be your desire, practise it, concern yourself with it, since it paves for you the path along which you can advance to divine virtue.

By Him who has given our souls the fourfold source of nature that never ceases! Every time you wish to do something, begin by praying to your Lord for success. If you keep to this and do not act contrary to these exhortations, you will become acquainted with the innermost essence of God's providence and that of His saints, and with all that concerns us human beings, what of it ceases one by one and what remains constant. You will become acquainted with the destined course of nature in everything according to one single model, so that you do not hope for something for which one cannot hope. You will know that men are to be pitied for their misfortune which they have voluntarily chosen for themselves; for they are close to the good things but do not perceive them, and they do not examine themselves concerning what they suffer. Some few individuals succeed in freeing themselves from evil. What they suffer of it affects their hearts and minds. They wallow in evil as if it were water, at different times towards different kinds of harm and different circumstances and in this way meet with countless misfortunes. For the matter which follows nature in wickedness [*Eris symphytos*] wounds unawares, and one should not aid it, but rather avoid it by pretending to imitate it.

Life-giving Father! Truly I say that you are able to avert many afflictions from them if you manifest to them the divine power [*sakīnah*] you have placed in them. However, you, man, must show yourself brave since there is a divine quality in man. The divine nature brings him to perception of every one of the things which, should you acquire a share in them, follow my counsels and heal your soul from all filth and hallucination, will let you be saved unharmed. Yet satisfy yourself with the nourishment we have mentioned; examine it and thus purify the soul and free it from imprisonment in the body; tell mankind what you know about each detail of it and appoint as supervisor over it the sound capacity for discernment. Then you will be free when you leave this body, and move about without ever returning to humanity and without suffering death.

14. Sayings of the sages on Alexander's death, from ath-Tha'ālibī, *Histoire des rois des Perses*, ed. H. Zotenberg (Paris, 1900), pp. 450–5.

Apart from the extensive report in Ibn Abī d-Dunyā's *Kitāb al-I'tibār*, Ḥunain appears to have preserved the longest version of this famous story. His version and others, such as those found in al-Mubashshir or the Istanbul MS Fatih 5323, however, all differ considerably from one another and from that of ath-Tha'ālibī. Al-Mubashshir points out that there exist many other aphorisms coined on this occasion. The *Kitāb al-Aghānī*,[3] IV, 43 f., has somewhat different versions even of the parallels to the verses quoted at the end of our excerpt. All this testifies to the immense popularity of this famous edifying tale. It remains to be investigated whether all the preserved material goes back to a single source or to several sources. Cf. A. Zajączkowski, in *Rocznik Orientalistyczny*, XXVIII (1965), pp. 13–57; S. P. Brock, in *Journal of Semitic Studies*, XV (1970), pp. 205–18.

When many philosophers and sages had gathered among the mass of people surging round Alexander's coffin, Aristotle said to them: 'Let us now express our feelings in words of wisdom which can serve to admonish the élite and stir the common people.'

He himself stepped forward, laid his hand on Alexander's coffin and said in a voice choked with tears: 'The jailer is now himself jailed, the slayer of kings himself slain.'

Then Plato stepped forward and spoke amid loud laments and wails: 'Alexander moves us by being still.'

Ptolemy stepped forward and said: 'Look how the sleeper's dream has ended and the cloud's shadow vanished.'

Diogenes stepped forward and said: 'Alexander never ceased to hoard gold until now gold hoards him.'

Dorotheus stepped forward and said: 'How much do men covet this coffin, but how little do they covet what lies in it.'

Balīnās [Apollonius of Tyana] stepped forward and said: 'Why can you who could control single-handed countries and men control none of your limbs?'

Ṭwbyq' [Tyana ?!] stepped forward and said: 'All this dominance of yesterday does not suit you since you are today so humbled.'

Democritus stepped forward and said: 'Why do you not abhor this narrow place since the whole world was not wide enough for you?'

Socrates stepped forward and said: 'You spoke more yesterday; today, however, you admonish more.'

Ghryws [Gregory ?] stepped forward and said: 'This lion used to hunt lions, but now he has fallen into the snare.'

Someone else stepped forward and said: 'Everyone harvests what he sows. So harvest now what you have sown!'

Someone else stepped forward and said: 'Golden ornaments are more beautiful for the living than for the dead.'

Someone else stepped forward and said: 'You have found rest from the occupations of this world. Now see that you find rest from the dangers of the next.'

Someone else stepped forward and said: 'What advantage was it to you to have slain so many people since you have now died so suddenly?'

Someone else stepped forward and said: 'We dared not speak in your presence. Now we dare not be silent.'

Someone else stepped forward and said: 'How complex was the object of your endeavours and how simple is your legacy.'

Someone else stepped forward and said: 'In life you caused men many tears and now you cause them tears in death.'

Someone else stepped forward and said: 'In the bathtub you were never as patient as you are now in the coffin.'

Someone else stepped forward and said: 'In quest of the light of life you ventured into darkness and did not know that it would lead you to the darkness of the coffin.'

Someone else stepped forward and said: 'You used to sleep at night in one place and take a nap in the afternoon in another. Why do you now restrict yourself to sleeping in a single place at night and in the afternoon?'

Someone else stepped forward and said: 'When you were able to act, we dared not speak. Now that we may speak, you are not able to act.'

Someone else stepped forward and said: 'The wind has uprooted the high tree. The shepherd has departed. The flock is lost.'

Someone else stepped forward and said: 'Follow another ruler, for your ruler here has departed and will never return.'

Someone else stepped forward and said: 'Now you know that you were born to die and built for demolition.'

Someone else stepped forward and said: 'You have travelled the length and the breadth of the earth till you entirely possessed it, and now all you possess of it are four cubits.'

Someone else stepped forward and said: 'Look how the high mountain has crumbled, the raging sea subsided, the rising moon fallen!'

Then Alexander's mother stepped forward and said: 'Dear son! I was able to wait for you when we were as far apart from each other as the east is from the west. Now that you are closer to me than my shadow, I have given up waiting.'

Rōshnak stepped forward and said: 'I did not know that my father's conqueror would himself be conquered.'

The Minister of Finance stepped forward and said: 'You ordered me to collect money, and now you hand over to others what I collected for you.'

The Treasurer stepped forward and said: 'Here are the keys to your treasure chambers. Command that I may be relieved of them before I am held responsible for something that belongs to you and that I did not take.'

The Head Cook stepped forward and said: 'The couches are put in places, the pillows laid out, the tables set up, but I do not see the host.'

The author of the present volume says: Abū l-ʿAtāhiyah frequently used the ideas contained in these sayings in his lamentations and ascetic poems. Plato's 'Alexander moves us by being still' he reproduced in the following verses:

> ʿAlī b. Thābit, a [dear] companion has departed from me!
> It was a great loss when you departed from me.
> Truly you have taught me the agony of death,
> And moved me towards it while you yourself are still.

He reproduced the saying 'Yesterday Alexander spoke more, but today he admonishes more' in the following verses:

> I have called you, dear brother, and you have given me no answer.
> Hence my call brings me mourning as a reply.
> It is sad enough that you have been buried and that I have then
> Shaken the dust of your grave from my hands.
> Your life has held admonitions for me,
> But today you admonish more than while you were alive.

He reproduced the saying 'Now you know that you were born to die and built for demolition' in the following verse:

Beget to die, build for demolition,
For you will all vanish!

15. The chapter on 'Sayings by a number of philosophers known by name for none of whom enough sayings are recorded to make a special chapter possible', from the *Mukhtār al-ḥikam* by al-Mubashshir b. Fātik, pp. 296–322, Badawī, with many variant readings from the manuscripts. The forms of the names are sometimes uncertain. A few Greek parallels were pointed out by H. Knust in his edition of the Spanish translation which reproduces this chapter in separate places ('Mittheilungen aus dem Eskurial', in *Bibliothek des litterarischen Vereins in Stuttgart*, CXLI [1879], 357_7–371_3; 395–7_{14}; 371_3–372_4; 397_{18}–400_{18}; 372_{21}–374_6). For some general remarks on the source situation in Arabic gnomology, see F. Rosenthal, 'Sayings of the Ancients from Ibn Duraid's *Kitāb al-Mujtanā*', in *Orientalia*, n.s., XXVII (1958), pp. 29–54, 150–83. Al-Mubashshir's chapter is not only based on anthologies but also contains excerpts from Greek writings on popular ethics available in Arabic. Its quotations of poetry undoubtedly derive from anthologies. A reprint of L. Sternbach's edition of the *Gnomologium Vaticanum*, which is frequently quoted in the following pages, appeared in Berlin in 1963.

1. Protarchus [Plutarch ?[8]] was asked why a certain man dyed his hair black. He replied: 'He does not want anyone to try to find the experience of the old in him.'

2. Balīnās [Apollonius of Tyana] said: 'When a fool prospers, he becomes all the uglier for it.'

3. He said: 'Humming melodies soothes a sad man's sorrows.'

4. Erasistratus was asked at what time one should have sexual intercourse. He replied: 'When one wants to weaken one's body.' [Cf. Diog. Laert., VIII, 9 (Pythagoras).]

5. Democritus was asked what made his knowledge superior to that of others. He replied: 'My awareness that I know little.' [Cf. *Gnom. Vat.*, no. 264, Sternbach.]

6. When he remarked that an obstinate sage was better than a just fool, one of his disciples said: 'A sage is not obstinate and a fool is not just.'

7. ʾsʾns [Aesop] had been taken prisoner, and someone who wished to buy him asked him about his family origins. He replied: 'Do not enquire about my family origins. Enquire about my intelligence and my knowledge.'

8. Archigenes had been taken prisoner, and someone who wished to buy him asked him: 'What are you fit for?' He replied: 'To be free' [Plutarch, *Apophth. Laconum* 234B, *Apophth. Lacaen.* 242D; Stob., *Flor.*, III, 466, Wachsmuth-Hense; *Gnom. Vat.*, no. 570, Sternbach (*Wiener Studien*, XI, 240)].

9. Someone else had been taken prisoner, and the man to whom he was offered for sale asked him: 'If I buy you, will you be of any use?' He replied: 'I am that even if you do not buy me' [Plutarch, *Apophth. Laconum* 234C; *Apophth. Lacaen.* 242C].

10. When someone abused Aeschines, the latter said: 'I will not get involved in a battle in which the victor is worse than the vanquished' [Stob., *Flor.*, III, 530, Wachsmuth-Hense].

11. He used to say: 'He who is ashamed of people but not of himself regards himself as completely worthless.'

12. Antigonus was overheard to pray to his Lord to protect him from his friends. When he was asked why he prayed for protection from his friends and not from his enemies, he said: 'I can protect myself from my enemy but not from my friend' [*Gnom. Vat.*, no. 107, Sternbach (*Wiener Studien*, X, 17 f.).]

13. When Sqlybws [Asclepius ?] was told that a certain man was ambitious, he remarked: 'Then he will be content with nothing less than Paradise.'[9]

14. Someone was asked what constitutes manliness. He replied: 'Not doing anything in secret of which one would be ashamed in public.'[10]

15. Anaxarchus was asked what he found impossible to give up. He answered: 'To shun ignorance, to desire knowledge and not to be ashamed during instruction.'

16. Agesilaus was asked what science children should learn. He replied: 'The sciences that they ought to be ashamed not to master when they are old' [Plutarch, *Apophth. Laconum* 213C–D; Diog. Laert., II, 80].

17. When someone praised Pindar for his disinterest in money, he said: 'Why do I need what is brought by luck, preserved by meanness and ruined by spending?' [Ibn Duraid, no. 54, Rosenthal].

18. Philo [?] was asked about the benefit philosophy had brought him. He answered: 'I do what I must do voluntarily, not because the law forces me to do it' [Diog. Laert., V, 20; *Gnom. Vat.*, no. 417, Sternbach (*Wiener Studien*, XI, 194); Maximus Conf. 825B[11]].

19. Democritus said: 'The most unfortunate being in the world is a sage subjected to the authority of a fool.' [Cf. Stob., *Flor.*, IV, 192, Wachsmuth-Hense ?]

20. A philosopher was asked who deserved most pity. He answered: 'Three kinds of people: A pious man subjected to a sinner's authority; he is always distressed about what he sees and hears. An intelligent man under a fool's control; he is always weary and grieved. And a noble man dependent on a mean man; he is always humiliated and degraded.'

21. Someone else said: 'An intelligent man's enmity harms you less than a fool's friendship.'

22. Someone else said: 'Whoever talks about people, people talk about him, and whoever does [or says] something frequently becomes known for it.'

23. Someone else said: 'Your hand is part of you even when it is withered.'

24. When someone menacing Euclid said: 'I will leave nothing untried in order to rob you of your life', he replied: 'And I shall leave nothing untried in order to free you from your anger' [Plutarch, *De fraterno amore* 489D; *Gnom. Vat.*, no. 278, Sternbach (*Wiener Studien*, X, 237 f.).]

25. Three philosophers, a Greek, an Indian and a Persian, assembled at a king's court, and he invited them to say something that would demonstrate their intelligence and their knowledge. The Greek said: 'I can refute what I have not said more easily than what I have said.' The Indian said: 'I wonder how a man can say something that will bring him harm if related in his name and be of no use to him if not related.' The Persian said: 'What I have said rides me, and what I have not said, I ride.'

26. Polemo [Aflīmūn] said to his companions: 'Use pure friendliness in dealing with free men; in dealing with subordinates use what they desire and fear; in dealing with the rabble use what terrorizes and humiliates.'

27. He was asked which was the best ruler. He answered: 'He

who masters his desire and is not enslaved by his passion.' [Cf. Stob., *Flor.*, IV, 257 Wachsmuth-Hense (Isocrates), as a closely related parallel.]

28. Timaeus [Timon[12]] was asked why he was always speaking only evil of men. He answered: 'Because I am not in a position to inflict evil on them.'

29. Hesiod said: 'A man is called good in the first degree if he does good on his own, and he is called good in the second degree if he accepts the good when he learns it from someone else' [*Erga* 293, 295; cf. *Nicom. Ethics* 1095b 10].

30. ʾrswrws [Aesop] said: 'Every man carries two bags of provisions round his neck, one in front and one behind. The one in front is for seeing the bad sides and mistakes of others, and the one behind is for seeing his own bad sides and mistakes' [Antonius Melissa 932B].

31. Khrwsbs [*leg.* Anacharsis] said: 'Vines bear three kinds of grapes: grapes of pleasure, grapes of intoxication and grapes of folly' [Ibn Duraid, no. 28, Rosenthal].

32. Democritus was asked how one best prospers in the world. He answered: 'Through luck.' [Cf. Pindar, p. 271, Schroeder; 343, Turyn.]

33. Zosimus [?] was asked to lend one of his friends money. He refused, and when blamed for it, excused himself with the following remark: 'I prefer to have a red face once than have it turn pale many times' [Ibn Duraid, no. 40, Rosenthal; cf. no. 158].

34. Ammonius said: 'Understanding is based on clarification, clarification on meditation,[13] meditation on questioning and questioning on definitions.'

35. Ammonius said: 'Three things alone can harm a ruler, namely, drinking wine, listening to music and conversation with women. All three ruin the mind.'

36. Ammonius said: 'The difference between a philosopher and a nonphilosopher is that the philosopher speaks through the intermediary of thinking and pays no attention whatever to the imagination. The nonphilosopher, on the other hand, speaks only through the intermediary of the imagination and does not use thinking.'

37. He said: 'If somebody is technically inclined, he must

constantly polish his imagination, and if scientifically inclined, he must constantly polish his thinking. For the technician's knowledge rests on the sensibilia while the scientists' knowledge depends on the intelligibilia.'

38. Theophrastus said: 'The educated man is the one who speaks of a man's good sides and keeps his bad sides secret.'

39. Demosthenes said: 'Man is a flame surrounded on every side by wind.'

40. Theocritus saw how a teacher who had a bad handwriting was teaching [writing], and asked him: 'Why do you not teach wrestling?' He answered: 'I cannot wrestle well.' Then he said: 'But you are teaching writing which you also cannot do well!' [Ibn Duraid, no. 44, Rosenthal].

41. Dywqwmys was asked how a person should behave so as never to be in need. He answered: 'If he is rich, he must be moderate, and if he is poor, he must work constantly.'

42. Nicomachus says: 'There is no greater educator than the intellect and no better warner than time. A clever man is one who accepts warning from the example set by another, before he himself becomes an example.'

43. Hipparchus said: 'Things caused last only as long as their nearest causes last. When the cause of love lasts, it itself lasts.'

44. Telemachus said: 'He who does not accept wisdom avoids it, not that it avoids him.'

45. 'nyq'nyws [Epiphanius ?] said: 'In the presence of a sluggard, one should not discuss the value of philosophical concepts. Animals notice only that gold and silver weigh heavily but not that they are valuable. Similarly, the sluggard, too, feels only that philosophical matters require a lot of toil and does not notice how valuable they are.'

46. Thales of Miletus was asked why men were not punished for evil thoughts but only for evil deeds. He answered: 'Because one intends that a man should do no evil deed whatever his thoughts may be, but one does not intend that he should not think.'

47. Sophocles said: 'You may not consider yourself a human being as long as wrath ruins your reason or you follow your desires.' [Cf. no. 144.]

48. Pindar said: 'What has been cannot be undone, whether

it happened justly or not. However, we can cure it, not by remembering it but by forgetting it' (Ol. II, 29–34 [16–20] = 12 f., Schroeder; 10, Turyn).

49. Archigenes said: 'I would blame myself should I not thereby praise myself.'

50. He said: 'If by saying "I do not know" I would not imply that I do know, I would say "I do not know".'

51. He said: 'A man honours himself if he speaks only of what he thoroughly understands.'

52. Plutarch fashioned an ox from clay and sacrificed it on the day when his compatriots used to sacrifice to their idols. He said: 'It is ugly to slaughter a living creature that breathes in honour of something that neither lives nor breathes' [Ibn Duraid, no. 15, Rosenthal].

53. He said: 'Truth is wholly beautiful, and the most beautiful truth is when a person who knows says concerning something he does not know: "I have no knowledge of it." When one hears someone say: "I do not know," he is a person who knows, and when one hears someone say: "I am a person who knows," he is ignorant.'

54. Deucalion said: 'If you cannot on your own acquire as much knowledge as the ancients, you must enrich yourself with their wealth. For they have left treasures of knowledge for you in their books. Hence, open them, study them and enrich yourself with them! Do not be like a blind man who holds a jewel in his hand but does not recognize it and cannot see its beauty!' [Cf. no. 125.]

55. Pindar [Phaedrus ?] said: 'I marvel at those who shrink from saying what is ugly but seek to do it, who boast of the beautiful but avoid doing it as much as they ought to avoid the ugly.' [Cf. nos 75 and 124.]

56. Democritus said: 'Patience is a strong fortress. Haste is the ruin of manliness and brings regret with it. Truth is the fruit of nobility. Greed is the excess of desires.'

57. Polemo [Aflīmūn] said: 'How little use is great knowledge together with an immoderate nature and a strong desire, and how very useful is a little knowledge together with a moderate nature and subdued desire.'

58. Crito said: 'When nature gains the upper hand, it annuls

knowledge and causes one to forget the consequence. Were knowledge firmly established, it would gain the upper hand.'

59. Timaeus said: 'He who resolves to be content with nothing and to believe in nothing, cannot be moved to change his attitude even if thousands of philosophers and rhetoricians were to assemble especially for this purpose, since he is content to be discontented and believes that he does not believe. Whatever they say is wasted on him, and their attempts to explain his difficulty would be strange. That he is little content with philosophy does not diminish its value, rather [does it show] that he is not up to it.'[14]

60. Dyqwmys was asked why the wealthy walked about haughty and boastful while scholars did not act so. He answered: 'Because scholars are aware of God and know that one cannot compete with His glory, while the fools do not know what they have to do in this respect.'[15]

61. He was asked whether it was better to seek wisdom or wealth. He answered: 'For this world wealth, for the next wisdom.'

62. Ariston said: 'Low people resemble mules which carry gold and silver and feed on straw' [*Gnom. Vat.*, no. 120, Sternbach (*Wiener Studien*, X, 23)].

63. He attended a banquet and was silent for a long time. When asked why he did not speak, he said: 'A fool is a man who cannot be silent' [Plutarch, *Apophth. Laconum* 220A].

64. The pious Aristides was asked why a certain man had so much to do with the ruler. He answered: 'Because he wants to rise high among men.'[16] When asked what aim he himself pursued, he answered: 'To guard myself from fools.'

65. Hieronymus [?] was asked why a certain person avoided him. He answered: 'It makes no difference whether he comes [towards me] or turns his back [on me].' On being informed that he had uttered threats against him, he said: 'He assumes that he is injuring me; he should rather benefit himself.'

66. When Pindar [Phaedrus ?] was informed that someone spoke well of him, he replied: 'I will certainly reward him for it.' They asked him: 'In what way?' and he answered: 'By making what he says come true.'

67. Pindar [Phaedrus ?] said: 'When the soul discards the burden of shameful deeds and banishes the cares which prevent the doing of good deeds, its tongue will surely be in a position to

captivate listeners and let them drink of the pure and sweet fountains of wisdom, and never will it happen to it that it has nothing or too little to give. It makes fools wise and nourishes children. Each time it distributes its wealth and gives it away, it becomes ever more and more.'

68. Timonides said: 'Who can assess the amount of the wealth of the soul, which is immortal and cannot be robbed, from which nothing can ever be taken away against its will, since it always generously bestows of its wealth on everyone to whom it sees fit to give something. He who enjoys its generosity then finds himself in one of two conditions: either he thrives on its gifts or he despises it and its wealth.'

69. ʾnyqṭws [Epictetus ?] said: 'Through wisdom in speech and gentleness in listening, the treasures and noble roots of the soul are manifest. Whoever is not of this kind, is, in our view, comparable to animals who have no power of discernment and can acquire neither intelligence nor a clear manner of expression.'

70. ʾsfsbws [Speusippus ?] said: 'If one undertakes to speak to fools and blockheads about philosophy, they will, owing to their total incapacity to understand details, do no more than resemble beasts of burden which are laden with gold, pearls and precious stones but understand nothing of them; rather do they complain constantly of the weight of their load, entirely unaware that it is better than any other load.'

71. Brṭws said: 'Scholars, philosophers, teachers and leading personalities who say and teach what does not accord with their actions deserve by right to be severely censured in public for what they have said but not done, what they have found worthy of censure in others but have not remedied in their own persons. Philosophical speeches turn nobody into a philosopher, only philosophical deeds. On the basis of their actions, philosophers are called outstanding and learned. What they are they demonstrate through their actions. Whoever is subject to shortcomings may not censure them, and sinners may not reproach them with being sinners.'

72. Polus [?] said: 'Had not the philosophers before us stored such treasures, undertaken such activity willingly in our interest, opened such gates for our departure and paved such paths for us to follow them, we should have been found just as deficient and

wretched as we were before the philosophers had banished poverty through wealth [?] and before the sources of poverty were silted up in front of us. We should have been considered no better than the blind who come across a pearl but cannot see its light and beauty, so that it appears to them like a common worthless thing.'

73. Bryqwnsw [*peri kosmū* ??] said concerning the love of women and lust for the female sex: 'They are debit accounts for fools and great storehouses of sin.'

74. Xenophon said: 'A vessel or measure cannot contain more than its capacity permits, and one cannot at will add more, since it would then flow over, but one can put in less. Thus hearts, too, can only contain of the treasures of wisdom as much as their capacity permits.' [Cf. no. 111.]

75. Pindar [Phaedrus ?] said: 'I marvel at those who say they hate shameful deeds but endeavour to do them, who love good deeds but shun them as if they were shameful and evil deeds. How can one describe someone who loves what he hates, hates what he loves and eventually regards the evil deeds he commits as good deeds, and the good deeds he does not do as evil!' (Cf. nos 55 and 124[17].)

76. Crito said: 'Who can walk straight ahead between conflicting ambitions which are like dark, towering waves constantly following one another, when the pure of heart look out for the safe and trustworthy courses along which ships are safe from shipwreck and dangers?'

77. ʾmʾrwn [a woman's name] said: 'Fate has indeed destroyed my entire fortune, but it has at the same time taught me to be extremely cautious.'

78. ʾnʾkhws [ʾrʾkḥws, Anacharsis ?] said to his companions: 'Arrange your affairs in this world as if it were something you will never part from, and prepare for your next life as if it were something you will never attain!'

79. The story goes that Basilius[18] said: 'Do not take from everybody all he has, but only that which appears praiseworthy. An apple is not only useful for its scent but also because one can eat it. A flower is useful for its scent, the oleander for its appearance, the date-palm for its fruit, the rose for its blossoms and for its scent. Therefore take the best he has, unless all he has is good; in this case take all! Furthermore, consider not only the capacity

of what you want to take but also your own capacity, namely, whether you are equal to taking it. The bee can suck honey from a flower, man cannot.'

80. Gregory said: 'Painters can reproduce external beauty with their colours and often even improve on it, but internal beauty none can reproduce save he who in reality possesses it.'

81. The story goes that King Eumenes—the name means 'austere'—invited his brothers one day and said to them: 'Dear brothers, if you treat me as a mighty king ruling you, I will behave towards you like a brother, but if you treat me like a brother, I will behave towards you like a ruler' [*Gnom. Vat.*, no. 293, Sternbach (*Wiener Studien*, X, 241)].

82. Melissus said: 'It pains me to have to watch frequently the vain efforts of these who lie awake in anxiety at night, undertake difficult journeys, risk mortal danger on the high seas or live far away from their native land only in order to acquire a fortune of which they know not who will inherit it after their death, while they do not care to strive after the praiseworthy treasures of wisdom whose owner knows no poverty, and which, when those dear to him inherit them, remain none the less still at his disposal wherever he may go, and never leave him. Scholars testify to this by the saying: So-and-so is not dead since his wisdom is not dead.'

83. Fryqnyws says: 'People who spread their wisdom among men who have not even reached the entrance gate to philosophy do not suit me. Whoever speaks a barbaric tongue cannot understand what people who speak languages foreign to him are saying. Thus the fool, too, does not understand what the philosopher says. How could he do so, since he does not know what philosophy is? Such a person regards the pearls spread out in front of him as pebbles and pumicestone. This is, however, detrimental to philosophical remarks uttered in his presence, and they become falsified when they are wafted towards such a fool and knock at the locked gate of his ear, without anybody opening for them. Hence the philosopher should always be aware how highly they must be esteemed and honoured, and he should not allow his remarks to reach the gate of the fool and suffer trouble and misery there. Not only do they suffer damage when a fool, who has no power of discrimination, rejects them, but he who makes them available to him in this way also suffers thereby.'

84. Pindar [Phaedrus ?] said: 'Just as from a body whose soul has departed, a stench penetrates the noses of those who bury it and are in its vicinity, similarly from the mouth of a fool who lacks wisdom, the second soul, no word comes forth that does not smell foully and harm the hearer. And just as the body is not conscious of the stench that proceeds from it, since it is dead, the fool also does not notice the stench of his words, since he has no power of discrimination.'

85. Gorgias [?] said: 'Blessed are the philosophers who are few! Everyone wishes to be called a philosopher. Yet by merely wishing he does not gain the name of philosopher, and the name does not thereby adhere to him. The name adheres to him who sincerely exerts himself for philosophy and patiently pursues it. I have the greatest respect for people who can teach and educate themselves. It is very easy to teach and educate others. The great difficulty lies in teaching oneself.'

86. Xenophon said: 'The philosopher must determine what he knows for certain and of what he is firmly convinced, and what has become decisive for him as a result. This he must then teach his disciples. It is shameful to teach others and ask them to do and like what one does not like oneself.'

87. Anacharsis was asked how a drunkard could be cured and induced to give up drinking. He replied: 'When he is sober, let him see how wine affects the drunkard, and he will dislike being similarly affected by it' [Diog. Laert., I, 103; Stob., *Flor.*, III, 522, Wachsmuth-Hense].

88. Diogenes[19] said: 'I have observed how people, when food is served to them, insist on bright lamps and plenty of oil in order to be able to see the foods with which they stuff their bellies and which do not stay with them. But they do not care for the nourishment of the precious soul and do not insist on making any preparations for it and on kindling the lamps of the intellect through knowledge and insight, in order to avoid errors in this way and be safe from the consequences of folly and blunders' [Stob., *Flor.*, II, 214, Wachsmuth-Hense].

89. Ywswywrs [Musonius[20]] said: 'Remember that pleasure is full of ugliness and remember that pleasure passes but ugliness remains!' [Ibn Duraid, no. 47, Rosenthal.]

90. Msqwlws [Musonius ?] the Athenian said: 'My true exist-

ence rests on my knowing the truth, yet I cannot describe it. I only know that it exists.'

91. Crito said: 'Through my knowledge that philosophers alone are not harmed by death, I have attained greater insight. He who has perfected himself in philosophy may wish for death. Yet he who does not master it must most zealously try to escape from death. For nothing resists death and escapes the grief it causes except perfection in philosophy' [*Liber de pomo*, pp. 206 f., 233 f., Margoliouth[21]].

92. Zeno said: 'What Aristotle says leaves us no possibility of deriving benefit from this world, enjoying a pleasure and hoping for lasting existence. He can only envisage death more confidently than we, though we are not afraid of it, because he has improved his own soul, which we have not done. If we had improved our souls as he has done, and expelled from them the greed, desire and anger that accompany them as he has done, we would be able to envisage death just as confidently as he.'

When Solon[22] said: 'My weariness of life does not induce me to summon death before it comes by itself,' Zeno asked him: 'Why do you hesitate since you are sure of great honour after death?' Solon answered: 'I am like a guard at a frontier region. If he stays at his post, he remains there in distress, and when he withdraws, honour awaits him.' Thereupon Zeno asked him how this simile was to be explained, and Solon replied: 'That which remains at its post is the soul of the philosopher. The frontier region is his body. The enemies are greed, desire and anger, which are opposed to the soul. The distress is their conquest and banishment through the soul. Honour is joy in the next world, to which the philosopher's soul withdraws' [*De pomo*, pp. 497, 501, Margoliouth].

93. ʾsfryʾs said: 'If I endured wisdom only in order no longer to be called ignorant and blind, it would be worthwhile' [*De pomo*, pp. 207, 234, Margoliouth].

94. Dorotheus [? Zeno] said: 'If I endured wisdom only in order to escape the terrors and sorrows of death, it would be worthwhile' [*De pomo*, pp. 207 f., 234, Margoliouth].

95. Qrnyws [Crito ?] said: 'It is one of the most secure uses of philosophy that it has consolidated my worries and made them into a single worry' [*De pomo*, pp. 208, 234 f., Margoliouth].

96. Qrn'y's [Carneades ?] said: 'If there are only worried people in the world, then the most fortunate is the one who worries about what endures' [*De pomo*, pp. 208, 235, Margoliouth].

97. Phaedrus said: 'In this world everybody is at war, and the closest enemies most deserve to be fought.' Whereupon 'nkṭws [Archytas ?] said: 'The philosopher's closest enemies are those thoughts of his which harm his philosophy' (*De pomo*, pp. 208, 235, Margoliouth).

98. Fyrys [Pyrrho ?, Bryson ?] said: 'I blame people who say: "All men ought necessarily to be of one opinion." That is no good. If all men were of one opinion, everyone would want to be the ruler who commands and is obeyed. Who should then receive the orders and show obedience, if all were rulers and nobody remained who would be content with less than being a ruler, and who would carry out the ruler's orders? Whoever is trained in philosophy knows that it is best when the leader gives orders and he who receives the orders carries them out, just as it is best when the pupil learns and the teacher teaches. Human nature testifies to that.'

99. Democritus said: 'It is fitting for someone who comes to a strange land and knows nothing of its inhabitants to be quietly and peacefully his own spy and observe the way of life of local philosophers, to gather information about them and their teachings, and then to measure all that by his own standards. If through comparison of that which they have with what he himself has he perceives that what he has is better and superior, he should offer his philosophy there, so that they recognize the superiority of what he has and can borrow from it if necessary. Should he, however, find that what he has is inferior to what they have, he need not therefore grieve, but should take as much as possible from their tents[23] and move on.'

100. Theophrastus said: 'Intelligent tax collectors collect more by mild methods than they would gather by harsh and violent ones, just as the leech collects more blood without causing pain or making a sound than the mosquito with its sharp sting and awful noise.'

101. Sophocles said: 'Use guile before anything happens, for after it has happened, guile is limited [in its effect] and the mind is confused.'

102. Flyks,[24] the disciple of Pythagoras, said: 'Unfortunate the man who wrongs the unprotected and serves someone who is of no use to him.'

103. Sblʾqws [Simplicius ?] said: 'It is best if one abstains from all that is excessive and pursues what is right. A livelihood depends on improving one's financial position and having a fixed expense budget, for extravagance is the key to poverty and the door to impotence. Slowness leads to ruin. He needs wealth most who prospers only through wealth. Prosperity lies in seeking advice. To satisfy all men is an unattainable goal. Hence be not loath to arouse the anger of someone satisfied only with injustice. Accustom yourself to exercise patience, and you will be praised for it.'

104. Sophocles said: 'He who achieves power together with authority is like a drunkard if he has no intelligence. He despises beauty, avoids justice, is extremely boastful and vain and does the ugliest things. When he becomes poor and sober again, he knows he was intemperate and had abandoned truth and justice, and he is clearly aware what his intoxication meant.'

105. He said: 'He who looks with a sharp eye and a pure heart and gets rid of desires is successful.'[25]

106. He said: 'An intelligent and energetic ruler is accustomed not to be deceived by the fact that everything is in order and progressing favourably under his leadership and that there are few rebels. Otherwise, he would no longer be concerned for his soldiers, officers and aides, whom he would not pay because he has so little need of them. Furthermore, in reliance on the prosperity of his subjects, he would follow a bad policy and treat his subjects unjustly. Thereby he would become defenceless should something unexpected happen. All would desert him and turn against him. Besides, such behaviour prevents him from lasting long and causes his realm to disintegrate.'

107. (ʾl)Nṭʾfyrs[26] was asked why he had so many enemies. He answered: 'Because I have given up to be intimate with them.' And when asked why he had withdrawn from men, he replied: 'That happened after I came to know them.'

108. Chrysippus [?] was asked why he bore it so patiently when people blamed him. He answered: 'All of us have reprehensible qualities, and I appear in their eyes as they do in mine.'

109. Democritus says: 'You must gather good men around you. You should carefully protect your friends and turn your enemies into friends'.[27]

110. Polemo [Aflīmūn] said to a painter who was decorating a bath house with [wall] paintings: 'Decorate it well, for bath houses are decorated for the benefit of the people. On emerging, they are preoccupied with contemplation of the beautiful pictures, and thus they do not hurry to put on their clothes and go outside. Otherwise, the cold air in winter and the warm air in summer would affect them.'

111. Xenophon said: 'A vessel filled to capacity into which one pours still more, overflows, and thereby something of its original content is possibly stirred up and flows away. Similarly, the mind is capable of absorbing only as much as it can hold; if it wants to absorb more, it becomes confused and possibly loses even some of what it had previously absorbed.' [Cf. no. 74.]

112. Pittacus said: 'When a man becomes very old, he finds it difficult to be a friend. That is because then a great deal works against him, time, luck and repute [? *doxa*]. They remain with none, but pass swiftly to others.'

113. Thales of Miletus said: 'When a man comes, he must know whence he comes and why he comes, and, when he goes back, whither he is going.'

114. Heraclitus said: 'He who endures evil that befalls him [from outside] and does not originate from himself, and avoids the evil that stems from his free will, and, in addition, always obeys God who is his Creator, the source of his being and the element of his substance, is the happy sage.'

115. He said: 'Whoever seeks something but does not attain it and wants to abandon it, should try it again; for fate may enable him to attain it at one time and refuse it to him at another.'

116. He said: 'An intelligent person is not deceived by the flattery and the sweet talk of his enemy; for the peacock despite his sweet voice eats snakes.'

117. He said further: 'An intelligent man is accustomed to look among evil men for friends with whose help he need not fear his enemies. For vinegar there is only its own worm,[28] and iron cuts iron.'

118. When Theophrastus noticed a youth silent for long, he

said to him: 'If you are silent because you have little education, you are educated, but if you are educated, you harm education if you are silent' [*Gnom. Vat.*, no. 333, Sternbach (*Wiener Studien*, X, pp. 259 f.)].

119. He said further: 'If you make an enemy of someone, do not make an enemy of his entire family. On the contrary, make friends with some of them. For that will prevent him from doing you harm.'

120. He said: 'Evil men and their help are needed for mutual advantage, just as the sandalwood tree derives advantage from snakes, and snakes from the sandalwood tree. The snakes profit from the scent and coolness of the sandalwood tree, and the snakes protect it from being felled.'

121. Sophocles said: 'If you punish your friend, he becomes your enemy, and if you punish your enemy, he becomes your friend.'

122. When Diocles the physician was told that someone had bought himself a medical book but did not intend to study it, he said: 'Books are an aid to the memory for those who study them; for others they are fetters' [*Gnom. Vat.*, no. 264, Sternbach (*Wiener Studien*, X, 231)[29]].

123. When he was asked why he did not like being together with his friends, he answered: 'Since I did not find their company praiseworthy, I have withdrawn from them.'

124. Pindar [Phaedrus ?] said further: 'I marvel at people who shrink from saying what is ugly but seek to do it' [Cf. nos 55 and 75.]

125. Deucalion said: [no. 54].

126. He said: 'God is served with ten qualities. (1) When you are given something, be grateful. (2) If a misfortune befalls you, be patient. (3) When you speak, tell the truth. (4) If you promise something, keep it. (5) If you are determined to do something, do it properly. (6) If you have power, forgive. (7) Begin with doing favours before you are asked for them. (8) Honour those who love you. (9) Pardon friends as well as enemies their mistakes. (10) Consider only as acceptable for them what you consider acceptable for yourself.'[30]

127. ʾysywdhs [Hesiod ?] said: 'Conclusion and investigation are comparable to the soul and the body. Both are linked with

one another. Namely, conclusion requires investigation. The assumption that it can exist without investigation or that investigation can exist without it rests on weak grounds. Such a thing can occur, but it happens only very rarely.'

128. When someone blamed Simonides for having lent money to an evil person, he said. 'I did not lend it to the man but to the need' [Cf. Diog. Laert., V, 21, etc.]

129. He said: 'One must honour the good in their lifetime and pray for them after their death' [*Gnom. Vat.*, no. 268, Sternbach (*Wiener Studien*, X, 233 f.)].

130. Menander said: 'Abundant occupation distracts from the existence of pleasures.'

131. Asked when philosophy had manifested itself in him, he answered: 'Since I began to despise myself' [Stob., *Flor.*, III, 558, Wachsmuth-Hense].

132. When Demosthenes the orator heard a youth tell impossible tales, he said to him: 'If someone tells you the like of it, do not believe him. If you think that you yourself have seen something like it, I do not believe you' [H. Schenkl, *Das Florilegium Ariston ktl.* (*Wiener Studien*, XI, 27), no. 90].

133. When somebody talked a great deal at a party, he said to him: 'Why did you not learn from whom you learned to speak, how to be silent as well?' [*Gnom. Vat.*, no. 207, Sternbach (*Wiener Studien*, X, 213)].

134. He said: 'Shame is to beauty as the gate to the city.' [Cf. Stob., *Flor.*, IV, 587, Wachsmuth-Hense.]

135. He was asked how he had acquired more knowledge than all other men. He answered: 'Through spending on oil for the lamp what others have spent on wine' [Ibn Duraid, no. 13, Rosenthal].

136. Aristophanes said: 'A victory through words without deeds is no victory, but a defeat. On the other hand, a victory through deeds, even if they take place without words, is a true victory.'[31]

137. Anaxagoras said: 'Just as death is something bad for anyone for whom life is good, thus it is something good for anyone for whom life is bad. Hence it must not be said that death is good or bad. It is good or bad according to the prevailing circumstances.'

138. Melissus said: 'Nobody is rich whose wealth is preserved

for him for only a brief period, whom another can deprive of his wealth and whose wealth does not remain after his death. Wealth is rather what is permanently preserved for its owner, what nobody can take from him and what remains after his death—all qualities found in knowledge and wisdom.'

139. Heraclitus said: 'The greedy man has no peace, the avaricious no wealth.'

140. He said: 'Wise is he who controls himself, manages his qualities and subdues his desires.'

141. When some boon-companions of King Philip of Macedon advised him, after his victory over Athens, to destroy the city, he said: 'What could be more shameful than to do something that would turn our victory into a defeat?'

142. He asked the misanthrope and ascetic, Antipater, why he spent his life so entirely without anything, since after all, he did not know what would happen later. He answered: 'So that I should not be too much affected when something occurs' [Schenkl, *Das Florilegium Ariston ktl.* (*Wiener Studien*, XI, 38), no. 148].

143. When the mother of Thales begged him to get married, he said that the time for it had not yet come. When a considerable time had elapsed, and she pressed him again and again, he said: 'The time for marrying is over' [Diog. Laert., I, 26; *Gnom. Vat.*, no. 318, Sternbach (*Wiener Studien*, X, 251)].

144. Sophocles said: [no. 47].

145. He said: 'Whoever strives for more than he needs gets distracted from that which is of use to him.'

146. Euripides said: 'The tongue swears falsely, but the intellect does not swear falsely. That is the meaning of our assertion: whoever swears and lies, swears and lies, if he does so with his tongue, but if he does it with his intellect, he does not swear and lie. Hence, endeavour to achieve harmony between your tongue and your intellect' [Hippolytus 612].

147. Theognis said: 'Do not ask God for something that you have; for God gives everyone what suffices him. You should rather ask God for something that you do not have—that what you have may suffice you.'

148. Brsqs said: 'Since the common people assume that God is only to be found in the temples, they think that you must behave well and orderly only in the temples. But those who possess true

insight and know that God is to be found in every place must behave everywhere as the common people do in the temples.'

149. Protagoras said: 'Since the tongue is an instrument for the interpretation of ideas that enter the soul, it must not be used for anything that has not entered the soul.'

150. Sophocles said: 'Whoever thinks[32] that he possesses only a natural life is unhappy. That is because he is like the shadow that swiftly vanishes, like the plant that withers quickly. He remains on earth for only a short while and lives like the wild beasts. Yet he who knows that he has a life of the soul as well, that he is immortal and remains forever imitates God in his actions and does only what is good.'

151. Plutarch said: 'How useful it is for us to watch our actions, to consider our being, to do or say nothing carelessly, thoughtlessly or aimlessly and to be completely blameless in all our undertakings' [*De capienda ex inimicis utilitate* 87D[33]].

He said further: 'If you wish to cause your enemy pain,[34] do not call him a fool, a liar, a slanderer, but show that you yourself are the opposite of all these. Be considerate, honest, merciful and just to everybody. If you rashly accuse him of lying, avoid being yourself a liar. Consider what you do and do not be like the man to whom one says: "How comes it that you are a doctor and nevertheless covered with sores?" If you call him a fool, be wise yourself. If you call him greedy, keep back from desires yourself. For there is nothing uglier and more shameful than an accusation that can be raised against the accuser himself' [*De cap. util.* 88C–D].

Antisthenes said: 'He who would like to be praised for his actions must have honest friends or foes whom he fears; for the former keep him from stumbling, and the latter restrain him from evil' [*De cap. util.* 89B].

Plutarch said: 'Since the voice of love is subdued and cannot reprove rudely and loudly, but rather uses gentle words mixed with flattery, we must seek truth from our enemies and listen to it' [*De cap. util.* 89B].

He said further: 'There are people who, when one abuses them, do not first consider whether they did not deserve it, but immediately revile those who abused them in return. They resemble two wrestlers who wrestle with each other and upon whom one throws ashes. They do not shake it off, but throw it back at the one who threw it at them, and everyone gets soiled. This also applies to anyone who abuses in return instead of shaking off the insult' [*De cap. util.* 89D].

152. Plutarch said: 'Do not neglect your friend's affairs and despise none for whose help in need and participation in good times you hope. How exceedingly harmful that kind of thing is! If your wall collapses, it is only the wall that suffers damage. But if you lose friendship and friends, the damage is enormous. Your friend becomes an enemy; instead of advantage one receives harm from him, and you are not safe from his mischief and enmity.'

153. He said further: 'Whoever is inflamed by anger forgets everything, till he is like a house on fire full of noise and smoke, so that one cannot see or hear anything inside it, or like a ship driven by the wind or hurled high by the waves, and nothing can be done for it from outside. When the soul is excited by anger, external admonitions are of no use to it, and it[s fire] cannot be extinguished' [*De cohib. ira* 453F–454A].

'If somebody considers a little anger unimportant, it can lead to his being inflamed by violent anger, just as flames flare up readily in straw and firewood and eventually burn down great castles and forests. In many instances, silence extinguishes anger; for whoever robs fire of its fuel, extinguishes it, and he who is silent extinguishes anger' [*De cohib. ira* 454E].

He said further: 'A drunken man cannot recognize the ugliness and filth of drunkenness while he is drunk, until he perceives it in others. In the same way, a man who is angry cannot recognize the ugliness of anger, unless he perceives the effect of anger on another. Just as a shrunken face, a yellowish tinge of the nose and sunken eyes are signs of a patient's [imminent] death, the change of a face in anger is a sign of the [imminent] death of the mind' [*De cohib. ira* 455E].[35]

'Just as one can deduce the depth and extent of boils from the size of the swelling, so can one deduce the distemper in their hearts from the words of angry people. This is proved by the fact that women lose their tempers more quickly than men, sick people are more bad tempered than the healthy, and the aged remain angry longer than young men. This shows that anger stems from weakness and folly of the soul, not from its strength and courage' [*De cohib. ira* 457A–B].

He said: 'A bad tempered man, who quickly flies into a temper, should not acquire very valuable and rare vessels, furniture and utensils, whose loss or breakage would highly excite him' [*De cohib. ira* 461E–F].

'Satisfaction with what one possesses makes us pleasant in intercourse with our relatives and friends' [*De cohib. ira* 462A].

154. Anacharsis the Scythian [*Saqlābī*] attended a gathering of sages. He got involved in a discussion, and one of those present said to him: 'Keep your mouth shut, Scythian.' Whereupon he replied: 'My shame is my origin. Your shame is you yourself' [Diog. Laert., I, 104].

155. He saw that a man was worried, and said to him: 'Stop musing, for it causes waste of time.'[36]

156. Agis was asked why there were evil people. He answered: 'In order that men might be distracted from thinking about their own wickedness by what they tell of them.'

157. They asked ʾyrwthyqs [Hierotheus ?] what the pleasure of the soul was. He answered: 'The contemplation of the bliss of eternal life, which provides a feeling of security for souls and rest for hearts, as well as the realization of the true nature of the supernatural through thoughts in the breast and the vision of the innermost mysteries through reflection.'

158. Someone asked Zosimus [?] to lend him money. He refused, and when somebody blamed him for this and said that that man had shamed him, he replied: 'He did no more than make my face red once. Had I lent him the money, he would have made my face pale many times.' [Cf. no. 33.]

C. METAPHYSICS

'Plato's disciples are divided into three groups, namely, Seekers of Illumination, Stoics and Peripatetics.

The Seekers of Illumination [*Ishrāqīyūn*] among them have cleared the tablets of their intellect from all records of earthly existence. Hence the rays of the lights of truth from the tablets of the Platonic soul have illuminated them without the mediation of remarks and the intervention of allusions.

The Stoics [*Riwāqiyūn*] are those who used to sit in the portico of his house and derived wisdom from his remarks and allusions.[37]

The Peripatetics [*Mashshā'ūn*] are those who used to walk alongside his stirrup and receive the pearls of his wisdom. Aristotle belonged to them, and it is frequently claimed that the Peripatetics are those who used to walk alongside Aristotle's stirrup, not Plato's' (al-ʿĀmilī, *Kashkūl* [Cairo 1380/1961], I, p. 312).

The philosophy of illumination was propagated in the twelfth century by the great mystic Shihāb-ad-dīn as-Suhrawardī, and it is in fact essentially of Neo-Platonic origin. Of all Greek metaphysical systems, Neo-Platonism appealed most to Islamic thinkers. Even in pre-Islamic times it had been intimately connected with Near Eastern monotheism. It was not very difficult for its doctrine of emanation to be reconciled with monotheism and mysticism. Translations of their works or, rather, of elaborations of and commentaries on them made all the great Neo-Platonists familiar to the Arabs. Much Neo-Platonic thought also came to them through the Aristotelian commentaries, though Aristotle himself, since he represented the doctrine of the eternity of the world, was less acceptable to the Muslims in metaphysical matters than Plato. Yet the doctrine of the First Mover was considered entirely on a par with that of the First Cause, the One Pure Good.

The basic fund of Muslim theological ideas was developed by the Muʿtazilah and in the struggle of the 'orthodoxy' against them in the eighth and ninth centuries (cf. above, pp. 4 f.). A good example of the final results of this development on the rationalist level is Ibn Rushd's 'Incoherence', which is available in the English translation of S. van den Bergh (London, 1954). All of it was borrowed from metaphysical theories of Hellenistic origin. Sometimes these theories were already strongly Christianized before they reached the Muslims. Old inherited religious conceptions such as those of angels, jinn and an inescapable destiny persisted almost unchanged in the popular faith of Islam. However, even these primitive demons became a kind of spiritual and intellectual beings, at any rate for scholars and educated men. They had a secure place in the process of emanation which permitted the interpretation of destiny as Providence based on the emanation of divine power.

The First Mover and the intellect

1. From Alexander of Aphrodisias, *The Principles of the Universe*, ed. ʿAbd-ar-Raḥmān Badawī, *Arisṭū ʿind al-ʿArab*, pp. 266–70_{13}. The rather faulty text of the Istanbul MS Carullah 1279, 56a–57b, has been compared with Badawī's text.

If movement is eternal, the First Mover, if he is one, is also eternal. If the Mover is many, the eternal things are also many. One must assume, however, that the First Mover is one and not many and that the things are finite and not infinite. For since the accidents are always single things in themselves, it is best and most fitting to assume that in natural matters the finite is preferable to the infinite wherever possible. It is sufficient for us that the one and eternal which existed before all things is immovable and the start of the movement of all other things and that the cause of the eternal movement is also one.

Alexander says that Aristotle then brings a proof for this, as follows:

> What I say clearly has the necessary consequence that the First Mover is something one and eternal. For it is clear that movement must of necessity be lasting, and if it is lasting, it necessarily follows that it is continuous, since a lasting movement is something continuous, while one which takes place by degrees is not continuous. Yet though continuous, it is still one in relation to the one mover and the one thing that moves.

Alexander says: If the thing that moves [the mover ?] by way of its desire is one, since the entire divine body which moves in a circular, continuous and regular movement does not move only through those things [?], one should accept providence [*pronoia*] for the things beneath the sphere of the moon, with their free choice of and disposition for it, as the reason for it. In this way, it is in fact possible for a thing around which bodies move in a circle to remain eternal in its kind, since the forms of the movers may be numerous and, though not entirely separate in kind, still different from one another through priority with respect to substantiality and nobility, as Aristotle has explained in his *Meta-*

physics, since originally no thing has priority over those substances. Among those substances which are higher and nobler than all other substances, we find a difference according to their nobility and priority. It is a justified supposition that something better than something else is not better because it shares in its opposite. The fiery flame which is less hot than heated iron is not less hot because of an admixture of cold, just as a body that is less fertile is surely not less fertile because it shares bad matter. Hence we can assume that the noblest of these things, which deserves the highest priority, is the mover of the sphere of the fixed stars and that through it he also moves the things whose movement originates from it. Next comes the mover of the second sphere, the third and so forth, so that the differing speeds of the spheres' movements are caused by the difference between the moving causes. We have previously explained the nature of this difference.

A difference between incorporeal things cannot, as many people assume, result from a body. For one should not maintain that one incorporeal thing cannot be different from another; for it is incorporeal because the nature of incorporeal things, like that of bodies, is not one. The various kinds of the category of substances prove this. We must believe that all spheres have souls, that each individual sphere has its special soul and that it moves with its natural movement because of the desire peculiar to its nature. The nature of those things, that is, the souls, ⟨. . .⟩,[38] since the form of the divine body is the most perfect of all forms, and the souls of divine bodies do not require the various eternal bodies at all for their activity. The First Mover who perceives and desires through the intellect moves the thing that moves towards Him only because it is intellectually perceived, just as the lover moves the beloved without himself moving, since He is not a body and is entirely free from elementary matter and separate in every respect. When the beloved causes the movement of the lover, [it is as if] something whose essence desires sets its own essence in motion and that whose essence desires is something good. This situation corresponds exactly to that of the First Mover. Consequently He must move His essence if it is to be possible for Him to recognize and know His essence intellectually.

This Mover causes not only the activity of the divine living body corresponding to Him and its peculiar perfection, but He also causes the habitation of the earth through human beings. Supreme happiness, including all that is praiseworthy, is the perception of that thing by means of the intellect; for man's true perfection lies in philosophical speculation, as has been explained elsewhere. For the principle and beginning of speculation is the perception of divine things through the intellect. All things that take part in the speculation attain the perfection due to them, which man describes as true perfection, through the actions proceeding from them and through what has been intellectually perceived. Nothing that does not possess intellectual perception can absorb any good that is truly and absolutely good, since true perfection exists only in what possesses intellectual perception.

The First Mover is an eternal, immovable, incorporeal substance; He is better than all existing things and the causer of the first, eternal movement. The causer of this movement is Himself only set in motion through intellectual perception of what can truly and actually be perceived intellectually. For that which can actually be perceived intellectually is itself actual intellect, because intellectual perception takes place through the acquisition of what is intellectually perceptible, and that which the intellect acquires through perception assimilates to it, and thereby becomes identical with it. Hence one says that what perceives intellectually perceives its own essence intellectually during intellectual perception, since it then becomes identical with it during the process.

The first to move is again truly and actually perceived by the intellect. Since it is described as something 'truly and actually', it also has existence. For it is an intellect better than the intellectually perceived, and something actually intellectually perceptible is identical with the intellect, since it is itself actual intellect. This means that in a state of intellectual perception the intellect is identical with the intellectually perceptible and that, in respect of the intellectually perceptible, the intellect is then something that actually perceives intellectually, since the actual intellect, in respect of what is actually intellectually perceptible, is identical with the intellect originating from the action.

Of intellectually perceptible things which have existence only together with matter, none is absolutely and through its own nature actually intellectually perceptible, but only when it is intellectually perceived and, through what is intellectually perceptible in it, separates itself from the matter with which it jointly has existence, is it actually intellect and intellectually perceptible. Since it is not absolute intellect and also not identical with what is intellectually perceived by it, it is only in a state of intellectual perception that it becomes one with the intellect.

The form that is completely separated from matter and potentiality, since it is, owing to its own nature, intellectually perceptible, exists constantly in actuality. We may describe it as intellect in its essence, not because of something different from it, which it perceives intellectually, but rather because it can be actual intellect by virtue of its essence and because actual intellect is such only through intellectual perception. Accordingly, the form behaving in this way, that is to say the constantly actual form, must be identical with the intellect. And since the substances whose actions are good are also constituted thus, and good actions can exist only in good things, one must assume that the activity of this intellect, that is, its intellectual [actual ?] perceiving, extends solely to what is best of all existing things. The First Intellect, however, is better than all of them. Hence, since it perceives its own essence intellectually, what is intellectually perceived by it must be better than all existing things, since it progresses to something intellectually perceptible which is not its own essence. Something shameful follows from this, namely, that this progress must be accompanied by a movement. Something that perceives many things intellectually is not the best, but rather that which perceives good things continually. Hence, the intellect must constantly perceive its own essence intellectually. For in this way it is simple, immovable and enduring in the same condition for all times. . . .

2. From Ibn Rushd's commentary on the *Lambda* of the *Metaphysics* 1073a 3–10, according to the edition of M. Bouyges (Beirut, 1948, *Bibliotheca Arabica Scholasticorum*, VII), III, pp. 1626–8. Ibn Rushd says (1392 f.) that he had a commentary of Alexander of Aphrodisias and a paraphrase of Themistius at his disposal.

Here he points out what the preceding arguments have shown him, namely, that there is an eternal substance which does not move and which is separate from all material elements. That it is a substance, that it is an intellect, that it causes movement just as the beloved moves the lover, that it also possesses all other demonstrated qualities of that mover—that is something which has become evident here in this book. That it does not move and that it is separated from matter, that has become evident at the end of the eighth book of the *Physics*. He also points to it in the words: 'It has emerged that that substance can have no dimension, but is something which has neither part nor divisibility.' By this he means: It has become evident in natural science that that mover cannot be a power in a body or a body, since it has no parts and is indivisible, either essentially or accidentally, while every body has parts and is divisible.

Then he stated the reason why it cannot happen that it should either essentially or accidentally have parts. For he says: 'Since it causes movement for an infinite period of time.' By this he means: Thus it must possess an infinite power.

Then he says: 'No finite thing has an infinite power.' By this he means: That which has an infinite power is of necessity no body, since every body is finite and nothing finite has an infinite power. Hence the syllogism can be constructed in the following way: The first mover has an infinite power. Every body and every power in a body is finite. Hence, according to the second figure, the first mover is neither a body nor a power in a body.

Since a body must of necessity have a finite power, since every body is finite and corporeal powers are divisible through the division of the body, he here undertakes to state the cause of this and hence says: 'Every dimension is either infinite or finite.' By this he means: Every power must of necessity be in a finite body; for if it were infinite, it would have to be either in an infinite body or in a finite body. But there can be no infinite body. Hence the power is in a finite body. And if an infinite power were in a finite body, that body would have to be in motion in the present, according to what has been set forth in the eighth book of the *Physics*, since he only refers to these things briefly here. This is what he points out in the words: 'For this reason it is not in a finite dimension and there is nothing infinite, since there is no infinite dimension at all.' By this he means: The reason why infinite power exists neither in a finite nor in an infinite body is, in the case of the infinite body, due to the fact that there is no infinite body and, in the case of the finite body, to the fact that the power is divisible through the division of the body and whatever is divisible through the division of something finite is finite.

The First Cause

3. From the *Liber de causis*, ed. O. Bardenhewer, *Die pseudo-aristotelische Schrift Über das reine Gute, bekannt unter dem Namen Liber de causis* (Freiburg, 1882), pp. 95–103; ed. 'Abd-ar-Raḥmān Badawī, *Neoplatonici apud Arabes* (Cairo, 1955), pp. 20_{10}–25_{2}. For a long time, only a single Arabic manuscript was known. For another in Istanbul, cf. *Journal of the American Oriental Society*, LXXXI (1961), pp. 8 f.; according to Fuad Sezgin, its original is in Ankara. Cf. further *Orientalia*, n.s., XXI (1952), p. 471. Bardenhewer's emendations of the Arabic text, where they are based on medieval translations, have frequently been taken into account. For the *Liber de causis*, cf. G.-C. Anawati, *Prolégomènes à une nouvelle édition du De causis arabe*, in *Mélanges Louis Massignon* (Damascus, 1956), I, pp. 73–110.

It was already recognized by Thomas Aquinas, and it may well have been vaguely known in Arabic tradition, that the *Liber de causis* is an adaptation of the *Stoicheiōsis theologikē* of Proclus. Chapters XIX–XXIII of *De causis* translated here correspond to Proclus, paragraphs 122, 127, 115, 134 and 142. The correspondence is sometimes literal and sometimes remote. Paragraph 115 is very different and its relationship to the Arabic is doubtful, but it appears in fact to be related.

The First Cause guides all created things without mingling with them, since guidance in no way weakens its uniqueness which is exalted above every thing, and since the nature of its uniqueness, which keeps it apart from things, does not prevent it from guiding them. For the First Cause is firm, constant through its pure uniqueness, and lasting. It guides all created things and causes power, life and the goods to emanate upon them in accordance with their potential and capacity.

The First Good causes the goods to emanate evenly upon all things. However, each of the things absorbs from this emanation only as much as it is, through its being, capable of absorbing. The First Good has achieved the uniform emanation of the good upon all things because it is good by virtue of its being, its identity and its power, inasmuch as it is a good and the good and identity are one and the same. The First Identity has become uniformly an identity and a good; and it has likewise achieved the even emanation of the good upon things, without it emanating more upon one thing and less upon another. The goods and virtues differ only by reason of their recipients who absorb them not equally but in varying degrees.

Again we say: Between any agent acting through its being alone and what is effected by it there is neither a bond nor any other intermediary. The bond between agent and effect is merely something additional to the being. That means, if agent and effect created are connected by an instrument and the agent acts not through its essence or some of its qualities and its being is something compounded, such an agent acts through a bond [alien to its being] between itself and its effect; the agent would then be distinct from its action and would not be guiding it correctly and completely. On the other hand, an agent which has no bond between itself and its action is a genuine agent and a genuine guide; it makes things with an accuracy which could not possibly be any greater, and gives its action the best guidance, since it guides a thing through its very action. It acts through its identity, which simultaneously exercises guidance. It has therefore succeeded in guiding and acting perfectly and in a manner that admits neither variation nor inaccuracy. Actions and guidance through the first causes vary only according to the merit of the recipient.

The First Cause is self-sufficient. It is supreme wealth. This is proved by its uniqueness, which is not scattered in it but is rather a pure uniqueness, because it is simple to the highest possible degree. The person who would ascertain that the First Cause is supreme wealth must envisage compounded things and examine them thoroughly. He will then find that all that is compounded is imperfect and deficient. It needs either something additional or the things from which it has been compounded. On the other hand, the simple thing, that means the one which is a good, is one and its uniqueness is a good. The good and the one are one and the same, and that thing constitutes supreme wealth. It causes emanations but receives none in any way. All other things, whether intelligible or sensible, are not self-sufficient. They need the truly one which effects the emanation of the virtues and all the goods upon them.

The First Cause is above any name that one could use, since neither deficiency nor perfection alone apply to it. What is deficient is clearly not perfect and cannot engage in a perfect activity because it is deficient. And what is perfect cannot, in our opinion, even if self-sufficient, create anything else or cause emanation from itself. We can accordingly repeat that the First Cause is neither deficient nor perfect but it is above perfection, since it creates things and causes the goods to emanate upon them in a perfect manner, for it is an infinite and inexhaustible good. The First Good thus fills all worlds with what is good. Yet every world absorbs from it no more than it is capable of absorbing. Hence, it is now fully clear that the First Cause is far above any name that one could use.

Every divine intellect knows the things inasmuch as it is an intellect and guides them inasmuch as it is divine. For the special property of the intellect is knowledge. Its full perfection depends on its being knowing. God is the guide, for He fills the things with the goods. The intellect was the first to be created. It resembles God most closely. It has, therefore, succeeded in guiding the things beneath it. Just as God causes the emanation of the good upon the things, the intellect causes the emanation of knowledge on the things beneath it. Yet although intellect guides the things beneath it, God has priority over the intellect in respect of guidance; He guides the things in a higher sense than the intellect, since it is He who has granted the ability to exercise guidance to the intellect. This can be proved by the fact that those things which are not subject to the intellect's guidance can be guided by the intellect's Creator, since nothing can evade His guidance, for He wants all things to obtain His good. Not every thing longs for the intellect or desires to obtain it, but all things long for the good that springs from the First and fervently wish to possess it. Nobody doubts that.

The First Cause exists equally in all things, but all things do not exist equally in the First Cause, for although the First Cause exists equally in all things, each thing accepts it only according to capacity. Some things accept it in a single way, others in many ways; some accept it permanently, others temporarily; and some accept it spiritually and others corporeally. Such differences in receptive capacity are due not to the First Cause but to the recipients. Since they are varied, receptivity is also varied. The originator of the emanation is one and unvaried. He causes the equal emanation of the goods upon all things. Since the First Cause causes the equal emanation of the goods upon all things, the things must be the cause of the varied effect of the emanation. If the things are the cause of the varied effect of the emanation [of the good] upon the things, there can be no doubt that all things do not exist equally in the First Cause. It is thus clear that while the First Cause exists equally in all things, all things do not exist equally in it. A thing shares in the First Cause and enjoys it in accordance with its proximity to it and the extent of its receptivity for it; for it shares in the First Cause and enjoys it only in accordance with its own existence. Existence is to be understood as knowledge [gnosis]; for it is according to its knowledge of the First creative Cause that a thing shares in it and enjoys it, as we have explained.

The soul's vision of the divine world

4. From the Arabic Plotinus tradition according to the *Theology of Aristotle*, ed. F. Dieterici, *Die sogenannte Theologie des Aristoteles* (Leipzig, 1882), text, pp. 8 f.; (Leipzig, 1883), trans., pp. 8–10; ed. ʿAbd-ar-Rahmān Badawī, *Plotinus apud Arabes* (Cairo, 1955), pp. 22–31₃. Cf. G. Lewis's English translation of the Arabic Plotinus texts in the Plotinus edition of P. Henry and H.-R. Schwyzer (Paris-Brussels, 1959), II, pp. 225–7, to *Enn.* IV, 8.

Often have I been alone with my soul. I have discarded my body and become like an incorporeal, abstract substance. Thus I enter my essence, return to it[39] and leave all other things behind. I am at one and the same time knowledge, knower and the known. In my essence I see a beauty, a splendour and a radiance which surprise me and leave me speechless. I know that I am part of the noble, excellent, divine world, the possessor of active life.

When I was sure of this, I let my reason ascend from that world to the divine world. It is as if I had succeeded in finding a place in it and a link with it, and thus found myself above the entire world of the intellect, and appear to be standing in that noble divine place. There I see a light and a radiance which neither tongues can describe nor ears comprehend.

When I drown in that light and radiance and cannot endure it, I cast myself down from the intellect to thought and reflection. When I arrive in the world of thought and reflection, thought obscures that light and that radiance for me, and I am amazed how I could leave that sublime, divine place and reach the place of thought, since my soul had possessed the power to leave its body in order to return to its essence and to ascend to the world of the intellect and thence to the divine world, until it eventually reached the place of radiance and light, which is the cause of every light and radiance. It is amazing how my soul alone could have appeared to me full of light while in the body as always, and without having left it. I have, however, thought about this for a long time and reflected on it. Then I became somewhat dismayed and remembered Heraclitus who ordered investigation of the soul's substance and the longing for ascent to that highest noble world. He said: He who desires it and ascends to the highest world necessarily receives the best reward. Hence nobody ought to abandon his studious desire for ascent to that world, even when tired and strained; for in front of him lies rest beyond which tiredness and strain are no longer there. With this remark Heraclitus wished to spur us on to search for the intelligibilia, so that we may find and perceive them as he found and perceived them.

Empedocles has said: The souls have been in the high, noble place, and when they sinned, they fell down to this world. He himself also reached this world only in flight from divine wrath. When he came down to this world, it was to help souls whose intellect had fallen into confusion. So he became like a madman and shouted at people as loudly as possible and bade them abandon this world with everything in it and proceed to their first, highest and noblest world. Furthermore he bade them implore God for help and thus regain their previous rest and well-being.

Pythagoras agreed with this philosopher, when he called on men to do the same as the latter had called on them to do. But he addressed them in parables and riddles and in such a way ordered them to leave this world and abandon it and return to the first, true world. . . .

Divine Providence

5. Chapter XVIII, About Eternal Providence, of the *Metaphysics* of 'Abd-al-Laṭīf al-Baghdādī, according to the Istanbul MS Carullah 1279, 173b–175a.

God's Providence extends over the high and the low world. It finally overlooks nought deserving any degree of perfection, where previously it had been impossible for it to give it what it deserved. We have already stated that the high world, in accordance with its fitness, has a larger share of this Providence and besides, needs no intermediary. The low world has a much smaller share in it, since its matter cannot endure more of it. If it could endure more, there would be neither greed nor envy nor deficiency here. The share which occurs in the low world reaches it through the mediation of the high world.

We do not claim that Providence and order are primary, which could mean that Providence creates a causal relationship for its recipients[40] whereby the noble would come into being because of the ignoble and the earlier because of the later. Such a claim would be shameful and absurd. Nor do we claim that Providence comes by pure accident from any possible direction, without the existence of anyone to provide an entrance for its essence and without his knowing what proceeds from him. Both assumptions are unworthy of the First Principle or of the first noble body. We claim neither that God's activity aims primarily at the order and welfare of the world, nor that these matters come to pass without His knowledge and without His will and consent. Nor do we claim that the existence of these things has a cause other than Him. Rather do we claim that their existence and order follow from His existence; for He is entirely good. All men agree on this, just as they agree what His goodness and His good are. He does what is good like the fire which warms everything near it, though its existence and warmth do not exist because of what it warms but in order to preserve continually its own special nature. Thus, too, it is with God. For He gives all existing things as much goodness and rank as they wish and are able to accept. If, in addition, we were able to assume that the fire knows and wills its own nature and the warming and illumination proceeding from it, the comparison would be complete. However, this is as far as we go in making things understandable; the student must understand a hint and be able to supplement the rest by himself.

The divine power reaches the hylic things beneath the moon's sphere to this extent, but voluntarily and with [their] consent. The bodies beneath the moon's sphere are connected with Him [God] and in touch with Him. Hence they succeed in borrowing something of the power emanating from Him and in ending near Him [?]. Hence we claim that everything that subsists naturally contains a divine power, which is active and protects all that is passive and inclined to allow itself to be protected, and we say that every natural thing can be called a divine work, and nature a divine craftsman.

Furthermore, since the noble circular movement dissolves the elements in various ways and brings them to ferment and through straining divides them into different kinds and distinct levels, it is not possible that they should all assume a single form. Some develop so that they breathe while others do not breathe. Among the first some are rational, and some of these are better than others. These, then, are the most perfect of all the things that by nature subsist in mortal bodies. Were it possible for everything formed by nature to possess reason, this would, indeed, be the case. Nature creates forms in the best order and proportion and does so without reflection or thought. He who reflects sometimes acts right and sometimes wrong. Nature, on the other hand, never happens to err, because it draws on the First Power for aid, and the latter never commits an error. Yet its substratum [namely, that in which nature is active] is something possible, and the execution of its activity encounters obstacles, whereby defects and evils result. Man has been given the intellectual power for the removal of all kinds of defects. It enables him to practise the activity which impels him to acquire the happiness which is appropriate for him and every single individual. It enables us to know the divine things, and by virtue of their knowledge, man is superior to everything in the world of generation and decay and attains happiness; for in this way he knows goodness and the good and the one who practises it. This knowledge is the greatest good that man can attain. Some men fall short of this power and are not sufficiently prepared for it, either by natural inclination or by custom. This derives from the fact that they do not use the power given to them for the acquisition of virtues and the knowledge of the divine things, but, on the contrary, for the acquisition of vices and defects. It is unjust to ascribe such vices and obstacles to Providence and to say that they stem from it. Although we have been created in possession of the power necessary for the acquisition of the virtues, it is not possible to attain them without instruction and training. Thus we have been given the power for the acquisition of the virtues, while their acquisition has been left to our will and our acquisition, just as the appropriation of foods and the like have been left to us. If we were able to accept the virtues from nature without this power that has been given us for their acquisition, evil would no longer find room anywhere, and we would not differ as to eminence and knowledge. Yet, since this is impossible, nature's efforts aim at inducing us to accept the virtues. It follows from this that we accept the vices as well. For whatever has an opposite must, of necessity, be able to accept this as well, and vices are the opposite of virtues. Since we have been created primarily for acceptance of the virtues, it follows that we are also able to accept their opposites, the vices. Hence, we must not blame Providence for the manner in which it has given us the power for the acquisition of the virtues. We should rather blame those who were given this power but have not acquired any kind of virtue through it and, instead, occupied themselves with the acquisition of the opposite of the virtues. Thus it may happen that someone is given a knife in order to kill his enemy or to cut off something useful to him, but cuts himself with it instead.

Thus there are three possibilities open to Providence. Firstly, it can from the very beginning withhold this power from us, so that we would then be in the same situation as all other animals. Secondly, it can give us the virtues directly; we should then be in the same situation as the angels and the heavenly bodies, and that is impossible in the world of generation and decay. Thus, only the third possibility remains for it, namely, to give us the power for the acquisition of the virtues and to leave success to our will and choice. By this means, we are superior to all other animals in ability, and we also differ from one another, so that there are among us rulers and ruled, kings and slaves.

There are many kinds of things that prevent the attainment of happiness and the acquisition of the virtues. They can lie in nature, as, for example, a naturally defective disposition. They can stem from custom or intercourse with evil people, and they can also derive from bad conduct or lack of knowledge or a mentor.

This is Aristotle's view of Providence, and we say that it agrees with what observation teaches us about the world, when we examine it and consider its parts and its conduct.

Democritus, on the other hand, belongs to those who hold that the world consists of indivisible particles and that the diversity of existing objects originates from the diversity of the formations of these atoms and their entanglement with one another. That is absurd. In their view everything is a result of chance, and they consider the idea of a Providence as absurd. However, an examination of existence shows this to be false. We can manifestly observe how the existing things are subject to a fixed order and arrangement and individual proportions. We see that the seeds of plants and animals always reproduce the same kind. From a date stone no fig tree grows, and no horse develops from human seed. Every part of animals and other things has its fixed size which it does not exceed. Furthermore, warnings of things to come, based partly on divine revelation, partly on dreams and soothsaying, demonstrate that they are wrong. Their view leads to the inevitable conclusion that nothing can have nobility or an ultimate good and that there can be no difference between man and beast.

The view of Plato and Zeno is the opposite of the previous view. For they assume that nothing in this world is outside Providence and that everything is filled by God and that He penetrates all things. This is excellent and very true. It is the view to be followed by the great mass and one in which one must believe. It leads to orderly political life and social harmony. The prophets have proposed it and the divine books expressed it. In my opinion one must believe in it; for all things have to do with Providence and do not stand outside it. Yet some things fall primarily under Providence, while others do so secondarily, while still others fall under it through consequence and result and compulsory connection; there are many degrees for what results and how the process takes place [?].

This view leaves room for critical consideration and examination. For if all things fall under Providence, where do evil and harm come from? And how does it come about that some men merit praise and reward and others blame and punishment? All actions based on reflection as well as education and the use of instruments become futile. Religious precepts, politics, instruction and different kinds of education also become futile. There remain, on the other hand, contradictions and bad notions of the common people. They are enforced on them in their confusion when they see that worldly goods remain withheld from great men and evil men receive them undeservedly. The philosopher's [Aristotle] teaching removes all confusion and doubt of this kind by assuming that Providence gives men power and various kinds of predisposition but leaves acquisition to the individual. The Qur'ān speaks of this in several places. Thus God says [Qur'ān 90. 8–10/8–10]: 'Have we not made two eyes for him and a tongue and two lips and led him on both roads?' That means on the path of good and evil. The eye serves for insight, the tongue for speech. These are the powers and instruments. Man's duty is predisposition and acquisition.

We have, indeed, said earlier that customs and ways of life exert a strong influence on the acquisition of virtues and vices. Now we also claim that tempers, too, exert a not inconsiderable influence in this respect. The choleric temper is predisposed to different qualities of character and ways of life than are to be found with the melancholic and phlegmatic temper. The sanguine temper inclines its owner to love amusement and emotion[al music] and to be greedy in eating, drinking and copulation. The melancholic temper has its own rules as well, and such is also the case with the phlegmatic temper, which may derive from an original disposition, but also from illness. It is accompanied by a bad character, [excessive] hardness and softness, etc., and disappears when the symptom of the illness from which it stems disappears. The moderate temper, which inclines to the earthy and the ripe, fiery and radiant, is the temper of quiet, of slumber, of sound thinking, of correct views, and of good and successful counsels. It is the temper of the prophets and great philosophers. God has never chosen an ignorant saint, a foolish prophet, a silly man or one devoted to desires and pleasures.

Damage and destruction of what perishes before it matures have various reasons, which are largely described in my following statements. The world of generation is built on contrasts, contradictions and oppositions. This all began with the deposit of specific and characteristic powers in the elements. Fire burns and moves upwards; water does the opposite. The earth is cold and dry, the air the opposite. Contrary elements mingle, and the existing things result from them. By nature they strive to gain the upper hand. The elements surround the existing things. Sometimes they strengthen one of the elements of the combination; then this element triumphs and effects the dissolution of the combination. Sometimes they weaken it; then the opposing element becomes stronger and effects the dissolution. Sometimes part of worldly Providence is strengthened by the movements, corresponding to its own power, of some stars, sometimes it is weakened by an opposite movement. Sometimes it decays and becomes putrid. Sometimes it increases or decreases. From this various kinds of corruption derive, for example, floods, fires, pestilences, plagues and great wars. Sometimes the movement of a star and its position in the zenith opposite a certain place on earth causes a wind which drives the clouds together or cools them, raises dust or results in hail. One compound object perishes in this way, while another remains unharmed. This causes certain effects, and these in turn have other consequences. There are so many details here that one cannot enumerate them all. The last consequences are said to arise by chance and on their own. However, one should not believe that they have no causes. It is merely that their causes are not primary and that they have no attainable goal. They do not belong to what happens necessarily and in the majority of cases.

V

NATURAL SCIENCE

The tradition of Aristotelian philosophy is responsible for the fact that 'natural science' in Islam comprises all the disciplines that primarily rely on data based on sense perception. Hence, it deals not only with the rudiments of what we nowadays call physics, but it also includes zoology, botany (possessing strong connections also with medicine), mineralogy and meteorology. Standard works of antiquity existed in Arabic translation for all these branches of learning. On the other hand, 'natural science' excluded sciences like astronomy and music which were considered based on mathematical foundations belonging to the realm of the abstract intellect rather than on sense perception. Geography also formed no part of 'natural science' if only because its main purpose was the mathematical–astronomical description of the earth. While medicine originally was a natural science in the sense the term is understood here, its practical aspects made it a field so large and diversified that it always had independent status in Islam just as had been the case among the Greeks and is the case in the modern world. Alchemy, magic and related subjects were always regarded as bridges between the natural and the supernatural sciences.

Within this large agglomeration of subjects, the reflections of Muslim scholars regarding the basic problems of physics are of the greatest interest to the historian of science. These problems were first posed by the Greeks. Their fundamental importance was fully recognized by their successors in the world of Islam. They applied to the study of such concepts as time, place, vacuum and atomism the only means at their disposal, logical speculation. Observation of facts and explanation of single natural phenomena played a somewhat subordinate role. They found a certain measure of constant attention among scientists and highly educated laymen, but the study of them remained comparatively sterile. In general, the Greek achievement in the realm of natural science can be said to have been at least as accessible to the Arabs as it is to us.

The subject of natural science

1. From Abū l-Barakāt Hibatallāh al-Baghdādī, *al-Mu'tabar fī l-ḥikmah* (Hyderabad, 1357–8/1938–9), II, 5_{23}–7_{1}. Abū l-Barakāt's work is based on Ibn Sīnā, but, on the whole, he appears to have been a quite independent thinker. S. Pines's articles on him are fundamental (cf. *Encyclopaedia of Islam*,[2] I, pp. 111–13).

'Nature' is the term applied by some people to every corporeal power, that is to say, to every principle of an activity that proceeds from the bodies in which it exists. Nature is said to be a first principle which sets in motion that which contains it; its immobility is essential, not accidental. This is more general than our '[movement] in one direction or in different directions' or also '[movement] through cognition or not through cognition'. Accordingly, the word 'nature' expresses a compulsory setting-in-motion, not one that comes about through cognition and will. Here there are contradictions between designation and meaning as well as between meaning and designation. One can generally agree with the first mentioned understanding provided one does not understand by 'nature' all that essentially causes motion; for that would include what is called the soul and its nature. Therefore, natural things are the things linked with this power, either because they are substrata of it and of such things as the bodies emerging from it, which are called natural bodies, or because they represent influences, movements and formations proceeding from it, such as colours and shapes.

Natural sciences are those sciences that speculate about these natural things. They speculate about mobile and immobile bases and from what, whereby, whence, whither and wherein natural movement and natural immobility arise, furthermore, which corporeal things fall in the realm of the senses, as well as their conditions, which of their movements and actions are sensually conditioned and which power and essences that are not sensually perceptible effect movement and activity in them. Such knowledge is derived in the first instance from the most obvious of such phenomena, and then one advances to the more and more concealed. The most obvious for us is that which is best recognizable and comes first, even though by nature it comes later. We can observe actions and conditions with our senses and thereby draw conclusions as to powers and active principles, although by nature these come earlier. Accordingly, what we can best recognize and what comes first for us comes later by nature, and what comes later by nature comes earlier for us. In the study of logic we proceeded methodically in such a way that we acquainted ourselves with the essences of the principles as they appear in composite things and then deduced from them how these principles appear in simple and individual things. In this manner, in our quest for cognition we pursue what is best recognizable for and closest to us, though the subsequent purpose and the necessary result [are what we actually want to study], and thereby we reach what is best recognizable as far as nature is concerned, namely, the active principle. On such a basis one attains cognition.

In the sciences, on the other hand, we use the knowledge which is first available to us, which is sometimes the cause of an effect, and sometimes the effect of a cause. In natural things one begins with the sensually perceptible and, indeed, with what is most apparent of it, and arrives at the intellectually perceptible in the end and, finally, at the more and more recondite intelligibilia.

The problem of movement

2. Abū l-Barakāt, *al-Mu'tabar*, II, pp. 28–34. Cf. also chap. VIII, no. 3.

One speaks of several aspects of movement. Thus there is local movement, which means a movement through which what moves is transferred from one place to another. Then there is positional movement, which means a movement through which the position of what moves changes and its parts undergo a change of place within parts of the place where it is, without being entirely removed from its place through its movement, for example, the movement of the waterwheel and of the millstone. Furthermore, there is the movement of growth and decline, whereby what moves becomes larger or smaller. Again, there is the movement of change, for example, movement whereby something becomes warm or cold.

Some things actually exist in every respect, while others exist partly in actuality, partly in potentiality. There is nothing in existence that exists potentially in every respect but has essentially no reality at all, as will soon become clear. Everything potentially in existence is destined to pass on to the actuality corresponding to its potentiality. There is no potentiality for what cannot possibly become actual. The transition from potentiality to actuality can take place suddenly, as, for example, the illumination of a house by means of a lamp, or it can take place gradually, as is usually the case. For the most part, it takes place in kinds of existing things, since there is no kind which does not constantly undergo the transition from potentiality to actuality. In the case of substance, such a transition shows itself, for example, in the emergence of man from a drop of sperm. As for quantity, it shows itself, for example, in growth after deficiency. As for quality, it shows itself, for example, in the appearance of blackness after whiteness. As for relationship, it shows itself, for example, in the father's transition, in respect of paternity, from potentiality to actuality by begetting children. As for locality, it shows itself, for example, in reaching a place after one had previously not been there. As for time, it shows itself, for example, in the transition of morning and evening from potentiality to actuality. As for position, it shows itself, for example, in lying down and standing upright. Likewise, it also shows itself in financial status, for example, wealth after poverty; in activity, one may write after having previously not written; and in passivity, one may be interrupted or uninterrupted. The movement caused by such a transition from potentiality to actuality refers only to a gradually occurring transition, for example, the reddening of an unripe date, and not to a suddenly occurring transition, such as, for example, the illumination of a house by a lamp. It also has its special kinds of existing things in which it takes place, among them quality, as one speaks, for example, of the unripe date reddening after having previously been green, and doing so very slowly and gradually until it is at last red. Or take quantity, for example, something that grows; take locality, for example, reaching a place where one had previously not been; take position, for example, the change of locality of parts of what moves through a circular movement from parts of the place where it is.

Aristotle defines movement as the first perfection of something potential as something potential [*Physics* 201a 10 f., Arab trans., ed. ʿA. Badawī [Cairo, 1964–5], I, p. 171, cf. Simplicius, 413 f. Diels]. For example, something white is potentially black, and its transition from whiteness to blackness represents the perfection of this potentiality. For, if this takes place gradually through a movement which the white also potentially possesses, and the white as long as it remains white is an actual white that remains actually white while it potentially moves towards blackening and becomes potentially black, then blackness is the perfection of its whiteness as being potentially black. Movement is the perfection of its immobility as potentially moving. However, the movement is something that comes to it not by itself. It comes to something through something in something. It comes to the body through the blackening in the whiteness. It is the first step in the transition from potentiality to actuality. The movement of change from whiteness to blackness is a primary perfection of the white as being potentially black. The same applies to locality, position, etc. Hence he has defined movement as the first perfection of something potential as something potential.

In a logical definition one must not define something in terms of what is less known or known to the same extent. Otherwise one could define movement as the transition from potentiality to actuality in time and justify it approximately as follows: Things can exist potentially and actually. What exists potentially is what passes into actuality. Its transition from potentiality to actuality may take place in time; one then says that it moves, and the transition is called 'movement'. Yet if the transition does not take place in time but suddenly, it is not called movement but simply transition and alteration. Hence, one calls the transition and the alteration which take place in time, 'movement'. One says, however, that if one wants to define time, one defines it in terms of movement, as we shall mention. How can one then define movement in terms of time? Thereby that clear definition is replaced by a definition that requires explanation. It is easier to explain what movement is [than time; hence time should not be injected into the definition of movement].

Now, I say that it has frequently been said that something may primarily be known defectively and generally as well as imperfectly and incompletely. Such is the case, for example, with regard to ordinary people's knowledge of movement and time. Everyone recognizes what they are in a general and unspecific way. He counts days and nights and recognizes time as something past or future, even if he does not understand it completely and logically and does not ask himself whether it is a substance or an accident, what causes it and what is its substratum, beginning and end. Time is better known in such general terms than movement according to its specific, complete, scientific definition. On the other hand, movement according to scientific, complete knowledge is better known than time. Hence it does no harm if time in its primary general terms forms a restrictive component of the explanation and definition of the word movement. When one subsequently understands the quiddity, purpose, agent and substratum of movement perfectly, time, too, becomes thereby truthfully defined. It is not unusual that something becomes known through itself—that means that one attains perfect knowledge of something through defective knowledge of it—and that defective knowledge of something leads on to perfect knowledge of it, as has been briefly treated in connection with the science of demonstrative speculation, and it is therefore not unusual that one knows something through something else which one only knows generally and defectively. Correctly applied, these remarks can also prove useful in other branches of knowledge.

The movement best known and most worthy of the term 'movement', which is most widely applied to it, is local movement. Hence, it must be treated first. The underlying idea correctly understood will offer guidance towards the understanding of other kinds of movements.

As regards movement in locality, primary knowledge shows that what moves leaves one place and occupies another, in that it is in contact with another body or confronts it and then gives up that contact or confrontation and comes in contact with another body or confronts it. That such a movement exists is evident through sense perception, but how it achieves existence, what kind it is, what it means, that demands subtle speculation. The existing local movement of which we speak here can, indeed, be either the [original] contact of a body with the body from which it moves away, or the termination of this contact or the start of another contact with the body towards which it is moving, or all these three things together. Neither the original nor the second contact alone is movement. Otherwise, there would be no difference between movement and immobility, and movement would not be opposed to immobility; for immobility is the nonexistence of movement in something that ought to move. The termination of contact is nonexistence and is not an existential idea. Were it to represent movement, then movement would be nonexistence and not something existing, unless the termination of contact were to be another contact; however, the latter contact, like the former, would also not be movement. Furthermore, if the first and second contact and the termination of the first contact were together to form movement, then movement would not be something existing that starts, since starting cannot exist together with termination. The first contact together with the termination is nonexistent, and termination itself is a nonexistent idea, and the second contact that starts is immobility and corresponds to immobility, since it is no movement. But how could nonexistence and a nonexistent idea together produce something that exists? Again, if movement were the sum of the two contacts, the starting and the terminating, it would also be something that cannot achieve existence, for the terminating movement has no existence in common with the starting one. Consequently, movement would be neither something that starts and exists, nor one of the components [of the described complete process], nor would it be different from immobility nor the opposite of immobility, which it is, after all, generally known to be on the basis of the meaning of the words 'movement' and 'rest' [immobility]. But it can also be assumed that something outside the components [of the described complete process] is a local movement. Hence, movement is not something that starts and exists in the sense in which we are accustomed to say of individual things that they exist and start.

Manifestly, however, the mind, on the basis of the evidence of the senses, believes in the existence of movement and regards it as an idea that is the opposite of immobility. There is nobody among us who would not say when he finds something first in one place and then again in another that it is something that moves and that it must previously have moved. Otherwise, he would have to say that it is something that is immobile while knowing full well that if it were something immobile, he would not find that it has left the place where it had previously been and reached another place and that it could then be found by him separated from the place where it had previously been. But that is the meaning of 'not being immobile', and local things that are not immobile may move, so that that thing has undoubtedly moved. And whatever has moved has possessed movement and contained it. Consequently, movement exists, and yet it has been claimed that it is something that has no existence. That is an obvious difficulty.

The mind, however, is able to recognize the truth and to overcome this difficulty and to believe that it does not constitute a paradox. For we must realize that we infer something according to its attribute or attributes known to us not only as to whether it possesses that attribute so that it can be inferred accordingly, or as to whether it possesses all those qualities together at a given time, but also as to whether we know it [to have such a quality or qualities] either at the given time or earlier or later or as to whether all of them are found together or separately. For our inference finds them all together in the mind as well as in the soul. Thus, when we find that one body is in contact with another, our mind is certain that it is in contact with it, and we always remember it thus, especially whenever we have anything to do with it, since that is the most obvious. Then, when we find that it has another contact with another body, we, under the influence of the second contact, no longer think of the first contact, and it disappears from us in a way that resembles a complete termination of its existence. In this manner, the meaning of termination, that is to say, the disappearance of the first contact, is related in our mind to the first contact, and the second contact subsequently with both [that is, with the first contact and its termination]. One is a nonexistent idea, which has no individual existence, namely, the termination. The second idea, namely, the first contact, no longer exists. Only the third idea, namely, the second contact, exists. The entire process, however, can be grasped by the mind, though the individual components themselves cannot as such be grasped at the given time. We have not inferred that it exists at a given time, but rather that it exists absolutely and implicitly, either at the given time or earlier or later, and we claim that the total process is something that exists, that is, that it has existence; for it does not include within it anything that does not deserve to be called existent, though not together and at the given time, since the first and the second contact undoubtedly have existence, but not together, and the termination of the first contact is something which the mind infers from something nonexistent, which is perceived by means of existential observation, a negative [*sālib*] occurrence.

Accordingly, every component of movement undoubtedly has existence, even if it is an inconstant existence unconnected with the existence of one of the other components. It is not the same whether something has no existence at all or merely no constant existence. Now, if all components of movement have some sort of existence, then their sum, too, has existence, even if the entire process is not always present; for a sum cannot be something different from its components. In this sense movement is said to exist, and one must also understand it in the same way when one says that everything that exists and occurs together with movement exists. This has a different meaning here than [the expression existence] as applied to heaven, earth and other existing things and their attributes which have constant existence. We deduce their existence, in fact, only after having perceived some part of them as existent and before one has perceived it as nonexistent. First the thing exists, then we perceive it, and when we have perceived it, we infer its [existence]. Repeated perception confirms the inference, and that confirms the existence. The fact that something occurs continuously and exists does not influence our inference concerning existence, even if, according to our inference as to its [existence], the matter would not exist, provided only that the inference occurs before perception of nonexistence.

Since the meaning of 'existence' is not the same for everything that is described and explained as existent, the First Philosopher [Aristotle] has established existence not as a genus for the kinds of existing things but rather as a homonym that can be used with different meanings. When one of the ancients, namely, Zeno [Aristotle, *Physics* 239b 5 ff., Arab trans., II, 713; Diog. Laert. IX, 72], says that movement has no existence, he may have represented this idea merely because 'existence' [read: 'movement'] includes ideas not a single one of which can assume an existence on its own in the world of existence; for the starting existent is not to be united with the terminating nonexistent, and it is these two where movement originates, whither it proceeds and between which it emerges and finally becomes a single existent. What, then, is the position with regard to nonexistence, which must be meant by termination? Here we have the view of an extremely conscientious investigator, even though it is his paradoxes, whose incorrectness is generally known, that have made him a much admired and imitated model of philosophers, since they have not understood what he meant by them, and he himself has not explained them. Perhaps he used 'existence' only for something that possesses permanent existence, while every movement, as well as everything whose existence is connected with movement and only together with it continually happens and takes place does not possess any permanent existence. It only exists while it takes place, both of which belong together in it.

The remaining kinds of movement must be regarded in this light. In positional movement, there is a terminating position and a starting position, and, in general, an exchange of positions. In change, there is a terminating quality and a starting quality and, in general, an exchange of quality, for example, something white that becomes black gradually and in time. Yet, here the process takes place in an additional quality, in contrast to other [movements] where what is first there together with what is added later persists, while here [?] it does not persist. In the movement of size, for example, in the case of something growing that in time passes from a small size to a large one, it is a matter of a movement that, like the qualitative one, contrasts with the local and the positional in that the first size of what grows, together with what is added later, remains preserved. In the opposite case of decrease this is not so. Here we must assume that the size established with respect to what decreases stands as such at the starting point, and the final result stands at the final point, and we do not regard the former as part of the latter in both places, but the one as one thing and the other as another; thus the resemblance with other movements in respect of starting and final points remain.

One must know that movement consists of six things, namely,

(1) the mover, (2) what moves, (3) the whence, (4) the whither, (5) the wherein, for example, the distance over which the movement extends, and (6) time. The whence, whither and wherein are components of the meaning of 'movement'. Time is demanded by the mind, or it enters into the constitution of the meaning, and so does what moves. The mover and his being different from what moves demands an explanation, and this is the suitable place for it. . . .

Views on the vacuum

3. Abū l-Barakāt, *al-Mu'tabar*, II, 44_{10}–47_{24}. *Fārābī's Article on Vacuum*, ed. N. Lugal and A. Sayili (Ankara, 1951), may be compared.

The emptiness and fullness of places can be observed by means of things to be found in them, which either occupy them or keep away from them, as in the case of a wine jar and wine, a house and residents. Hence the idea has become established in the human mind that such an empty or full place exists prior to what fills it or leaves it empty. Hence it has been said that there is an empty vacuum, which exists prior to every single thing that occupies or fills a place, that all existing bodies in that vacuum either are immobile or move, and that it cannot be [entirely] filled with existential bodies, since, were it densely filled, their movements would cease, because all that moves can only move in a vacuum.

Then the space between sky and earth was investigated, and it was found that the winds move and blow there. The study of that moving [object] revealed that in its being it resembles space; it does not bar the glance from access and constitutes no obstacle for what fills or what breaks, which moves within it or against which it moves. For example, the winds blow against mountains, walls, trees and similar objects, which break the oncoming winds through their solidity. That [object] moving in space has been called 'air'. Even when it is immobile, it exists in space, and it becomes sensually perceptible when it is stirred to move, by means of fans, for example.

Observation has shown that the air either fills this space or is identical with the space which is regarded as the vacuum. Yet it has been argued against this as follows: if air were identical with space or filled space, it could not move, and the winds could cease to blow. Thus, for instance, water which entirely fills a bottle and leaves no empty space in it cannot move in it, but if it does not fill it completely and some space remains, it can move in it and make waves. Now the winds do indeed blow and move the air. Accordingly, its movement takes place in a vacuum. The empty space and the moving or immobile air do not differ during the process of vision in respect of the object of vision and the fact that they do not bar the glance from access to the objects of sight behind them. There is, however, a difference between them as regards the sense of touch. It perceives the air by means of a certain resistance it offers, moving or causing movement, cold and warmth. Space, on the other hand, our sense of touch cannot perceive in the same way and through the same things. Therefore, we make a distinction in our perception and our mind between vacuum and air. That is quite natural. Compressed air in inflated skins makes them extremely hard and moves them from the bottom of the deep water towards the surface, which they seek to reach and where they subsequently float upon the water with great power, which is sufficient for carrying the heavy loads fastened upon them. So we now know what air is and have established that our sense of touch shows that there is a difference between air and empty space, though we cannot perceive it with our sense of vision.

Then the interior of empty vessels was investigated, and it was found that where they appear to be empty they are filled with air. Water and other things can enter only when the air goes out. If it does not go out, nothing can enter. Our attention is drawn to this by the fact that, when the inflowing water fills the openings [?] of the vessel, so that the air when going out presses on it, then the latter makes an audible sound through colliding with and breaking through the water, especially in vessels with narrow openings. If the openings are so narrow that one cannot pour water through them, and the vessel is placed in the middle of the water, the air can be observed coming out in large and small bubbles, according to the size of the opening, and a gurgling sound is heard. This is particularly noticeable in the vessel called clepsydra. It has an opening above through which water can flow in, and one or more holes at the bottom. One fills it with water, closes the opening and suspends it in the air, not slanting but straight, so that the weight of the water comes to rest on the hole or holes at the bottom. Then the air cannot break through the water and rise upwards through the hole or holes at the bottom of the vessel, and the water cannot flow out until the opening in its position above is opened. When the hole above is opened, the water can then flow out through the holes below, but as long as the opening above remains closed, it cannot flow out. This shows that the water is prevented from flowing out by the fact that the air is shut off and finds no entry. If then the opening above is opened and air streams in, the water begins to flow, and the air follows and takes its place. There never remains a vacuum. Were a vacuum possible, the water would flow from the holes below even during the closure of the opening above. The bodies continually exert in their movements, through proximity, attraction and repulsion upon one another and never separate from one another, unless another body comes between them. No body moves without the repulsion of the bodies in front of it and the attraction of those behind it. Coarser bodies attract the finer and more tender ones and repel and break through them. This cannot happen in reverse.

There are diverse views about the vacuum. Some scholars are of the opinion that it exists. Others, again, are of the opinion that it does not exist at all. Each group uses arguments which must be investigated by the scholar who seeks the truth. He must exclude the false and verify the correct ones.

The assumption that space is altogether a vacuum and that air is to be defined merely as moving winds while immobile air is content to belong to the vacuum has already been recognized as incorrect through our remarks about the effect of fans and inflated skins. And the assumption that something that leaves a space empties it and that the space then constitutes a pure vacuum has been refuted by our reference to the clepsydra and to vessels in which one can observe that the air comes out when water flows in and vice versa, and indeed, in the same proportion.

It would be beneficial for scientists if they would listen to a certain argument and answer it, namely, that from movement. It states that if there were no vacuum, nothing would move, since bodies can only move in empty space. This is a famous and widespread argument, which the mind quickly accepts. With it they attempt to refute the assumption of those who do not admit the existence of a vacuum in view of the obvious succession of water and air and all further statements in this respect. They claim that the succession of water and air is possible only in a place which has the same volume as they, and is wholly or partly empty and, when empty, exerts attraction. They attempt to prove this by refuting the clepsydra proof. They say, in fact, that, if we suck out a bottle vigorously and stop up its opening immediately after the suction and do not open it until we have laid it in water with its opening downwards, then one can see how the water flows upwards and no air comes out at the time. This happens because it flows into an empty space due to our sucking the air out. If we had not sucked out the bottle and not thereby removed some air from it, then the water on flowing in ought to have been accompanied by air coming out and would not have flowed upwards. It did this only because of the attraction of the vacuum. The air which must have come out so that the water could flow in is that which we have previously sucked out. As much air as we have sucked out, so much water had flowed in and, attracted by the vacuum, been forced upwards.

According to their view, attraction in natural bodies arises from the vacuum, which feels the need to attract things to it in order to be filled with them. They explain the desire for nourishment felt by living creatures and the attraction which trees exert on water by a vacuum which, when empty, necessarily longs for something that fills it. Living creatures whose belly is empty long for food and quickly devour it, just as that bottle attracts and devours the water quickly.

Furthermore, it has been said that we can observe how bodies thicken or dissolve. They thicken when the vacuum is small and dissolve when it is large. We can observe, for example, how water heated in a pot fills it and overflows or causes it to burst. A vessel can also be filled with ashes and then, in spite of the ashes, with water. Were there no vacuum, it would not have enough room to be filled twice. The water penetrates into the vacuum between the ashes or the ashes that within the water, or both penetrate mutually into each other's vacuum. Everything that grows, grows because nourishment penetrates [into the vacuum] between its parts. There is no penetration into something full, but only into a vacuum.

Hence, as we have established, the vacuum is something sensually perceptible as well as something intellectually perceptible, in which things found in places succeed one another, even though it is never entirely free from them. It is a reality which is different from that of what fills it and succeeds one another in it, just as the reality of a body differs from that of colours, shapes, etc., which succeed one another in it. Its existence is proved by the movements which cannot arise in a densely filled space but only in a vacuum. When something moves in what is full, it must either repel it and thus move it or it must penetrate into it. Hence it follows from the movement of moving things in the existing world either that the vacuum exists or that the bodies can mutually penetrate into one another or that, when a single moving thing moves, the whole world is set in motion by its movement, and all that is full is stirred in a manner corresponding to its stirring. Visual observation, however, demonstrates that the third case is incorrect; for there are bodies that move, while other adjacent bodies are immobile and not moved by their movement. Hence, there remain only the other two cases, or one of them, namely, the mutual penetration of bodies and the vacuum. As will be seen, the mutual penetration attests to the existence of the vacuum. Hence the existence of local movements in bodies attests to the existence of the vacuum.

Problems of meteorology

4. Excerpts from a work of Theophrastus, ed. and trans. G. Bergsträsser, *Neue meteorologische Fragmente des Theophrast* (Heidelberg, 1918, *Sitz. Ber. Heidelberger Akad. d. Wiss.*, phil.-hist. Kl. 1918, 9). Not quite complete English translation in C. Bailey, *Titi Lucreti Cari De rerum natura* (Oxford, 1947), III, pp. 1745–8. On the much more detailed Syriac original of the Arabic text, cf. H. J. Drossaart-Lulofs in *Autour d'Aristote . . . offert à Monseigneur A. Mansion* (Louvain, 1955), pp. 433–49. It has now been edited and translated by E. Wagner and P. Steinmetz, *Der syrische Auszug der Meteorologie des Theophrast* (Wiesbaden, 1963, *Abh. d. Akad. d. Wiss. und d. Literatur, Geistes- und Sozialwiss.* Kl., 1964, p. 1).

I have found a work in Syriac by Theophrastus which I here present in abbreviated form. We ask God for help.

Thunder: Thunder arises in seven different ways, namely,

1. When two deep clouds meet and collide, a noise arises

through them, just as, when we hollow [?] the palms of our hands and clap them, they produce a powerful noise.

2. When a wind enters hollow clouds and circulates in them. We can observe how a wind which blows and enters a cave produces a powerful noise.

3. When fire falls into damp clouds and is extinguished. We can observe how a hot iron produces a powerful noise when the smith dips it in water.

4. When wide, icy clouds are violently split by the wind. We can observe how the wind produces a powerful noise when it beats strongly against a papyrus leaf.

5. When a wind penetrates clouds with long hollow spaces. We can observe how, when slaughterers blow into the intestines, the passage of the wind produces a noise in them.

6. When a strong wind is enclosed in hollow clouds, and they burst. We can observe how a bladder produces a powerful noise if one blows into it until it bursts.

7. When thick clouds rub against one another. We can observe how millstones produce a noise when they rub against one another.

Lightning may arise for four reasons, namely,

1 and 2. Through beating together and friction. We can observe that fire comes from stones when they are beaten against one another, and pieces of wood give off sparks when they rub against one another, as do flints.

3. When fire gathers in damp clouds, and their thin portions catch fire. We can observe how a kind of flame is produced when the smiths hurl a heated iron on to the water.

4. A fire may be enclosed in the clouds, and the clouds then contract so that it falls out, or they pull apart and burst like a sponge or a woollen fleece containing water. When they are compressed or pulled apart, the water they contain comes out. Thus clouds gather or press together and, when they are pulled apart, lightning emerges.

Thunder can be latent for three reasons, namely, either (1) because the clouds do not hold fire enclosed within them or it is too little and not enough to produce lightning or (2 and 3) in two different ways, namely, either because pulling apart and the friction in the clouds take place quietly until, finally, the fire slides out and the noise remains enclosed or because the clouds dissolve or gather, and thus lightning is produced without being accompanied by noise. We can observe that when sponges are pulled apart or pressed together, water emerges without making a noise thereby.

A stroke of lightning is either a fiery wind or a windy fire; for when it falls on dry leaves or firewood, it sets them afire, and when it falls on gold or silver, it melts them. It is fire which produces these effects of a stroke of lightning. Furthermore, a stroke of lightning does not consist of coal-like fire but of flame-like fire; if it falls on the earth, one does not find any coal, but rather where the stroke of lightning falls one usually only sees its effect, and these effects correspond to the properties of fire, since in our opinion a stroke of lightning is finer than other flame-like kinds of fire which cannot pierce a wall or penetrate the earth. The stroke of lightning which can penetrate any sensually perceptible substance cannot be seen, since our glance is split by its fineness. Nobody has ever seen it. Its effects are visible, but it itself is invisible.

A stroke of lightning arises in two different ways. When fire is enclosed in the clouds . . ., for example . . . [or] because it [?] is fine and because when it[1] rubs against the clouds and emerges and approaches us violently with a great effort, it is set afire like lead shot from a sling; when it rubs against the air, it becomes warm and is set afire. They say that if a stroke of lightning falls on a purse containing gold coins, it does not damage the purse but damages and melts the gold coins. This can be explained by the purse possessing something that dissolves and disintegrates, so that the stroke of lightning finds a passage for itself. Among the gold coins, however, it does not find a passage, hence they resist it until it damages and melts them while it does not damage the purse.

The story goes that if a stroke of lightning falls on a man, it kills him by passing through his body into the earth.

In the Syriac manuscript at my disposal there is a discussion of the causes of rain, which I have not abbreviated, as it agrees with my own opinion . . . [lacuna].

. . . What collects from steam and forms drops, like fine steam rising in the bath and, if it finds no exit, forming drops.

Snow, they say, comes about when clouds contract from cold before they completely change to water. Before the particles of water unite and while [the water] stays firmly [in the clouds], it divides into very small drops, which are kept apart by the air. This is evident from the fact that we can clearly see in the snow a large quantity of air previously enclosed in it. This is shown to us by its lightness. Also, when it is pressed, it can be compressed, and it becomes less when it dissolves into water. Furthermore, its white colour derives from the amount of air enclosed in it. The same applies to all bodies in which a great deal of air is enclosed; they are white [*abyaḍ*], as, for example, foam and oil beaten together with water.

Hail comes about when drops of water change and contract owing to dampness [read: cold]. Hailstones are round, either because their corners have been broken off or smoothed in their fall—for hail comes from an element that is not round by nature, namely, water—or because cold contracts hailstones in this particular condition [evenly] from all sides.

Hoar-frost and *ice* come about when the dew contracts from the cold. Ice is white owing to the air enclosed in it, since what becomes snow above, becomes hoar-frost below.

Winds, they say, are produced either from above or from below. Whatever is produced from below comes either from the water or from the earth. We can observe how gales come down from clouds and we can see winds blowing from the water and from the mountains. Wind is set in motion either because of its lightness when it tries to rise upwards, since, we could say, for example, that it is a vapour and that what is fine in it predominates, or because air sometimes contracts in an eastern place, at other times, however, in a western, northern or southern. When it contracts somewhere there, and then finds no empty space, it moves from one area to another opposite, because the vacuum forces it to do so, and draws with it vapours from the water and from the earth, until finally no space is left. Thus we can also observe, when we lay the opening of a pipe on the water and draw out the air that is in the pipe through suction and ⟨. . .⟩, how ⟨the water flows in through the suction⟩ under the vacuum's pressure until no empty place exists in the pipe. In the same way, winds are produced from below.

Winds produced from above come about when the water above the clouds dissolves into wind or, furthermore, when many vapours come forth from the earth. When they then collide with the clouds or with the above-lying air, they suddenly seek to return downwards, and a storm begins, for example, the tornado which descends from the sky upon the sea and sometimes even pulls ships upwards. It is called *prēstēr*, which means whirl[wind]. It arises from the clouds when winds meet hollow clouds. Then, if they clash with them, they extend right down to the sea below and simultaneously draw water and ships upward, since a strong wind, when it clashes with something, retreats violently and repels the air in its retreat. When thus repelled until it finds no empty space, the water and the ships rise up together with it. The wind casts the ships it had lifted up down again without destroying them, provided this does not happen suddenly, but it abates gradually. Nevertheless, ships are wrecked when, for some reason or other, the wind [suddenly] lets the ships drop.

The *halo* around the moon comes about when the air becomes so dense that it is set in circular motion round the moon; for, when the rays [??] find the air dense, then the place opposite the moon becomes fine, since the finer that part of the air becomes, the thicker become the parts in its vicinity. Hence the air to be found in the vicinity of that part forms a halo.

I say: the radiance of the moon penetrates the vapours in its vicinity in straight lines, which leads on all sides [evenly] to the form of a circle. When the vapours are light, more of the moon's radiance penetrates them, and the halo is therefore wider; if, on the other hand, they are dense, not much of it penetrates them, and the halo is therefore narrower. When a strong wind blows dividing the dense [vapours] and rain comes, the halo disappears.

Earthquakes have four sorts of causes, namely,

1. Through cavities in the earth, for example, caves or hollows which collapse. This they do when the earth dries up and crumbles or when it becomes damp and disintegrates. We can observe how,

on stony ground, a single rock rolling away from its place shakes up all the rocks.

2. Through water that is enclosed in a cavity of the earth. When such water is set in motion, either because it has found a narrow exit or for some other reason, it moves the earth, just as a ship is moved by the waves.

3. Through many winds enclosed in the cavity of the earth. When they escape through a narrow exit, the earth trembles. Hence there are sometimes noises during an earthquake.

4. Through fire enclosed in the cavity of the earth. When it rarefies, the air enclosed in the earth's cavity, dissolves it and disintegrates it, then the air needs more space; it splits the earth and causes it to tremble.

They say that earthquakes are of different kinds. There are vibrations when part of the earth's cavity collapses. There are landslides and collapses when the wind emerges violently, clashes with part of the earth and then, when it draws back violently, clashes with another part. Landslides alone come about when the wind only emerges but does not return, either because it pursues the air or because it is weakened above before it clashes with another part of the earth.

VI

MEDICINE

The Muslims distinguished between scientific medicine and the so-called 'prophetic medicine'. The latter, codified in a number of books, was a collection of home cures ascribed to the Prophet Muḥammad as well as to other ancient Islamic authorities; it was aligned to magic and superstition. The former, scientific medicine, was intensively cultivated in both its theoretical and its practical aspects; it constitutes the zenith of cultural life in medieval Islam and has been deservedly much admired. It is well known that it is entirely dependent on the medieval heritage of classical antiquity, apart from comparatively scanty Indian influences.

Hippocratic and Galenic medicine was based upon the humoral theory. The humours or natures of the body determined health or disease depending on their normal or abnormal relationship towards one another. This theory was dominant in the West till the nineteenth century. It was never replaced by any other theory in traditional Islam. Medicine was mainly seen as anchored in theory, and it was generally not pursued empirically; there were some creditable exceptions among whom ar-Rāzī was outstanding, who believed in empiricism at least to some degree. The dependence of Muslim medicine on that of classical antiquity extended to all medical specialties, even to a field such as ophthalmology in which Arab physicians were able to register great advances.

It is particularly significant that Muslim medical deontology, the ethical basis for the physician's scientific activity and human worth, was determined by that of classical antiquity. By and large, his social position may also have been determined by classical precedent. These influences affected the physician as an individual. The rules for ethical conduct of the medical profession inasmuch as it affected society as a whole had been less important for Greek paganism than they were for early Christianity. Thus Christian intermediaries provided the first and decisive stimulus for Muslims to become aware of medicine's duties to society. Among them it proved extremely fertile, as Islam was particularly receptive to all ideas concerning the well-being of society. The hospitals which were founded and maintained to take care of public health were the most visible result.

As set forth in the Introduction, medicine played a particularly prominent role in the process of Islam's adoption of the Greek heritage. In consequence, almost the entire Greek medical literature became known to the Muslims to the same extent as it is known to us. In addition, many other works not preserved in Greek were known to them and are thus available to us through their Arabic versions. Some practically unknown late Hellenistic physicians are more familiar to us through quotations by Arabic authors than from Greek writings. Again, ar-Rāzī's name must be mentioned as his work is our most prolific source. The careful collection of the fragments preserved in Arabic can contribute to our knowledge of the history of ancient medicine.[1] Since the medical literature preserved in translation but not in the Greek original is so large, the following samples have been mainly restricted to such material, but regrettably, here as elsewhere, they are necessarily too few.

Medical ethics

1. The Hippocratic Oath, as quoted in the history of medicine by Ibn Abī Uṣaibiʿah, *ʿUyūn al-anbā'*, I, 25_{18}–26_{3}.

I swear by God, Master of life and death, giver of health and creator of healing and every cure, and I swear by Asclepius,[2] and I swear by all God's saints, male and female, and I call on all of them as witnesses that I will fulfil this oath and this condition.

I believe that he who instructs me in this science[3] takes the place of my fathers. I will let him share in my livelihood and, should he need money, I will give it to him and let him participate in my income. I will consider the generation of his descendants as equal to my brothers and I will instruct them in this science, should they need to learn it, without payment and without condition. I will allow my children and my teacher's children and the pupils who have accepted this condition and are sworn to the medical *Nomos* to participate together in exhortations and learning and all that has to do with the science, but for nobody else will I do so.

During the entire treatment, I will strive, as far as it is possible for me, to benefit patients. Things that may harm them and do them wrong I will avoid to the best of my judgment. I will not give a lethal medicine if asked for it nor give such counsel. Similarly, I do not believe that I may give women an injection to induce abortion. In my treatment and my science I will keep myself pure and clean. Also, I will not make an incision for someone who has a stone in his bladder, but will leave it to those who perform this operation professionally.

All the houses that I enter, I will enter for the benefit of patients, being in a condition far removed from injustice, wickedness and voluntary and deliberate corruption in general as well as in respect of sexual intercourse with women and men whether free or slaves. Things concerning people's activity which I observe or hear during the treatment of patients and at other times and which ought not to be discussed outside I will avoid, since I believe that one should not talk about such matters.

He who keeps this oath and does not corrupt it in any respect will be privileged to perfect his treatment and his science most excellently and beautifully and will be constantly praised by all men in future. The opposite applies to him who breaks it.

2. The medical *Nomos* of Hippocrates would seem to owe its origin to the mention of a *Nomos* in the 'Oath'. It appears in Ibn Abī Uṣaibiʿah, I, 26_{3-14}, in the following form:

Medicine is the most noble of all the sciences. However, the inadequate understanding of those who practise it has caused men to be deprived of it. For in no city does one find anything to blame in it, except for the ignorance of those who claim to be physicians but are not entitled to be called physicians. They resemble the shadow-figures presented by actors in order to entertain people thereby. As these are forms devoid of reality, thus, there are many physicians in name, but only very few in actuality.

He who wants to study medicine must possess a good and suitable natural disposition and a great interest entirely directed to the study of medicine. The natural disposition is most important, since the student if he possesses the suitable natural disposition readily accepts instruction and does not resent having his mind formed and producing beautiful fruits, comparable to plants in the soil. The natural disposition can be compared with the soil, the utility of the instruction with the seed, and its educational effect with the seed falling into the good earth. Once [the students] are preconditioned for medicine to this extent and then go into the cities, they become physicians not only in name but in actuality.

Medical knowledge is a good treasure and a proud possession for whoever has it, a rich source of private and public joy. Medical ignorance, on the other hand, is an evil and a bad possession for practitioners, something joyless, something that constantly causes fretting or rashness; the fretting proves their incompetence and the rashness their scanty acquaintance with medicine.

3. The testament of Hippocrates known by the title 'The Arrangement of Medicine', from Ibn Abī Uṣaibiʿah, I, 26_{14-26}. For corresponding Greek texts, cf. K. Deichgräber, *Medicus gratiosus* (Mainz-Wiesbaden, 1970, *Abh. d. Akad. d. Wiss. und d. Literatur, Geistes- und Sozialwiss. Kl.* 1970, 3), pp. 88–107.

The student of medicine must be a free man by descent and good by natural disposition. He must be young, and be of moderate size and have well-proportioned limbs. He must be equipped with a fine mind and be well-spoken and know how to give sound advice. He must be chaste and courageous. He must not be greedy for money and must know how to control himself in anger, while not abstaining completely from getting angry. He must not be dull-witted either. He must feel compassion and sympathy for the sick and be capable of keeping secrets, since many patients inform us that they suffer from illnesses about which nobody else should know. He must bear with abuse since some people suffering from phrenitis and melancholic mania confront us physicians with calumnies. We must bear with this and understand that it is not their fault, but is caused by their unnatural illness. He must have his hair cut moderately, that means not have it completely shaved nor let it hang down over the shoulders. He must not cut his fingernails too short nor allow them to grow beyond the tips of his fingers. His clothes should be white, clean and soft. He must not walk too fast, since that is a sign of levity, nor too slowly, since that indicates mental sluggishness. When called to a patient, he should sit down with crossed legs and ask him quietly and slowly, not nervously and excitedly, about his condition. Such a manner, clothing and conduct are, in my opinion, better than all others.

4. An explanation of the first aphorism of Hippocrates by Ibn Hindū, *al-Kalim ar-rūḥānīyah*. The passage is missing in the printed text and is translated here from the Istanbul MS Aya Sofya 2452. Cf. F. Rosenthal, 'Life Is Short, the Art Is Long', in *Bulletin of the History of Medicine*, XL (1966), pp. 226–45.

'Life is short, science long, empiricism dangerous, decision difficult, time sharp.' The author [Ibn Hindū] says: 'Every single one of these words is an exhortation for the physician.'

By the words: 'Life is short, science long', he encourages the compilation of medical books; for the life of the single individual is too short to produce the science of medicine completely, but if everyone produces a part of the science and one is joined to the other, then the science reaches completion or approaches it. The science of medicine is, in fact, only long when measured against the lifespan of the single individual. Many long lives together, on the other hand, are more than enough for the science.

By 'empiricism is dangerous' he means to say: When it is not accompanied by theory. For empiricists study obvious things and use whatever they consider beneficial for the treatment of an illness. Yet illnesses may be similar in their form but require different kinds of treatment. A wound caused by iron must be treated with medicines which cause coagulation. However, if the wound from the bite of a mad dog is sealed at the very beginning, this leads to death, since the poison is thereby confined in it. Analogical reasoning [theory] together with empiricism is what one must use.

By the word 'decision' in 'decision is difficult' he means theory [drawing conclusions through analogical reasoning] and thus attempts to encourage subtlety in the application of theory and the thorough study of the symptoms of illness, since most illnesses are concealed and not obvious to the senses.

By 'time is sharp' he encourages alertness and attention in every situation. For the physician may order the treatment of an illness, and it may have changed in the meantime into an entirely opposite or different illness, before the treatment is undertaken.

Humoral pathology

5. From 'Alī b. Rabban aṭ-Ṭabarī, *Firdaus al-ḥikmah*, ed. M. Z. Siddiqi (Berlin, 1928), p. 40.

Man derives his nourishment from the four natures, since he inhales *air*, drinks *water*, eats food like meat, grain [corn] and fruit, which are transformations of *earth*, and all these contain particles of *fire* as well.

The foods which derive from water, become *phlegm*, those that derive from air, *blood*, those that derive from fire, *yellow bile* and those from the earth, *black bile*.

The foundation of medical knowledge: Theory or empiricism?

6. Galen, *On Medical Experience*, ed. and trans. R. Walzer (Oxford, 1944), paras IV, X, XIII, 4–5, XXXI. Cf. also above, no. 4.

If you affirm this, we ask: What is more varied, complicated and manifold than disease, or how does one find that one illness is identical with another in all its characteristics? Is it in the number of its symptoms, in their power or in their extent? For if a thing possesses an identity, I believe that it must possess that identity in all such characteristics, since, if one of them is missing, the entire thing is spoilt, and it loses its identity because of not possessing that missing characteristic.

However, let us give way to them in this case and admit to them that a certain disease which now develops is identical with that former disease in all such characteristics. Nevertheless, even if we admit that, it may still be possible that the one is identical with the other two or three times, but not very many times. Besides, even if it were possible that it happens very many times, it would not be possible that one and the same person could observe it every time, and if someone who now observes it is different from him who observes it at another time, this does not mean that one must assume that it has been observed very many times, since something observed and perceived must be constantly, continually and uninterruptedly observed by him who observes and perceives it. On the other hand, since the position with regard to the matter to be observed is as I have described it, many people must observe it. How can anybody know whether something he now observes is identical or not with something observed in the past, if he himself has not observed both? In order that they should not think that we wish to harm them and enjoy quarrelling with them, when we proceed so carefully and engage in such hair-splitting, we wish to give way to them in this matter as well and admit to them that it is possible that any particular disease with all its symptoms can be identical with another disease and that one and the same person can observe it very many times.

Furthermore, I say that this affair which you wish to settle with your remarks is extremely repellent and ugly. For you attack empiricism because it is concerned with the storage of details, as well as for other reasons, and you praise and extol the analogical reasoning from the known to the unknown [theory], since thereby one can learn whatever one wants to learn according to a comprehensive, general method. For example, in order to treat a patient with diarrhoea, it is more useful and helpful to know that constipating medicines are useful to him than that quinces and pomegranates are useful to him. For the two latter items are, in fact, included in the general principle, just as many other things are, so that it includes almost everything that is useful for people with diarrhoea. If the empiricist were to enumerate not only approximately three but even fifteen kinds of remedies which are useful for them, he would still not have mentioned all, since what he omits is more than what he mentions. And if someone were also to concede to them that they might mention in their books all medicines applied by physicians, which is impossible, nobody would be able to keep all this in memory without being able to appeal to a general principle on which to base himself and without all these things having something in common in which they resemble one another.

It follows of necessity from their statement that it is the special characteristic of theory to make all its discoveries at once and that it is the special characteristic of empiricism to discover something gradually. It is their duty to tell us whether they think that the whole of medicine had suddenly at one moment been discovered and become known, thus agreeing that Hippocrates had been the first to become familiar with the whole of medicine in his age—and the necessary consequence of such a statement would then be that Hippocrates had done something useless and superfluous when he set down the observations and perceptions he wished to remember in the *Epidemics*—or whether they think that Hippocrates discovered many things and that his successors later discovered a not inconsiderable number of other things, so that we find that some things have already been discovered, and one can hope that others will be discovered in the future. If they think that, it is much more probable and appropriate that such gradual discoveries are made through empiricism and not through theory. And if that is so, which we, however, believe not to be the case, then not only is the claim that nothing can be discovered empirically wrong, but, on the contrary, the claim that everything can be discovered empirically is true and correct.

It also belongs of necessity to all the conclusions that follow from the argument of the theorists [the Dogmatists] that research as to the way in which medicine was discovered is vain and superfluous. You theorists believe, in fact, that such [medical-historical] investigation is useful, because one needs it for the discovery of that which had not yet been discovered in the past; thus you can undertake it after all and in this way discover what you want to discover. But if everything has already been discovered by means of theory, we need not discover anything further in the future. Accordingly, research as to how remedies applied for healing in medicine were discovered is also worthless and vain. Besides, that [in the first place] you admit and agree with us that very many things apart from those already discovered have not yet been discovered and [secondly] that in what exists we must pass from the one to another similar one demonstrates clearly even to unintelligent people, and all the more to all others, that medicine has not been discovered by theory. I do not know how it has happened to us that these statements made in passing have made it immediately clear that nothing at all has been discovered by analogical reasoning from the known to the unknown, though we had not intended that at all but had rather intended to explain that not everything has been discovered by means of such analogical reasoning.

Further statements of a similar kind serve the same purpose. If nothing has been discovered by theory and empiricism together, it is permitted to the humoral pathologist to do everything without needing empiricism in any way, and to treat bodies only according to what theory indicates to him, in a way that is no worse than the treatment given by one who combines in himself the knowledge of both things. On the other hand, a man who bases his treatment only on what experience indicates to him can know or do nothing technical at all. However, that is not the case. Rather, if humoral pathologists would know the discussion, argumentation and theory of the whole of medicine, but lacked empirically acquired knowledge, they could not carry out one single medical procedure, even the most minor one, correctly. On the other hand, we have frequently found that someone who allows himself to be guided exclusively by simple experience in the practice of medicine progresses as a physician and achieves great competence. This proves clearly that empiricism does not require theory at all, and that theory is of no use for medicine in any respect. Discussion and argument have already become excessively prolonged here, but through them the way has been paved for several things required for our later exposition.

As far as I am concerned, I am surprised at our present-day sophists who do not readily heed Hippocrates when he says that, with regard to food and drink, one needs experience, and who do not like to give themselves and their followers the good advice to accept what the common people, and even more the élite, generally accept. Namely, if everything is known only by means of theory and nothing is known empirically, how then is it possible that the common people who do not master theory can have any kind of knowledge or how is it that it is generally accepted and that among the physicians not only Hippocrates but also all his successors, Diogenes, Diocles, Praxagoras, Philotimus and Erasistratus, advocate it? All of them concede that they have acquired their entire medical knowledge through a combination of theory and empiricism. Diogenes in particular and Diocles have discussed in detail the point that one can only know the effects of food and drink empirically. Hippocrates had established this apodictically and stated that it belongs to the empirically known things. If one turns to Praxagoras, Philotimus and Erasistratus, one also finds that even though they allot more room to theory than do all the other early physicians—they are, however, confused in some respects, for example, that purslane is a remedy against bluntness of the teeth, and similar matters—yet they admit that food and drink belong to the things empirically knowable. Their contradictions and doubts refer to things that are more varied, confused and complicated.

I would like to teach you in as few words as possible that empiricism suffices to discover all means and methods of healing. Nobody, I say, who investigates natural things, knows sufficient about the practice of medicine, if he does not make use of experience. A person who uses only experience can practise medicine with the greatest competence and in exemplary fashion, without using the reasoning from the known to the unknown that is called *analogismos*. And nobody who combines the two and uses them together has ever made any branch of medicine better than it was before. Hence, the reasoning from the known to the unknown called *analogismos* does not suffice for the discovery of the things used for healing, neither entirely on its own nor mixed with something else.

Now in order to curb you and bind your mouth with a muzzle so that you feel constricted and hemmed-in from all sides, I am ready to concede to you that everything can be discovered through the reasoning from the known to the unknown which is called *analogismos*; but then I follow it up with a proof that we do not now require it for anything useful. You claim, I say, that I, when I recognize something truly and correctly with the aid of things known through observation which serve as indications that lead me to my final conclusion, can thereby discover other unknown things and from these previously unknown things, discovered by means of those things known through observation, deduce something concerning the things to be used for healing. To this I would say: I do not intend to go beyond these moderate assumptions. I declare them permitted and accept your assertion that where such indications exist, the treatment must be absolutely correct. I also accept everything that you proclaim who consider possible the discovery of medicine from its entire [theory]. For example, you do not deny that one should bleed a young man who suffers from pneumonia and has a strong pulse. And if you say that, in contrast to the theorists, not a single empiricist can give a reason for the blood-letting, we say: You do not understand how to treat the case any better and thus you are in no way superior to us. Otherwise, show it to us! For we say that it is not impossible that there are young men with a strong pulse who benefit from blood-letting and that beyond that nothing obliges us to investigate the reason why blood-letting benefits them. You who pronounce on the reasons for the effectiveness of the things used for healing do indeed chatter and babble more than we do, but against disease you can do no more than we can.

We want to concede to you in friendly fashion that you have discovered and know through theory why one must bleed a patient with that disease. But we say that we are not familiar with the theory and do not know what it is. Nevertheless, one can apply what one has discovered and knows. Now consider in what way you are superior to us as regards the application of the things used for healing. I claim that you have no superiority over us. The facts show this clearly. Hence, you are now not superior to us in respect of the application of the things used for healing, even though one admits to you in friendly fashion that all the things used for healing have been discovered only through the reasoning from the known to the unknown called *analogismos*.

In the preceding discussion we have shown that empiricism also suffices for the discovery of the things used for healing. This discussion here at the end of our entire discussion interrupts your chatter and stops you from chattering once and for all. One has, indeed, conceded to you in friendly fashion that all the things used for healing were discovered through theory, but later it has been shown that we do not now need it in any respect.

Anatomy

7. On the vivisection of animals from the ninth book of Galen's large work on anatomy, ed. and trans. M. Simon, *Sieben Bücher der Anatomie des Galen* (Leipzig, 1906), pp. 18–20, trans. pp. 13–15; English trans. W. L. H. Duckworth, M. C. Lyons and B. Towers (Cambridge, 1962), pp. 15 f.

[For methodical reasons] I think that here too it is best if I add in this book what one can observe with one's own eyes in the brain during the vivisection of animals, in order that the brain may be treated here exclusively and exhaustively.

For this purpose, I say, one must prepare either a pig or a kid, and for two reasons. Firstly, in order not to have to see how ugly a monkey looks when he is dissected alive and, secondly, in order to have an animal which cries out very loudly when dissected, which a monkey does not do.

Undertake the experiment which I will describe to you on a young animal of tender age and then on animals weak with age. It will be found that there is a great difference here between young animals and those weak with age. The dissection must be undertaken on both animals in exactly the same manner. Every incision you make must be as straight as it would be in the case of a dead animal. The incision must be made unsparingly and pitilessly and so deep as to uncover the skull of the animal and expose it in one stroke. This is done by severing the membrane surrounding the skull [pericranium] together with the skin. Such an incision frequently produces such a great flow of blood that one is afraid to dissect further and complete the dissection. However, you need not be frightened by this; for the flow of blood in these places can be stopped with very little effort. You need only to pull the edges of the severed skin upward and to both sides. Besides, you can also tie off with your fingers the vein from which the blood flows, by pulling the skin to the side. In this it is also useful to have an assistant who would take hold together with you and help you to tie off what you must tie off in the described manner. Furthermore, it is good to have a hook on which you can hang and twist the piece from which the blood flows. Also, in such a dissection you need not confine yourself to this, but instead you can turn the place round, roll it up and pull it off or away or do whatever you want with it. You can do that just as well with the hook as with the fingers.

When you have treated both edges of the severed skin as I have described it to you, proceed to peel the membrane around the skull [pericranium] from the bone. For this employ the knife resembling the myrtle leaf. Then separate from the skull the bone at the top of the head without thereby piercing the thick membrane [dura mater]. Study meticulously what occurs in the brain in respect of the membrane [dura mater] and what you can now observe with your own eyes. Then you will see that as long as the animal does not scream, the whole brain gently rises and falls with a movement resembling the pulse in all the beating blood vessels, that is, the arteries. But when the animal screams, you can see how the brain rises more strongly till one can observe clearly that it is higher than the bone. It appears to the eye as if it rises more strongly for two different reason, firstly, because the observer observes the two edges of the bone and does not understand that the severed bone was higher than they, secondly, because it is now easier for the brain to move towards a place to occupy it. Before you severed the bone, the skull was the border which it could not overstep. Herewith, I have described to you briefly and concisely the reason for this procedure.

Pharmacology

8. The special problems of the adoption by the Muslims of ancient pharmacology, according to the famous report of Ibn Juljul, preserved in Ibn Abī Uṣaibiʿah, II, 46_{29}–48_{10}. Cf. also M. Meyerhof, in *Quellen und Studien zur Geschichte der Naturwissenschaften und der Medizin*, III (1933), pp. 72–4. The same report also describes the historical background of the Arabic translation of the history of Orosius, the only ancient Latin text whose Arabic translation is preserved, cf. G. Levi Della Vida, 'La traduzione araba delle storie di Orosio', in *Miscellanea G. Galbiati*, III, (Milan, 1951), pp. 187–203 = *Al-Andalus*, XIX (1954), pp. 257–93. For the Arabic Dioscurides, cf. E. J. Grube in the *Festschrift* for E. Kühnel (Berlin, 1959), pp. 163–94. For another translation, cf. A. Dietrich in the *Festschrift* for E. Heischkel and W. Artelt (Stuttgart, 1971), pp. 69–78.

Ibn Juljul has explained the terms for simple remedies in the work of Dioscurides from ʿAin Zarbah and clarified their hidden meaning. At the beginning of his book on the subject he says:

The work of Dioscurides was translated from Greek into Arabic in Baghdād under the ʿAbbāsids in the time of Jaʿfar al-Mutawakkil. The translator was Iṣṭifan b. Basīl [Stephen, the son of Basilius]. Ḥunain b. Isḥāq, the translator, checked his translation. He [probably Ḥunain and not Iṣṭifan] corrected it and licensed the study of it. In all cases, where Iṣṭifan knew the current Arabic term corresponding to the Greek, he translated the Greek term into Arabic. Otherwise, he left it untranslated in the hope that after him God would send someone who would know it and could translate it into Arabic. For the inhabitants of various localities have only freely chosen conventional terms for individual remedies; they name them on etymological grounds and for some other convention. Iṣṭifan therefore relied on the fact that after him there would one day be men who knew the individual remedies whose names he himself had not known in his own time, and they would assign to them the terms used in their age, so that one would attain full knowledge. . . .

This work arrived in Spain in the translation of Iṣṭifan, partly with Arabic identifications, partly without them. It was used, as far as it was intelligible, both in the East and in Spain, until the time of ʿAbd-ar-Raḥmān b. Muḥammad an-Nāṣir, then ruler of Spain. He conducted a correspondence with King Armāniyūs [Romanus],[4] the ruler of Constantinople, I believe, in the year 337/948–9, and the latter sent him very valuable presents, among them the book of Dioscurides written in *ighrīqī*, that is, *yūnānī*,[5] with wonderful Byzantine illustrations of the herbs. Together with it he also sent the work of the historian, Orosius, a wonderful history of the Rūm with historical information from olden days, stories of the earliest kings and useful information. In his letter to an-Nāṣir, Armāniyūs wrote that one could profit from Dioscurides' book only if there was somebody who understood Greek well and knew the individual remedies.

> If you have such a man in your country, O King, you can properly profit from the book. As far as the work of Orosius is concerned, you have surely in your country Latinists who are able to read Latin, and if you urge them to make the book available, they can translate it for you from Latin into Arabic. . . .

At that time there was no Spanish Christian in Cordoba who could read *ighrīqī*, that is to say, old Greek. Thus the book of Dioscurides remained in Greek as it was, in the treasury of ʿAbd-ar-Raḥmān an-Nāṣir and was not translated into Arabic. The book remained in Spain, but the translation of Iṣṭifan, which had come from Baghdād, remained in use. Then, when an-Nāṣir addressed a written reply to King Mārīnūs [!], he begged him to send him someone who spoke Greek [*ighrīqī*] and Latin in order to teach slaves to translate for him. Thereupon King Armāniyūs sent a monk named Niqūlā [Nicholas] to an-Nāṣir. He arrived in Cordoba in the year 340/951–2. At that time there were physicians there who were interested in scientific research and desired a translation of the unknown drugs from the book of Dioscurides. Ḥasdāy b. Shabrūṭ al-Isrā'īlī was the one most interested in scientific research and in such a translation, since he hoped thereby to gain the favour of King ʿAbd ar-Raḥmān an-Nāṣir. The monk Niqūlā was extraordinarily esteemed by him and very intimate with him. He explained the unknown names of drugs in the work of Dioscurides. He was the first in Cordoba to manufacture the *fārūq*-theriac with improved ingredients. Among the physicians of that time who were interested in improved identification of the names of the individual drugs in the work were Muḥammad, known as ash-Shajjār, a certain al-Basbāsī, Abū ʿUthmān al-Ḥazzāz, who bore the nickname of al-Yābisah, Muḥammad b. Saʿīd aṭ-Ṭabīb, ʿAbd-ar-Raḥmān b. Isḥāq b. Haitham and Abū ʿAbdallāh aṣ-Ṣiqillī, who spoke Greek and knew the individual remedies. . . .

All these people lived at the same time as the monk Niqūlā. I knew them, as well as the monk Niqūlā, already during the lifetime of al-Mustanṣir [read: an-Nāṣir] and mixed with them during the time of al-Mustanṣir al-Ḥakam. At the beginning of the latter's reign, the monk Niqūlā died. Through the research of these men concerning the names of the drugs in the work of Dioscurides, such sure knowledge of the individual remedies was obtained, especially in Andalusian Cordoba, that no further doubt remained and the individual remedies and the correct, faultless pronunciation of their names became known, with the exception of a few of them, about ten quite unimportant remedies. . . .

I very much desired and made a great effort to attain accurate knowledge of the materia medica, which serves as the basis of the compound remedies and, finally, God noticed that it was my intention to revive what I feared would get lost and lose its value for the human body and, in His benevolence, He gave me knowledge of it in adequate measure. God has created [the means for] healing and distributed them among the plants that grow on earth, among the animals that walk or crawl on earth or swim in the water and among the minerals that are hidden in the womb of the earth. In all of that there is healing, pity and kindness.

9. From the Arabic translation of Dioscurides, ed. C. E. Dubler and Elías Terés, *La 'Materia Medica' de Dioscórides* (Barcelona-Tetuán, 1952–9), II, p. 13 = Dioscurides, I, 2.

Āqūrūn [Greek *akoron* yellow flag]/*al-wajj* [galangal, here, however, to be understood in the sense of the Greek word]: Its leaves resemble those of the iris, but are finer, and its roots are not unlike those of the iris, but intertwined; they are not straight but bent and have nodules outside, are of a whitish colour, slightly sharp in taste and not foul-smelling.

The best *wajj* is white, thick, not corroded, full and sweet-smelling. The one originating from the city called Chalcis,[6] as well as the one from the land called Galatia and named *asplēnon* ['spleenless'], are of this kind.

The power of its root is hot and, if it is stewed and its water is drunk, it produces much urine. The root water helps against pain in the side [ribs, pleura], in the chest and the liver, against colic and torn muscles. It dissolves swelling of the spleen and helps against strangury and the bites of insects [reptiles]. It is as effective against pain in the uterus as iris water.

The juice of the *wajj* root clears obscurations of the eye.

The *wajj* root is a useful ingredient in electuaries.

Some fragments of Rufus of Ephesus

10. Some fragments of Rufus of Ephesus, quoted by ar-Rāzī with the indication of the titles of the works of Rufus from which they are derived. They are taken from the first fifteen volumes of the Arabic edition of the *Ḥāwī* (*Continens*), which is now complete in twenty-three volumes (twenty-five parts) (Hyderabad, 1374–90/1955–71). The corresponding passages of the medieval Latin translation, first printed in 1486 in Brescia, were reprinted by C. Daremberg and E. Ruelle, *Oeuvres de Rufus d'Ephèse* (Paris, 1879), apparently from the Venice edition of 1509 (abbreviated here as 'D.-R.'). The Latin text is helpful for the understanding of the very faulty Arabic edition and, in turn, can be corrected with its aid.

Whether we are dealing here with independent works or with chapters of one of the larger works ascribed to Rufus cannot be definitely ascertained, though the manner in which the Arabic refers to the titles suggests independent works. It is also not possible to arrange the individual fragments according to their position within the original works. Moreover, we are faced here with the familiar difficulty of being unable to determine definitely where a quotation ends and whether it might not be continued later after an interruption.

(a) *On Melancholia*, I, 74–7 (454–7 D.-R.), V, 80 (480 D.-R.), 185, 188 (480 and 482 D.-R.), VI, 86 (486 D.-R.), VIII, 34 (also VIII, 87) (491 D.-R.). [Further quotations can be found I, 135, 162, 180, V, 70, 120, VI, 115, 133, VII, 227, XIV, 248, XV, 72, 212, XIX, 192, XXII, 58.]

Rufus says in his book about the black bile: melancholia must be treated from the very beginning. Otherwise treatment is made more difficult by two circumstances, namely, because the humour has settled in and because it is then difficult for the patient to accept [medicines].

The beginning of melancholia is indicated by fear, anxiety and suspicion aimed at a particular thing while nothing abnormal is apparent in every other respect. They imagine, for example[7] . . . some are afraid of thunder or wish to think constantly about death or continually want to wash themselves or hate a particular food, a particular drink or a particular kind of animal or imagine they have swallowed a serpent, etc. Such symptoms last for a time; then they become stronger, and the symptoms of real melancholia appear and become increasingly more pronounced. If you perceive any symptoms of this kind, hasten to begin treatment.

When abscesses appear on the body of a melancholic, this indicates his imminent death. Such abscesses appear on both sides, on the chest and externally on the body. They possess a very painful heat and, with their itching and other manifestations, resemble carbuncles.

Men suffer from melancholia more frequently than women. Yet women who suffer from it have stronger phantasies and anxieties. Children do not get it, youths and young men rarely. On the other hand, elderly and old men especially get it, in particular the old; for melancholia is fairly typical of old age, since the old are naturally depressed, little inclined to merriment and moody. They are always worried and suffer a lot from flatulence. All these are symptoms of melancholia.

Winter is the season least favourable for melancholia, since the digestion is good in winter. Next comes summer, since it purges the stomach and dissolves the superfluities. One whose stomach is not purged suffers from very heavy rumblings in it. In melancholia it is harmful to drink much thick, black or new wine, eat tough meat or camel's flesh and avoid physical exercise[8]. . . .

Melancholia produces much thought and worry. Sometimes it can happen that melancholics are addicted to dreams and forecasting future events, and they predict them accurately. . . .

When someone falls ill with melancholia, often only the most experienced physicians can recognize it in the beginning. For a skilful physician knows how to distinguish a bad mood, despair and worry at the beginning of melancholia from symptoms caused otherwise. . . .

A sign of incipient melancholia is the craving to want to be alone, without any cause or visible need for it of the kind that the healthy can sometimes have, because they love scientific research or want to keep secret what must be kept secret.

One must look around for a common sign and then start treatment immediately, since melancholia can easily be treated at the beginning, but once it has settled in, it is extremely difficult to treat. The first sign from which you can conclude that someone is suffering from melancholia is that he becomes angry, sad and anxious more quickly than usual and likes to be alone. If this is combined with the accompanying circumstances which I am about to describe, you can feel confirmed in your supposition. For the patient cannot open his eyes properly, as if he were day-blind. The eyes of melancholics are somewhat rigid, their lips thick, their complexion brown, little hair on their body, their chest and adjacent parts of the body strongly developed, their belly below shrunken. Their movements are powerful and quick, and they can do nothing slowly. They lisp, and their voice is thin. They speak quickly, with a swift movement of the tongue.

Not every melancholic vomits or shows a black liquid in his excrement. Rather, phlegm appears most frequently. When something black appears in the stool, it shows that something like it predominates, and a large amount of it is present in the body. Their sickness then abates slightly, though with some the illness abates with the excretion of phlegm rather than with the excretion of the black liquid. The black liquid betrays its presence by vomiting or in the stool or urine or by abscesses and various kinds of rashes on the body or by the bleeding of haemorrhoids. Frequently, they also have varicose veins. Those among whom no black liquid appears are more difficult to treat. Even when the excretion of phlegm gives them relief, the black liquid still exerts control over them, and one must try to purge it. Usually melancholia does not arise from the presence of a large amount of black bile in the body, but by its penetrating the whole of the blood just as urine does when its sediments do not settle. When the black bile settles, it does not cause melancholia even when present in large quantities. . . . When it moves from the blood, whatever it is like, to the exterior of the body, for instance, through a rash or black scabs, or when it is discharged from the body, for example through urine, through black stool, through swelling of the spleen, or through varicose veins, no melancholia arises[9]. . . .

Their craving for sexual intercourse is also a proof that the black bile contains a lot of wind. Persons of excellent natures are predisposed to melancholia, since excellent natures move quickly and think a lot. . . .

Those suffering from melancholia find improvement and relief of their condition through purging, belching and vomiting[10]. . . .

In the Melancholia Rufus has reported many views which state that a surfeit of cold in the stomach arouses the appetite and a surfeit of warmth removes it. The appetite is stimulated by drinking cold water, while warm water calms it. It is also stimulated by the [coldness of] winter and of the north wind. . . .

He who travels in heavy snow feels his appetite so powerfully stimulated that he feels a ravenous hunger [*būlimūs*]. Cold water produces more of an appetite than wine.

Rufus in the Melancholia: He who suffers from excessive appetite must be treated with warming things and wine. All he eats he must eat warm, and preferably sit by the fire. He may not drink anything cold, since that arouses the appetite.

Rufus in the Melancholia: Ravenous hunger attacks people who travel in severe cold and heavy snow. Its treatment consists of warming with food and wine and sitting by the fire.

Rufus in the Melancholia: Two thirds of a dirham [drachma, about three grams] of camomile in honeywater, when drunk, purges the black bile.

Rufus in the Melancholia: Whoever has an ulcer in the intestines may have a stool of black liquid [*chymos*], which is an indication of death [or, according to the parallel passage: whereupon death follows].

(b) *On the Treatment of Children* (or *Infants*). This title is identical with *On the Upbringing of Infants*, but the title quoted in I, 162, 182, *On the Treatment*, presumably refers to another work. The passages translated are: III, 55 f. (470 D.-R.), 201 (474 and 475 D.-R.), VII, 6 (494 D.-R.), 273 (491 D.-R., compare also 531).

Rufus on the Treatment of Infants: A moistened piece of wool soaked in alum or old date wine or honey and lupine is put into the ear. . . .

In the ears of children there is some moisture, which the ignorant regard as pus, but it is only an excretion of food. When you see this, take care that they are not suckled at night. Then that moisture will largely disappear, and the ear becomes dry.

Rufus on the Treatment of Children: Black mouth thrush is fatal to children. It occurs frequently in Egypt,[11] hence it is also called the Egyptian boil. In the case of mouth thrush that is not black[12] crushed roots of iris or dried roses, saffron, pepper, myrrh, gallnuts and frankincense are sprinkled into the children's mouths. This simple compound is beneficial for the infant. It is helpful to add honey to it. After the child has been treated with it, he is given mixed honey or sweetened pomegranate juice to drink.

Rufus on the Treatment of Infants: Women who want to stop the milk by taking drugs injure and harden their breasts thereby, and are finally obliged to have them opened by the lancet. Basil [*Ocimum basilicum L.*] stops the milk of goats when they feed on it.

On Rearing Infants: When you allow milk to curdle and sprinkle asafoetida into it, it dissolves it immediately. Hence it is most suitable for somebody in whose stomach milk tends to curdle.[13]

(c) *On the Slimming of Fat People*, VI, 281, 287 (493 D.-R.), IX, 96 (500 D.-R.), X, 298 (509 D.-R.), 330 (510 D.-R.)

From Rufus's book on the Slimming of Fat People: a good and moderately fleshy body possesses the most perfect and reliable health. . . .

Beans keep the body moist. If you put iron dross, thyme and seeds [?] in cow's milk from which the cream has been removed and which has not yet turned into buttermilk, but is just about to turn into buttermilk, and then drink it, it makes the body fat.

Rufus on the Slimming of Fat People: Fat people cannot endure overexertion,[14] hunger and indigestion and have discomfort from them and become gravely ill. They have a predisposition to this, especially for strokes, epileptic fits, foul-smelling sweat, heartache, breathlessness, diarrhoea, fainting fits and high fever. When they fall ill, they are not immediately aware of it, because of the slowness of their sense perception, and thus it happens that they only seek treatment after the illness has already affected them severely. Their illnesses become bad because their cavities are narrow, their breathing is weak and it is difficult to bleed them owing to their abundant fat and the slenderness of their veins. Sometimes purgatives kill them, and even when they do not kill them, they weaken them, and this is unpleasant in their case. They have plenty of phlegm, which is the worst humour, and little blood, the best humour. They can hardly get rid of their illness, and when they do get rid of it, they do not recover quickly, and their bodies only return to their original healthy condition after a long time.

Rufus on the Slimming of Fat People: When the uterus of a fat woman no longer contains any moisture and becomes warm, she can become pregnant. But usually she does not become pregnant, and when she does become pregnant, she has a miscarriage. But even when she does not have a miscarriage, the foetus is weakly and puny.

From Rufus's book on the Slimming of Fat People: Fat people do not desire sexual intercourse and cannot perform it frequently.

From Rufus's book on the Slimming of Fat People: A fat person is not eager for sexual intercourse and cannot perform it, even when he is at least slightly [?] eager for it.

(d) *On Milk or Milk Drinking*, I, 102 f., IV, 102, VI, 58 (485 D.-R.), VII, 272 f. (491 D.-R., cf. n. 13).

Rufus on Milk: Fullness of the stomach is very harmful for the head. We know this because vomiting, sleeping and digesting relieve and calm a hangover.

From Rufus's book on Milk Drinking: When they suck mother's milk, they have stool quickly, and their abscesses on the lung heal quickly. (The following remarks may perhaps also be attributable to Rufus.)

Rufus on Milk Drinking: Whoever wants to purge his belly must guard against quickly filling himself again with food, since an empty belly fills up quickly.

From Rufus's book on Milk Drinking: Whoever drinks milk should not overstrain himself because that makes it turn sour; for overexertion turns coarse food sour, how much more so milk. One should not consume more of it before the first helping has gone down and been followed by belching.

(e) *On the Bath*, VI, 238 (and very similarly 249), 247 f. (493 f. D.-R., cf. also 520).

From Rufus's book on the Bath: Shade and shelter keep moist. The sun makes thin. Drinking of cold water fattens, that of warm water slims. Abundant perspiration slims. Sexual intercourse slims. Vomiting and prolonged sleep slims. Eating once a day slims, twice fattens.

Rufus on the Bath: He who does not take care to pour water over his body dries out quickly, especially when the weather is hot and dry. Whoever sweats a great deal, his body becomes dry. Moderate vomiting keeps the body moist, but too much makes it thin, since moderate vomiting cleanses the stomach and produces good digestion. Long sleep makes the body thin, since it takes strength away from it, while moderate sleep makes it strong and fat. Staying up late in company after eating in the evening makes one extremely thin, is harmful and spoils the nourishment one has consumed. Eating once a day slims, ties up the stomach and stirs up bile. Eating twice a day has the opposite effect. Drinking hot water slims. Dry nourishment makes the body thin and ties up the stomach. Overexertion dries the body out and shrinks it, and vice versa.

(f) *On the Sale of Slaves*, III, 29 f., 31 (469 f. D.-R.)

Rufus on the Sale of Slaves: The older the abscess in the ear, the worse it is. Its seriousness can be deduced from the width of the earhole and the foul-smelling thin pus. In this case it can happen that part of the ear bones is exposed.

Rufus on the Sale of Slaves: When the flow of pus from the ear has become chronic, one must fear that part of the ear bone will be exposed, especially in the case of thin, foul-smelling pus.

[A further fragment may be added from the *Bustān al-aṭibbā'* by Ibn al-Maṭrān.]

Rufus tells in his book about the Sale of Slaves: Once I was brought a slave whose head was twice as large as it ought to have been in comparison with his other limbs. He lacked some bones in his head on the right side, approximately a third of the whole. Where they were missing the head felt soft, and one could even recognize some arteries at that place. He was confused and could not control the movement of his left foot.

Veterinary medicine

11. From the hippiatric work of Theomnestus, who probably wrote in the first half of the fourth century A.D., according to the very faulty Istanbul MS Köprülü 959, fol. 4b. The Greek text of the second

paragraph is found in *Corpus Hippiatricorum Graecorum*, II, 231 f. Oder-Hoppe.

We have found many of our cures for animals among the inhabitants of Pamphylia [?, Thessaly ?], who occupied themselves earlier than others with the study of horses. What we have learned from the inhabitants of Cappadocia, whose horses and pastures we have ourselves inspected, these in turn learned from the Greeks called Arcadians. We have also watched for a long time the veterinarians in the palaces of kings and seen a great deal of the treatment and training of horses in the army.

Before we study the illnesses of animals and their treatment, we must briefly say a word in description of horses and which horses are fit to be tethered and deserve to be tended. The horse that is fit for us to occupy ourselves with it must be strong and handsome. A horse's strength lies in its legs, and its beauty in its head, since the strength and beauty of a horse appear in these two parts of the body. However, one can also recognize a strong horse from the place in which it was born and the way it trots. As regards its birthplace, it depends on whether the terrain happens to be mountainous or stony and whether it is descended from a horse with such a life history. For it frequently happens that a horse has his weak feet from his father, that is to say, if the father mounts and impregnates a mountain mare [while he himself] has grown up in wooded, marshy terrain. Then she gives birth to something resembling the horse that had mounted her, in respect of lack of strength and [susceptibility to] illness, as occurs with the children of gouty parents and with horses called[15]. . . . One must not confine oneself to studying only the birthplace of a horse, but must also study the stallions and mares which have sired it, so that it might not be descended from a mountain stallion and a mare raised in wooded and marshy terrain.

VII

GEOMETRY, ARITHMETIC AND OPTICS

In Muslim civilization, knowledge of the mathematical sciences was based on the translated great works of classical antiquity. In Greek schools, these works required exposition and commentary in order to make them more intelligible to readers and listeners. This tradition continued in Islam. The revised versions were provided with explicatory material and also often contained material taken from ancient commentaries (which is particularly valuable for us where the originals are lost). Relying at first on sources of this nature, Muslim scholars later on made outstanding contributions of their own.

Especially significant was the Muslim contribution to algebra. In connection with it and with arithmetic in general, the classical heritage has been considered as secondary, and the primary inspiration has been sought in a direct Oriental tradition going back to ancient Mesopotamia. However, this is by no means certain, as is now also shown by A. Sayili's investigations in connection with his edition of *The Algebra of Ibn Turk* (*Logical Necessities in Mixed Equations*) (Ankara, 1962). Here, too, more credit than one was long inclined to grant it appears to belong to the classical world as the transmitting agent.

In explanation of Euclid's Geometry

1. From the commentary of an-Nairīzī, ed. R. O. Besthorn and J. L. Heiberg, *Codex Leidensis 399, 1. Euclidis Elementa ex interpretatione al-Hadschdschadschii cum commentariis al-Narizii* (Copenhagen, 1897), pp. 12–21; medieval Latin translation, ed. M. Curtze, *Anaritii in decem libros priores Elementorum Euclidis commentarii* (Leipzig, 1899),

pp. 28–32. An-Nairīzī's work is mainly compiled from ancient Greek commentaries. According to Maimonides, it could not be called a proper commentary, since it contains too much extraneous material (M. Steinschneider, in *Zeitschrift der Deutschen Morgenländischen Gesellschaft*, XLVIII [1894], pp. 220, 232). Cf. J. E. Hofmann, in P. Wilpert (ed.), *Antike und Orient im Mittelalter* (Berlin, 1962), p. 103; A. I. Sabra, 'Simplicius's Proof of Euclid's Parallels Postulate', in *Journal of the Warburg and Courtauld Institutes*, XXXII (1969), pp. 1–24.

Euclid says: There are five postulates.

Simplicius says: After Euclid had mentioned the definitions which point to the essence of each of the defined things, he proceeded in his discussion to the enumeration of the postulates. Generally speaking, postulates are that which is not conceded, but rather what the pupil is asked to concede[1] in order to secure thereby a firm foundation for himself and the teacher. This foundation can be something impossible, for example, the postulate which Archimedes wanted to have conceded, namely, that he was standing outside the earth; were this conceded to him, he would guarantee to demonstrate that he could move the earth. For he says: 'Youth, concede to me that I can go upwards and stand outside the earth, and I will show you that I can move the earth.' This happened when he boasted of having found the geometrical [-mechanical] power. Though this is something impossible, he wanted this postulate to be conceded and to have such a situation presumed for purposes of instruction. What one postulates is either something impossible, as stated, or something possible well known to the professors but unknown to the pupils, which must be applied at the beginning of instruction. The things to be proved are similarly known to the professors and unknown to the pupils. However, they are not stated as postulates, since they are not principles but can be proved.

Postulates are stated because they are principles. Some are stated just because they are necessary for instruction, for example, the first three postulates. Others demand some explanation in order that they may be considered true and accepted as they are.

They are distinguished from ordinary notions inasmuch as the latter are accepted as such, as soon as one thinks about them. The postulates, on the other hand, stand by their very nature in the middle between principles derived from primary knowledge and whose causes are unknown to those who apply them—such as definitions—and ordinary notions, which all men equally accept; for postulates, though not known to all men, are nevertheless well known to the professors of every discipline.

Some people assume that geometrical postulates are only intended for conceding the element [matter], since not all procedures can be carried out thereby. Hence, someone may attack the postulates from the element and say: 'I cannot draw a straight line on the surface of the water, nor any straight line which extends to infinity, since infinity does not exist.' He who makes such a claim assumes first of all that postulates are only required in elemental geometry. What, then, do they say concerning the equality of right angles? How do they wish to convince us that the postulate concerned originates from the element. The same applies to all the following postulates.

It is best to say that postulates are what the pupil does not accept immediately on hearing it for the first time and what is required in the demonstration. Some are impossible and cannot be accepted as easily as the first three, yet one would like them to be conceded, as I have explained, for purposes of instruction. Some are known to the professor and accepted by him, while at the moment they appear strange and unclear to the pupil. Hence one wants him to concede them; this is the case with the postulates after the first three. The usefulness of the first three postulates consists in the fact that the element [matter] is not weak and, hence, it neither hinders nor delays the demonstrations. The subsequent postulates are used for certain proofs.

Euclid says: Let it be postulated that we can draw a straight line from any point to any other point.

Simplicius says: He says this because between two given points there undoubtedly exists a distance which is the shortest distance between them. When we draw it, what we draw is a straight line whose two ends are the given points. It is not possible to draw a straight line which passes through three points, unless the middle point goes through the two end points, which means that the three lie on the same course.

It is also possible to draw an arc from any point to any other point. If we draw the straight line connecting the two points A and B, then construct an isosceles triangle ABG on it, and, taking the point G as the centre, draw a circle with the radius GA, it will pass through the point B, since the distance BG equals that of AG, and thus the line AB is an arc.

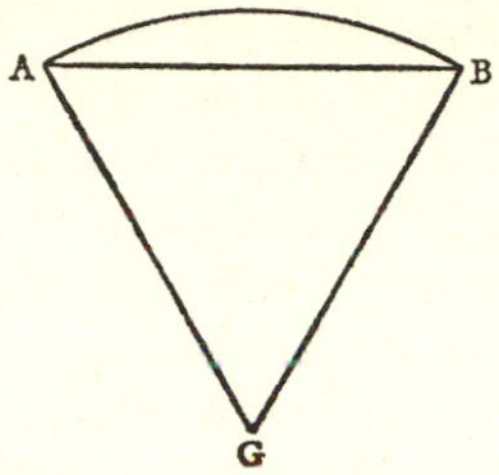

This must necessarily be postulated, since the element of geometry rests in the imagination; for were it in bodies which themselves possess the element, it would be careless to demand that it should be postulated that a straight line be drawn from Aries to Libra.

Euclid says: And that from a finite straight line we can draw a straight line which is straight and continuous with it.[2]

Simplicius says: Continuous is that whose ends are one. It is possible to draw a straight line, straight and continuous, so that it is altogether a single straight line. For it is possible that what one draws is continuous as a line, but not continuous as a straight line, namely, when it includes an angle. Conversely, it is also possible that both lines are straight but are not one single line, as happens when they are not continuous. We know by definition that the line is finite, for, if it were infinite, how would one then be able to draw it? Yet one can assume that the finite line can be extended to infinity, should that be necessary, in order that the line's inability to extend to infinity should be no obstacle for us in connection with any geometrical form.

That the line which follows the straight course of a straight, finite line is together with it a single line and not two, we wish to explain by the following method, after having first stipulated that one grants us one of the postulates, namely, the one immediately following here, that we can draw a circle from any centre and with any radius. Hence, let us assume a straight finite line on which there are A and B, and I say: The line which is drawn straight and continuous with it is together with it a single line. This can be proved as follows: If the line which is drawn straight and continuous with AB is not a single line with it, then we can draw the line ABG and the straight line ABD and describe a circle AGD around the centre B with the radius BA. Then the line ABG as well as the line ABD are straight lines and the diameter of the circle, since they pass through the centre of the circle, and both divide the circle in two parts, and hence the arc AGD equals the arc AG, the larger equals the smaller, which is an impossible contradiction. Therefore the line which is drawn straight and continuous with the line AB represents a single line together with it.

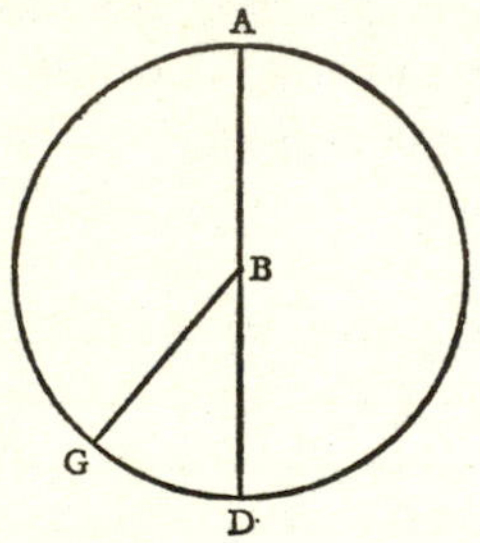

Euclid says: And that we can draw a circle from any centre and with any radius.

Simplicius says: By the radius with which the circle is drawn, he means the radius which is finite on both sides. If it is possible to draw a straight line from any point to any other point, and if a circle results when one of the two points of that straight line is fixed as the centre of the circle and the other point is led around in a circle until the circumference results, then it is obviously possible that one can draw a circle around a centre with any radius.

Even and odd numbers

2. Nicomachus of Gerasa, 13_7–14_{12} Hoche, according to the Arabic trans., ed. W. Kutsch, *Thābit ibn Qurra's arabische Übersetzung der Arithmētikē Eisagōgē des Nikomachos von Gerasa* (Beirut, 1959), pp. 19_{10}–

20_9. For an explanation of the second paragraph (the more divisors there are, the smaller they are), cf. the English trans. by M. L. d'Ooge (New York, 1926), pp. 190 f.

A number, strictly speaking, is a number of digits or a scattered quantity consisting of units. The first division of numbers is that even and odd numbers exist. An even number is one that can be divided into two equal parts, since no unit falls in between. An odd number is one which cannot be divided into two equal parts because of the unit falling in between. These two definitions are those of the common people.

On the other hand, according to the definition ascribed to Pythagoras, an even number is one which may be divided by one and the same thing [procedure] into something greater and smaller, into something greater according to measurement and into something smaller according to quantity, as the natural balance inherent in these two kinds demands. An odd number is one where this is not possible and which can only be divided into two unequal parts.

The ancients have defined both kinds of numbers from another point of view and said: An even number is one divisible into two equal and two unequal parts, except for the number two, which stands at the beginning of the even numbers and is divisible only into two equal parts. If one of the two parts belongs to one of the two kinds of numbers, no matter which, the other part must also belong to the same kind of number. An odd number is one which, no matter how it is divided, can always only be divided into two parts representing both kinds of numbers, and in it both kinds are found at all times always mixed with each other, or rather they exist in it always closely linked with each other.

If, on our part, we wish to define both even and odd numbers, we say that an odd number is one where the difference between it and the [nearest] even number in both directions, that is, greater or smaller, is one, and that an even number is one that differs from the odd number by one in both directions, that is, it is greater ⟨or smaller⟩ by one than the [nearest] odd number.

The theory of vision

3. The beginning of Euclid's *Optics* in the recension of Naṣīr-ad-dīn aṭ-Ṭūsī, printed in Hyderabad, 1358/1939, together with similarly

revised Greek mathematical writings in Arabic translation (*Majmūʿ Rasāʾil aṭ-Ṭūsī*). The Muslims were well aware of the fact that the theory of vision as caused by rays proceeding from the eye (the 'casting' of the glance, the 'sun-like' eye) was disputed, but it was natural for them to be greatly impressed by it, and it has therefore been chosen here for presentation.

With the assistance of the fiery bodies inside a transparent body, as, for instance, air and the like, which lies between the eye and the objects of vision, the eye produces a ray just as the fiery bodies themselves produce. This ray is in a way something sprung from the eye and coming forth from it. Then it serves the eye as an instrument of vision. According to its position, the conditions of visual perception differ and must then also be held true accordingly.

This ray has to be imagined as something joined continually to the eye in a straight line, and it must produce an infinite number of parallels running on straight courses.

The body of the rays is a cone whose vertex is at the eye and whose base lies at the end of the objects of vision.

Objects on which the sun falls can be seen, and those on which it does not fall cannot be seen.

What is seen from a large angle appears large and vice versa. What is seen from many angles appears manifold and what is seen from equal angles appears equal [the preceding four paragraphs correspond to *Optics* 3_{2-12} Heiberg].

I say: One must grant us that, if the directions of the rays differ in height and depth, in their position to the right and to the left, then the objects of vision are seen in different directions [3_{13-18} Heiberg]. That on which the ray falls more can be seen more accurately than that on which the ray falls less [$3_{19f.}$ Heiberg]. And that upon which the axis of the cone of rays falls is seen more accurately than that which surrounds it, since the ray is more concentrated there and more of it falls on it. What is nearer to it is seen more precisely than what is more distant [cf. $4_{10f.}$ Heiberg]. Hence an observer turns the axis of the cone of rays in the direction of what he desires to see or wishes to verify.

If the ray is reflected by a polished body, for example, a mirror, two equal angles appear there, one of which is called the angle of the rays and the other the reflected angle.

VIII

GEOGRAPHY AND ASTRONOMY

When medieval Muslim science had reached the end of its development in the sixteenth century, Ṭāshköprüzāde pointed out in his great encyclopaedia (*Miftāḥ as-saʿādah* [Hyderabad, 1328–56/1910–37], I, pp. 320 ff.) that geography is divided into four branches, namely, (1) geography proper as based on Ptolemy, which deals with the scientific description of the earth; (2) the knowledge of cities, countries, mountains and other geographical data, primarily of use to travellers; (3) knowledge of the distances between post-stations, which in fact is not essentially different from (2) and is represented by the same group of works, but emphasizes the value of geography for governmental and administrative purposes; and (4) the knowledge of remarkable natural phenomena to be found in the various zones. The last three branches had their predecessors in the Hellenistic world and, as we may well assume, also in eastern, mainly Persian-Sassanian, civilization. From them, Muslim scholars received their first stimuli of which they themselves may have often been unconscious; it was their own great achievement to have worked and written extensively on these subjects. On the other hand, Ptolemy's geography survived in direct and rather close dependence on it. The nature of the subject called for a kind of treatment comparable to that required in pharmacology. Geographical data pertinent to the world of Islam had to be integrated into Ptolemy's system, and geographical data mentioned by him had to be identified with those current in Muslim times. Since, in contrast to the situation in pharmacology, this was frequently of theoretical rather than practical interest, the latter task was usually disregarded. Scientific geography also furnished a particularly good illustration of how difficulties of translation successfully stimulated the spirit of independent scientific research among the Muslims (see below, no. 2).

Ptolemy also provided the basis for Arabic cartography, of which an example is given on plate IV. Dependence on Ptolemy is particularly clear in the representation of the course of the Nile, illustrated, for example, in Mžik's edition of al-Khuwārizmī and in K. Miller, *Mappae Arabicae*, Vol. VI (Stuttgart, 1927), plate 4; cf. also the map of the world, a colour reproduction of which appears in F. Rosenthal's English translation of Ibn Khaldūn's *Muqaddimah* (New York, 1958) as the frontispiece of the first volume.

Astronomy is closely allied to mathematical–scientific geography but, of course, covers a much wider field, and was much more intensively cultivated in Islam. In many respects, Muslim scholars went far beyond the astronomical heritage of classical antiquity. Al-Kindī's treatment of the introductory chapters of Ptolemy's great work on astronomy (known by the Arabic title of *Almagest*) must be regarded as an early, very modest attempt to make a new and important science known in wider circles.

Ptolemy's Geography *rearranged*

1. A brief excerpt (arranged here in tabular form) from the chapter about the countries in al-Khuwārizmī, *Kitāb Ṣūrat al-arḍ*, ed. H. von Mžik (Leipzig, 1926), pp. 103 f. It should be kept in mind that the Arabic original does not distinguish between the letters denoting 3 and 8.

	Longitude	Latitude
	for the middle of the country	
Spain [*al-Andalus*]	10° 0′	37° 40′
Epirus	45° 0′	38° 45′
Lycia	54° 0′	38° 30′
Cilicia	57° 0′	37° 30′
Mosul	68° 50′	38° 0′
Lusitania	8° 30′	41° 20′
Spain [*'sf'nyh*]	8° 30′	42° 20′
Gallia Narbonensis [*Tyrsn'*]	24° 0′	43° 30′

Vindelicia [? *'flyqyh*]	36° 0′	44° 40′
Macedonia	42° 0′	43° 30′
Upper Moesia	44° 30′	44° 0′
Lower Moesia	46° 0′	44° 30′
Thrace	47° 0′	42° 40′
Asia	52° 30′	43° 30′
Galatia	56° 30′	43° 0′
Cappadocia	56° 30′	41° 0′

The measurement of the circumference of the earth under al-Ma'mūn

2. From al-Bīrūnī, *Taḥdīd nihāyāt al-amākin*, ed. A. Zeki Validi Togan, 'Bīrūnī's Picture of the World', in *Memoirs of the Archaeological Survey of India*, no. 53 (n.y. [1938?]), pp. 65 f. Al-Bīrūnī states that his report is based on the *Kitāb al-Ab'ād wa-l-ajrām* by the astronomer Ḥabash who lived in the first half of the ninth century. For the problem, cf. C. A. Nallino, *Raccolta di Scritti* (Rome, 1944), V, pp. 301 ff., and for general information about astronomical research in the age of al-Ma'mūn, A. Sayili, *The Observatory in Islam* (Ankara, 1960), pp. 50 ff. Al-Bīrūnī's work was published by Ibn Tāwīt aṭ-Ṭanjī (Ankara, 1962) and by P. G. Bulgakov, in *Revue de l'Institut des Manuscrits Arabes*, VIII (Cairo, 1962/1964); English trans. Jamil Ali (Beirut, 1967), pp. 178–80.

Al-Ma'mūn had his observations made after he learned from Greek works that one degree was 500 stadia long. The stadion is one of the measures the Greeks used to measure distances. Al-Ma'mūn found that the translators did not know for certain what the generally accepted length of the stadion was. As Ḥabash relates on the authority of Khālid al-Marwarrūdhī, he therefore ordered a number of astronomers and skilled carpenters and coppersmiths to produce instruments[1] and choose a suitable place for measuring [the degree of longitude]. They chose a location in the plain of Sinjār in the region of Mosul, 19 parasangs [114 km] [distant] from its[2] capital and 43 parasangs [258 km] from Samarra. [The scholars] were satisfied with the evenness of the terrain and brought their instruments there. At a fixed site they observed the sun's height at noon. Then they divided into two groups. Khālid went with one group of surveyors and craftsmen northwards, while 'Alī b. 'Īsā al-Asṭurlābī and Aḥmad b.

al-Bakhtarī adh-Dharrā' proceeded with a number of people to the south. Each group observed the sun's height at noon, till in the end they found it differed by one degree, apart from the difference arising from the declination. During the march they measured the way by the yardstick and set up signposts on the way. On the way back they checked the measurements once more. The two groups met again where they had parted. Their finding was that one degree of the earth['s circumference] was 56 miles [112 km] long.

Ḥabash claimed to have heard how Khālid recited this report to Judge Yaḥyā b. Aktham, and he received the report from him by word of mouth. Abū Ḥāmid aṣ-Ṣaghānī reported it thus according to Thābit b. Qurrah. But according to the tradition of al-Farghānī, a further two-thirds of a mile [1.333 km] was added to the stated number of miles. I have likewise found all reports agreeing upon these two-thirds. I cannot explain the omission of the two-thirds on the ground that it goes back to the manuscript of Ḥabash's *Kitāb al-Ab'ād wa-l-ajrām*, since he calculated the circumference, diameter and all other distances on the basis of the stated number of 56 miles, and a re-examination shows that the result was in fact 56 miles for the measured degree. Hence it is much better to assume that the two different traditions [56 miles and 56⅔ miles] derive from the two groups. Here there is an uncertainty, which demands fresh examination and observation. Whoever wishes to conduct it must take the evenness of the terrain into consideration and beware of depressions[3] in it. For this purpose I chose the plain between Dahistān near Jurjān and the territory of the Ghuzz Turks. However, [political] conditions and, later, [my own] plans[4] have not proved favourable to the enterprise.

The earth does not move

3. The seventh chapter of the introduction to Ptolemy's great astronomical work in the recension of al-Kindī, *Fī aṣ-ṣinā'ah al-'uẓmā*, from the Istanbul MS Aya Sofya 4830, 76b–79a. On al-Kindī's work, cf. F. Rosenthal, 'al-Kindī and Ptolemy', in *Studi orientalistici in onore di Giorgio Levi Della Vida* (Rome, 1956), II, pp. 436–56. The last paragraph constitutes the beginning of the eighth chapter in the editions of the Greek text. This was already the case in the complete Arabic translation of the *Almagest* which was no doubt used by al-Kindī.

Seventh Chapter: Proof that the earth possesses no movement involving a change of place

The previous exposition has shown that the earth can neither possess movement towards any of the previously mentioned regions and directions, nor can it ever move in any way from its position in the centre—that is, in the centre of the universe. For the accidents that would arise if it were not situated in the centre of the universe would also arise if it possessed movement towards any region or direction. Hence he [Ptolemy] thinks that repetition of the causes of the movement towards the centre is superfluous, since it is clear already from what appears to the sense of vision that the earth is situated in the centre of the universe and that all heavy objects gravitate towards it from every direction. Simplest and nearest concerning the existence of what we have mentioned is just what we can observe, namely this: Together with the clear fact that, as we have mentioned, the earth is spherical and situated at the centre of the universe, our inclination as well as the special movements of all heavy bodies earthwards in all regions of the earth everywhere at all times proceed at right angles with the even, firm plane tangential to the objects that gravitate towards the earth. From what we have mentioned, it is clear that the objects gravitating towards the earth would reach the centre of the universe in their movements, were not the surface of the earth in their way, preventing them from going further; for the straight line that goes to the centre of the earth also constantly forms a right angle with the surface of the celestial sphere tangential to it.

Now, if all parts of the earth and all heavy objects proceed, as we have mentioned, towards the centre from every region of the world, something enclosing the centre of the universe must necessarily form from them, since they all possess the property of striving towards it as long as nothing keeps them away from it. What reaches it earliest must then be what encloses it. What moves towards it most slowly must be furthest from it, since it is deflected from it by what reached it earlier.

The erroneous view of those who are surprised that the terrestrial body does not rest on anything, that it stands still without settling and sinking downwards as a result of its great weight, he traced to the fact that they draw, for purposes of comparison, on accidents that are their own and not on those that specifically belong to the universe.

He accused them of ignorance of the [correct] manner and method of investigation. If only they enquired whether it was possible that such a heavy and large body could rest on anything other than a heavy or not heavy body, truth would be revealed to them and they would stop being surprised. For, if the substratum is a heavy body, it must itself have a substratum. And if the first heavy body, namely, the earth, with the heavy objects to be found on it, can only rest on a heavy body, it must likewise be true in respect of this heavy body which serves as a substratum that it cannot stand still, unless it has a heavy substratum itself. This can either be continued indefinitely—that is to say, an infinite number of heavy bodies—or it can have an end. Now we have pointed out in our *Physical Statements* that really there can be no infinite body. Hence the heavy bodies that rest on one another must be finite, all of them heavier than the earth and the objects to be found on it. One ought to be much more surprised, however, that, according to their view, in the relationship between the substratum and what rests on it, solely that which rests on the substratum should stand still in the light body, that is the air, since they can observe that every heavy object breaks through the air and finally settles underneath it. One should, therefore, not assume that air is the substratum of the earth and of all heavy objects, but rather that the earth by nature stands still. Its position must then be the one most suitable for standing still, namely, the centre of the universe.

When they discover that the size of the earth and of the heavy objects to be found on it corresponds to a dot in comparison with the body of the universe that encloses them, they will no longer be surprised. For it is more fitting for them to assume that a large, extensive, homoiomeric body can hold fast, restrain, repel and press [read *yaḍghaṭuhū*] from every direction, through equal and even support, a body small when compared to it, and that in the end it can make it stand still and prevent it from moving.

For instance, it can be observed how a speck of dust of sensually perceptible size stands still or moves slightly in the air, while, for one like a dot, it is more fitting not to move, since a dot is not sensually perceptible.

Since the preceding statement has established that the movement of the sky and the celestial body itself are circular, and our *Physical Statements* have made it clear that there can be no infinite body, it follows from our remarks that the body of the universe is circular and, since ⟨something infinite⟩ can never become a body, finite and moves in a circle.

For there is no justification for the description of part of it as higher or lower, as one can affirm about bodies placed upon one another. In their case, what lies at our heads can be described as higher and what lies at our feet as lower, just as what lies to our right is described as right and what lies behind us as behind and what lies to our left as left and what lies in front of us as in front. Since the earth lies at our feet, we speak of it as below, and since the sky lies above our heads, we speak of it as above. Right and left, in front and behind, differ depending on our position. If we face something on which we have previously turned our backs, we describe as back what we used to describe as front and as front what we used to describe as back. What lies under our feet we describe, like we did before, as below, and what is above our heads we continue to describe as above. Wherever we are on earth, we accordingly speak of the earth as below in relation to the sky and of the sky as above in relation to the earth. Yet, when we isolate the globe of the universe in our thought, it is something unique that has no relationship to anything else which would enable us to speak of it as below or above. If, on the other hand, one relates parts of the universe to one another, it happens that we can describe what lies at our head as higher and what lies at our feet as lower. Wherever we may be, the sky is above and the earth is below. The sky is highest at the zenith of the celestial body. The earth is highest where it is nearest to the sky and lowest where it is most distant from the sky. Accordingly, the lowest part of the earth is that where it is most distant from its visible surface, which is the highest part of the earth, since it is nearest to the sky. And the lowest part of the universe's body is the centre of the earth, which is the centre of the universe, and the highest part of the body of the universe is the surface of the body of the universe, since above is that which is furthest from below, while below is that which is furthest from above.

As we can observe, whatever moves by nature moves in one of

two senses, namely, either straight on or in a circle. The circular movement is that of the most distant body, since by its nature it moves in its place. The straight movement, on the other hand, is that of the four elements, earth, water, fire and air. Hence, as long as they remained in the middle, that is, in the middle of the sky which moves in its place, it has been the nature of those four elements to stand still in their place and not to move, since something that moves straight cannot move if it is to remain in its place and not change it, since through its straight movement it vacates a place and occupies another, while that which moves in a circle vacates no place and occupies no place except its own. However, that whose nature it is to stand still in the place, it is also its nature to let itself be guided compulsorily by what possesses movement by nature and moves it from its place, while by nature and not by compulsion it returns to its place and stands still there.

Among these things that move straight, we can observe two that move towards the middle of the universe, as we have previously defined it, namely, water and earth [cf. Theon of Alexandria, *Commentary on the Almagest*, p. 426, Rome], since through their movement they touch at right angles the even plane tangential to the terrestrial globe. The other two, namely, air and fire, move as we can observe, away from the middle and intersect the even plane tangential to the terrestrial globe at right angles at a point tangential to the earth. Earth moves, as we can observe, most readily towards the middle of the universe, and fire away from it.

Thus it is correct that the following heavy bodies repel by their weight those that have preceded them in their movement towards the middle of the universe and that then the heavy bodies stand still without moving in the middle of the universe. All smaller bodies move towards the terrestrial body if they are distant from it, and are then attracted to it, while the earth itself stands still and remains fixed in every direction and receives all heavy bodies that fall on it. Now, if the earth, the greatest and heaviest of the heavy bodies, would share with the other heavy bodies in the movement of the heavy bodies moving in the direction of the bodies moving earthwards, it would, in view of its greater weight and size, hasten downwards well in advance of the other heavy bodies advancing towards it, and the living creatures and all the heavy bodies to be found on earth would be separated from it and be carried in the air, since, on account of its excessive weight, the earth hastens in front of them; the earth itself would fall down and move away from the sky enclosing it. These and similar phantasies and conjectures are a sign of stupidity. Whoever utters them deserves to be ridiculed by fools and pitied by scholars.

Some people have said that the sky stands firm and does not move and that the earth moves round a single axis—namely, the equinoctial axis, round which the line of the equinox moves—and that the earth moves round this axis from west to east and makes a single rotation in a day and a night.

Others, again, say that sky and earth move together in their movements, but, as we mentioned previously, round the same axis and in such a way that they can catch up with each other.

The difference between the two movements is the period of one day and one night. This is the case when the earth's movement eastwards is faster than the sky's movement. As we can observe, the stars thus appear to rise on the horizon and to advance westwards. Hence there have been people who assumed that since they had no reply with which to refute the view of those people, they were right. They have admitted the correctness of their view and regarded it as necessary. It escaped them that it is not impossible that the view of those people in general, in respect of the visible behaviour of the stars in their courses, how they overtake one another and rise and set, may be correct. Yet, in respect of what appears and occurs among us and in the air, their view is obviously a tremendous mistake and reveals their folly as clearly as possible. Even if we were to grant them what contradicts nature, namely, that the light, fine, homoiomeric—that is, the sphere—either does not move at all or does not move counter to the movement of what is by its very nature counter to it—namely, the coarse—nevertheless the falsity of their view is completely and clearly proved by what obviously takes place in the air during the movement of the less light and fine, namely, during the movement of living creatures, clouds or things that are thrown or shot. For we can observe that the movement of those objects is faster than the movement of the sphere. While we remain in our place on earth, the clouds sometimes go past us eastwards. If we shoot an arrow or throw a stone to the east, it precedes us towards the east. Now, if the earth were to move eastwards, clouds, birds, shot arrows or thrown stones would move faster than it, since they separate from the course of part of the earth when they start to move and they would move away from it to the east. Were the earth to advance faster than they, the arrow, when we release it, would be left behind us, we would overtake it on the way to the east and it would descend behind us. The same also applies to the clouds. We would never find them preceding us eastwards, but observe how they would meet us during their westward movement, because of the eastward movement of that part of the earth on which we find ourselves; for, in their opinion, the movement of the earth is the fastest of all movements. Obviously the opposite of all this is correct. If the earth's movement were faster than that of the sphere, yet still slower than that of the clouds, of flying and jumping creatures and all things thrown or shot on earth, which are by nature lighter than the earth and heavier than the sphere, then it would also be much more fitting if it were slower than the sphere. However, the movement of a body that is by nature heavy and dense cannot possibly be as fast or faster than that of a body light and fine by nature. Furthermore, if their view were true, one would not be able, for the reasons put forward above, to observe anything moving to the east. In addition, if the earth were by nature to move in a circle, a particle of earth, if we picked it up and then dropped it from the hands, would travel through the air in a circle together with the earth and follow its course without falling on the earth.

But if they assume, what is also unnatural, namely, that it possesses by nature two movements, a straight one which brings it to the earth and a circular one which moves it around corresponding to the circular movement of the earth parallel to our location, and that it falls on the earth, not at right angles but always inclined to the east, since it falls towards the earth because of its straight movement and leaves the original course of its fall on account of its circular movement and hence falls on the earth, not following its initial course but diametrically,[5] then appearance contradicts this. In addition, they assume, as we have reported of them earlier, that the movement of the earth itself is faster than all movements that take place on it. If this were the case, one would be constantly aware of the air moving counter to the movement of the earth, and we would thereby always feel how the earth, with us, breaks through the air; for we would then constantly feel that the air is streaking towards us from east to west, that everything outside the earth always falls westwards, and that if one of us were to jump up, he would never come down in the same place. Appearance contradicts all this. And if one of them assumes that the air moves at the same speed as the earth, this would have the same result as we have stated concerning the movements of things moving in the air, like clouds, thrown or shot objects, or birds. If they assume that those natural things are fixed and connected with the air as if they were intertwined with it, and that they move with it and do not oppose its movement, it would follow that we could not see them go forwards or backwards, but they would stay fixed in the air as if nailed to it. They would neither change nor fall into disarray, nor move and change places, whether in the case of clouds through their movement, in the case of birds through their flight or in the case of arrows, stones or particles of earth through shooting, throwing or falling. Appearance clearly and distinctly contradicts this. None of these would then have fast or slow movement, whereas sensual perception shows that there is all this. That is an impossible contradiction. Thus it is clear that the earth possesses no movement involving a change of place at all.

The chapters previously treated must necessarily be put before the subdivisions and details of mathematical discussions and what follows them, just as Ptolemy did, in that he mentioned them as main subjects and principles sufficient for scientists. As far as we are concerned, we have mentioned them for the explanation, clarification, and confirmation of our assumptions. This is indeed required. We shall add more to it with the aid of evidence which appears in the course of the following discussion in our book, as brought to light by means of proofs subsequently applied in astronomy.

IX

MUSICOLOGY

The classical tradition exercised a decisive influence on the Muslim preoccupation with musical theory, the ethos of music, and the history of musical instruments. The great work of R. d'Erlanger (*La Musique arabe* [Paris, 1930–59]) makes available in French translation the results of their interest in musical theory. The wide-ranging ethical effects of music have frequently been touched upon but so far less intensively studied; there is a good introduction on the subject by I. Sonne and E. Werner, 'The Philosophy and Theory of Music in Judaeo-Arabic Literature', in *Hebrew Union College Annual*, XVI (1941), pp. 251–319, and XVII (1942–3), pp. 511–73. The musical instruments of the Arabs have been studied in the works of H. G. Farmer, among them his *Organ of the Ancients* (London, 1931) and numerous articles in periodicals, conveniently listed in J. D. Pearson and J. F. Ashton, *Index Islamicus* (Cambridge, 1958), pp. 265 ff. Farmer's *History of Arabian Music* (London, 1929) remains a useful general introduction.

On the history of musicology and on music appreciation

1. Fragments from a work by Aḥmad b. aṭ-Ṭayyib as-Sarakhsī on music, as cited on pp. 234 f., 47–9, 21–5, of the Istanbul MS Topkapusarai, Revan Köşk 1729, containing a *Kitāb al-Mūsīqī* by al-Ḥasan b. Aḥmad b. ʿAlī al-Kātib. As-Sarakhsī's work is reportedly preserved in MS but has not yet been made available. For his views on music, as for those on other subjects, he depends on his teacher, al-Kindī. A French translation of al-Ḥasan's work has recently been published by A. Shiloah, *La Perfection des connaissances musicales* (Paris, 1972).

Not everything in musical science[1] can be proved by logical demonstration, since logical demonstration does not pertain to all sciences nor has it a place in them. Arithmetic's method of proof is the example [? *ʿibrah*], that is, counting, that of geometry logical demonstration directed towards experience [*iʿtibār*] and convincing, and that of music is experience, logical demonstration, comparison and convincing by means of what is most proper and fitting. . . .

The original occasion which is said to have led one of the ancients to study numerical relationships between percussing and percussed bodies was the following: That man once walked along the street of the copper and iron-smiths and heard sounds which, he felt, resembled a sound with which he was familiar and stood in a proportional relationship to it. He considered them and found them harmoniously composed. And while considering these percussed and percussing bodies, he found that they stood in the same proportional relationship that, he felt, belonged to those sounds. On his return, he tried out different proportional relationships on different bodies. Then, with the aid of his sense of hearing, he tried to discover in which of these relationships those harmoniously composed sounds were to be found, until it became clear to him. Thus he achieved what he wanted by means of proportional relationships, counting [*ʿibrah*] and sense perception.

Nicomachus mentions that Pythagoras had been the first to discover the relationships of sounds and that he had been that man.

The earliest beginnings are completely unknown. Al-Fārābī's statements on the subject suffice.[2]

Provided that this science is studied properly, and one pursues every unknown element in it until it is known exactly, it is the view of the philosophers that it is always to be regarded as nobler than all the other mathematical sciences. For they used to hold the view that arithmetic, geometry and astronomy were less distinguished than the science of the melodies. However, since the low-class common people were concerned with music in name alone, not with what it really meant, and hence they claimed musical knowledge which they did not possess and thereby earned money from people who knew nothing about it, this made music contemptible in the eyes of incompetent people. Competent people, on the other hand, did not hold that they should join people who were to be blamed for their faults and were ignorant and deficient. They acknowledged the real value of music. They regarded musical science with great admiration and treated those who practised it kindly and supported them.

It is told that Alexander Dhū l-Qarnain rose and gave up his seat to a musician. When his friends disapproved of his conduct, he said to them: 'I wished to honour only the music in him.' He used to prefer musicians because of the nobility of their art to all other artists and scientists and to say: 'It is not I who have distinguished them, their art has done so!' He allocated them seats of honour, and when something upset him, he summoned them, took a rod in his hand, beat time and reflected meanwhile until he saw things clearly. Then he dropped the rod, which was a sign for the musicians to depart, and they departed. He used to say: 'Every time I encountered an enemy, the measurement of my soul and the composition of its number [numerical proportions] showed me whether I would vanquish him or he me. Thus I could take preventive measures against all my fears and feel sure of my cause.'

The fact that a person is moved when he hears music, or pretends to be moved, is no proof that he possesses musical understanding. Rather, if someone is easily moved, it sometimes indicates more that he does not understand what he hears and possesses little musical knowledge. This becomes clear upon observing how someone who understands nothing of music, poetry, grammar and prosody shows himself moved as soon as he hears a little music so-called, no matter how incorrect, repulsive and faulty it is. On the other hand, when someone who understands grammar but nothing of music hears the same music, his emotion is diminished according to the number of grammatical mistakes found in the song. Finally, when someone who understands poetry, grammar, prosody and music hears the same music, he feels no emotion at all, but the impression made on him is that of an indecent calumny which one would rather not hear at all. Thus the people who understand least of music are moved most quickly by every little bit of music they hear, while those who understand very much of music and possess the most advanced musical knowledge are moved with the greatest difficulty and least satisfied with what they hear. Human capacity to be moved by music is a transitory one, and it is also quite right that most people do not possess it, but it is the special gift of people with perfect power of discernment. . . .

In order to be able to grasp the nobility of music completely, we need a strongly developed sense of hearing and power of discernment. Beautiful sounds, such as rouse beasts and ignorant men to emotion, also produce the same effect on experts. Yet only the latter, not ignorant men and beasts, possess the capacity to recognize the beauty and harmony of a composition and to know what is incorrect, dissonant and repellent, and thanks to this capacity music moves them. Hence those men who understand most about music are poorest as regards experiencing emotion through music, and those who understand least of it are richest in this respect. For the expert to feel genuine emotion all things that cause emotion must be simultaneously present. Otherwise, the deficiency disturbs him, and faults hinder him from enjoyment, while possible mistakes and defects do not pain an ignorant man. Hence the expert requires the most refined sense-perception and accurate knowledge of what is correct, in order to feel deep emotion, since knowledge of what is correct and the beauty of what is correct go hand in hand. Skilful musicians have this, provided they have a healthy nature and constantly practise music and the study of its proofs and logical arguments. . . .

Music is not one of the sciences that one can learn through study, not even under the guidance of a teacher who has the skill to arouse an understanding of music, nor through listening to many outstanding musicians. For music demands a receptivity in the soul in addition to a natural aptitude that is readily guided to music, a capacity to absorb quickly music that drifts by one, and an ingenious understanding of its difficult details and its proportionate relationships in the various positions of notes and keys and the various rhythms. Without the natural aptitude, instruction is of no avail here, and the natural aptitude is of no avail without instruction. If the ambitious musician has all this—a praiseworthy natural aptitude, a great receptivity, a skilful teacher, constant practice, uninterrupted leisure, complete devotion—he is rarely unsuccessful. But if only some of this is lacking, he is correspondingly less good.

If the musician possesses skill and great ability, and the listener has the corresponding musical understanding, perfect emotion is experienced. The music one hears goes to the heart. One feels exhilarated. The powers of the discerning soul come to the forefront. It assumes the form of expertness. It puts on the robe of participation in the music and takes part in the race for delight in science. It enthusiastically avoids the vices and endeavours to acquire the virtues and to become ennobled through them. It was previously considered cowardly, and is now brave. It was considered avaricious, and is now generous. It was considered afraid, and now makes light of anything that excites fear and despises all terrors and dangers. It has taken the robe of the virtues as an ornament and great confidence as a joy. It embarks on the sea of emotion and gallops along the racecourse of joy.

The ethical power of music

2. A remark by al-Kindī, according to Isḥāq b. ʿImrān, *On Melancholy*, from the Munich MS Aumer 805, 106b–107a. This version appears to be the oldest one preserved. Quoted in Ibn al-Jazzār, *Zād al-musāfir*, it was translated into Greek (C. Daremberg and E. Ruelle, *Oeuvres de Rufus d'Ephèse* (Paris, 1879), p. 583). Cf. also F. Rosenthal, *Journal of the American Oriental Society*, LXIX (1949), p. 150. 'Orpheus' is uncertain, although the Arabic letters are an exact transliteration of that name.

Yaʿqūb b. Isḥāq al-Kindī tells that the composer Orpheus has said: Kings let me attend their parties in order to derive enjoyment and amuse themselves through me. But it is I who am amused by them and enjoy myself, since I can change their ethical qualities and turn their anger into calm, their grief into joy, their depression into a state of relaxation, their rage into friendliness, their avarice into generosity, and their cowardice into bravery.

Greek musical instruments

3. From al-Khuwārizmī, *Mafātīḥ al-ʿulūm* (Cairo, 1349/1930), p. 136; English trans. H. G. Farmer, in *Transactions of the Glasgow University Oriental Society*, XVII (1959), p. 2. Cf. E. Wiedemann and

W. Müller, in *Sitzungsberichte der Physikalisch-medizinischen Sozietät in Erlangen*, LIV–LV (1922–3), p. 8 f.; H. G. Farmer, in *Journal of the Royal Asiatic Society* (1925), pp. 299–304, and (1928), p. 512, and *Organ of the Ancients*, pp. 59 f. Cf. also chap. X, no. 4.

Al-mūsīqī means 'composition of melodies'. The word is Greek. Musician and composer are called *al-mūsīqūr* or *al-mūsīqār*.

Al-urghānūn is an instrument of the Greeks and *Rūm* made from three large skins of cow's hide. They are firmly joined to one another. Above the middle skin a big skin has been fixed, and above this skin bronze pipes with holes in certain proportions have been fixed. From these, sweet, moving and exciting sounds proceed as desired by the user of the instrument.

As-salbāq is a string instrument of the Greeks and *Rūm*, which resembles the harp [*jank*].

Al-lūr is the harp [*ṣanj*] in Greek.

Al-qīthārah is one of their instruments which resembles the *ṭunbūr*.

4. From al-Kindī, *Kitāb al-Muṣauwitāt al-watarīyah*, Bodleian MS Marsh 663, pp. 229 f. For the manuscript, cf. *Journal of the American Oriental Society*, LXIX (1949), pp. 149–52. The passage appears on pp. 74 f. of the edition by Zakarīyā' Yūsuf, *Mu'allafāt al-Kindī al-mūsīqīyah* (Baghdad, 1962).

The *Rūm* have manufactured an instrument with three strings attached to it. For they found that everything that grows is divided into three parts, rational men, irrational animals and plants. And that which grows [read: living creatures] is likewise divided into three parts, through progenitors as among men, through eggs as among birds, through offspring as among beasts, just as there are also three kinds of plants, those one plants, those one sows and those one neither plants nor sows. They found that there are three cases, nominative, accusative and genitive. Similarly, there are three kinds of word composition, fine, coarse and moderate: the fine is the nominative, the coarse the genitive and the moderate the accusative. Furthermore, they found that nothing is free from three situations, beginning, end and decay. The most distinguished number is three, the first of the odd numbers. They found that there are three truths. Firstly, true is a statement proclaiming that something exists in the way it exists, or does not exist in the way it does not exist. Secondly, true is a statement which informs us about what a thing has and, negatively, what a thing has not. Thirdly, true is a statement which affirms what must be affirmed and denies what must be denied. They found that the Creator of the world is not free from three aspects. Either ⟨. . .⟩. Or He resembles him in one respect and is different from him in another respect. ⟨Or. . . .⟩ They found that the world's substance and accident are not free from three aspects. Either ⟨. . .⟩. Or each of them subsists through itself and does not need the other, which is incorrect. Or the accident subsists through substantiality, and the substance subsists through itself, which is correct. They found that there are only three things in the world, substance, plant and animal. Grammar, they found, must divide speech into nouns, verbs and particles. There are also three natural movements, two straight movements in the elements and a circular movement in the spheres. When they had thus found that three is a number which appears in manifold forms, they attached to it three strings and three frets.

The *Rūm* have attached four strings to it. That is the lute, the instrument used most frequently by the common people as well as by the élite, and the most expressive. According to the view of some scholars, it has been described by the Greeks. However, the Babylonians—that is, the Persians—claim it for themselves. They think that during the reign of Anūsharwān a lad named Falhwadh grew up, whose method and class were not attained by anyone before or after him. Apart from the lute they also ascribe to him the invention of many other musical matters.

With the lute the *Rūm* did not only aim at its musical effect but they also wished to demonstrate with it in what shape the world is joined together. For they found that the elements that effect the existence of living creatures and the growth of all that grows, and serve passively for the renewal of what is old and for the replacement for what is used up, are four, the two dry elements, fire and earth, and the two moist elements, air and water. . . .

X

MECHANICS

The balance of Archimedes

1. The report of Archimedes's famous discovery from the *Kitāb al-Baḥth*, one of the writings of the Jābir corpus. The text has been published by P. Kraus, *Jābir ibn Ḥayyān* (Cairo, 1942–3), II, pp. 306 f., 330 f. Cf. also the text of al-Khāzinī published by N. Khanikoff, in *Journal of the American Oriental Society*, VI (1860), p. 12 f. Al-Khāzinī quotes a work by Menelaus addressed to the Emperor Domitian. A German translation of the relevant passage from Menelaus is to be found in T. Ibel, *Die Wage im Altertum und Mittelalter* (Erlangen, 1908), p. 183. The mysterious king of our text appears to be Domitian rather than Mānāṭiyus, an author subsequently mentioned by Menelaus. Cf. further M. Clagett, *The Science of Mechanics in the Middle Ages* (Madison, 1959), p. 57.

A crown given as a present to King Mālīqiyādūs [Domitian ?] was the original starting-point for determining the weights of minerals mingled with one another and thus learning in what manner and to what extent the various components of a mixed or composite object are represented in it. It was a big heavy crown that contained most kinds of meltable and pulverizable substances such as gold, silver, iron, lead, diamonds, rubies of all kinds, emeralds, pearls, carnelians, amethysts and all remaining varieties of precious substances. The king wished to know the amount of each of the different substances contained in the crown, without being obliged to break it or alter its composition. He told his philosophers, his wazīrs and sensible men of all classes of his trouble. But all shied away from it and declared they were powerless to do so and lacked the requisite technical ability.

Finally, Archimedes heard of it. He was known to be an

accomplished philosopher, but in his time he was also incomparable and outstanding in geometry [engineering] in particular. When the king told him of his trouble, he replied that the matter was feasible. He solved the problem for the king and specified for him the amount of each substance contained in the crown. Thereupon various people who had previously considered the matter and shied away from it said to the king: 'Archimedes is an extremely skilful and cunning man. He feels sure that the king will not permit the crown he values so highly to be broken, in order to find out the true weight and quantity of each of the different substances contained in it.' This talk impressed the king, since it was plausible to sense perception and more in accord with basic human nature. For not all men are sharp-witted or self-sufficient, as has been related of Thales, Pythagoras, Socrates, Plato[1] and others, who had nothing to learn from others, but from youth and from the beginning were scientifically productive. So the king again spoke to Archimedes, who said: 'I do not doubt that people say something of the sort; for there are only quite unusually few who attain such a high level of science. Hence, since the king has lent his ear to their words, let him order an object to be made containing a mixture of different substances in quantities known only to himself alone and hand it over to me! I will then inform him concerning each of the substances in it.' Whereupon the king ordered various substances to be selected and mixed together. Archimedes was not allowed to come in contact with the craftsman. The object was brought to him, and he gave the king correct information regarding the quantity of all its components. In this way did the king recognize that Archimedes had spoken the truth and that he was greatly superior to his colleagues. He then commissioned him to undertake, if possible, the compilation of a textbook describing the process for him. Archimedes did that in a book entitled *The Weight of the Crown*. It is, however, a very difficult book. Few can understand it, in fact only those very familiar with geometry [engineering] and philosophy, and we have therefore written a commentary on it.

A lion spitting water or wine

2. Philo of Byzantium, *Le Livre des appareils pneumatiques et des machines hydrauliques*, ed. with a French translation by Carra de Vaux,

in *Notices et Extraits des Manuscrits de la Bibliothèque Nationale*, XXXVII (1903), pp. 27–235, cf. no. 18, pp. 57 f., 139–41. For the 'Greek sources of Islamic scientific illustrations' in general, cf. K. Weitzmann, *Studies in Classical and Byzantine Manuscript Illumination* (Chicago, 1971), 20–44.

A large vessel AB, resting on three or four pillars, is used as a water tank. One of the frontal pillars—or any other—contains within it a pipe Ṭ, which fits invisibly into the vessel until close to its upper end. Then one takes a beaker JK which is attached firmly to the two pillars, as well as a copper lion A, attached in

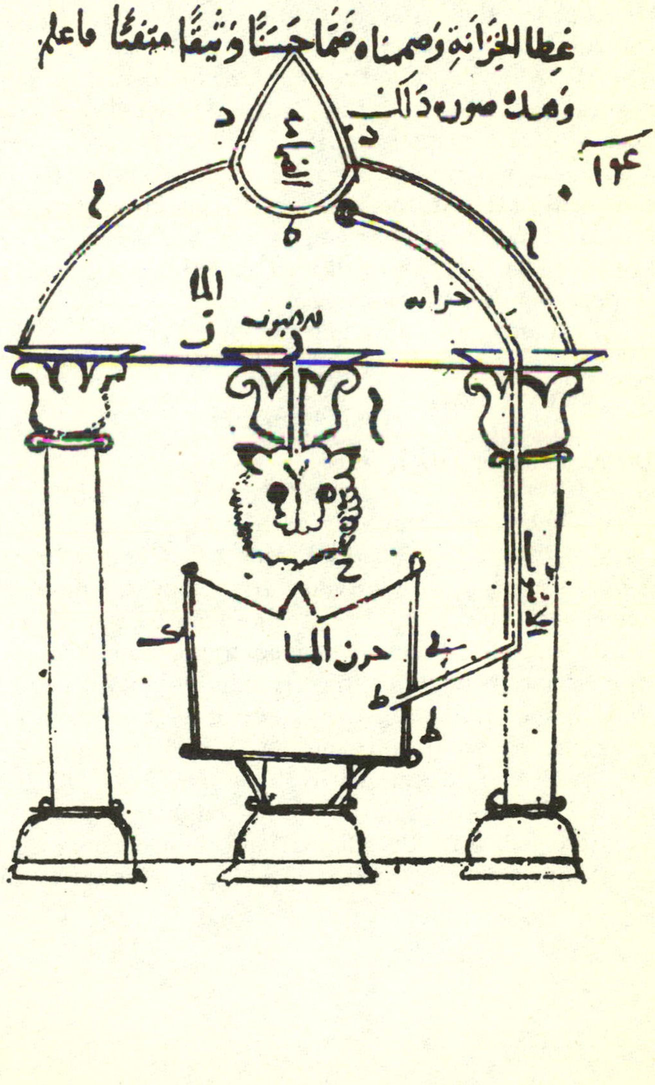

such a way that it apparently gazes down on the beaker. Then one similarly fits into one of the other pillars a pipe which leads into the lion and through him into his mouth, marked ZZ at the water tank and Ḥ at the lion's mouth, where the water comes out. Then one takes a lid DD for the top of the water tank, which is symmetrical all round and closes air tight. When we have completed this, we stuff up the lion's mouth with a finger and then open the water tank at the top, near DD, and fill it with wine until close to H; then we carefully and firmly replace the lid of the water tank. The entire apparatus looks like this: [see p. 233].

When we have done this, we open the lion's mouth, and the wine flows from the lion's mouth into the beaker and does not stop flowing until one covers the opening Ṭ. When this is done, the wine stops flowing from the mouth of the lion. The lion stops and allows nothing more to flow out until enough is taken from the beaker to expose the opening Ṭ. When this occurs, the lion again allows as much to flow out as was taken from the beaker, and this continues until no more is left in the water tank. The amount to be taken out so as to expose the opening Ṭ can be fixed by the manufacturer at will, two, three litres, or more, or less. This apparatus is extremely clear, simple, elegant and easily intelligible to anyone wishing to learn this science.

A whistling waterwheel

3. Philo, no. 62, pp. 114 f., 204 f.

A waterwheel can be arranged in such a way that it diverts water from a place where it stagnates and does not flow in from anywhere else. One makes a waterwheel from copper, whose opening [diameter] is a cubit in width and whose rim is a span in depth, and which has, in addition, two rims circling round on the outside, the distance between them corresponding to the depth of the first. The waterwheel is called A, the rim of stated depth B and the other two round rims Ḥ and D. Vessels of equal size are attached inside the waterwheel in the empty space BG between the rims. The vessels must be convex, similar to those in the drawing here. Let them be called H and their opening Z. In the place adjoining the above-mentioned place one attaches straight vessels Ḥ, similar to those in the drawing here, whose openings Ṭ are opposite those of the convex vessels. The waterwheel is set on beams in a quadrangular framework, whose bottom is immersed in a vessel filled with water. The surface of the water is indicated by the straight line JK.

Now, if someone turns the waterwheel in the direction of the curvature of the convex vessels, those quadrangular vessels rise filled with water and pour out that water at the straight line LM, provided that the convex vessels have been empty. If, then, somebody pours water on them from above, their weight makes itself felt, since they are situated on the longer periphery and pull up the quadrangular vessels which are full of water. The apparatus must be arranged in such a way that the water which flows out of vessels at LM weighs as much as that which is poured on the convex vessels, and since the appliance attached to the longer periphery dominates that attached to the shorter periphery, the waterwheel moves in a circle according to the inclination and movement given it by the water.

This apparatus can be arranged as we have described it. It is something quite wonderful, since the water never changes or diminishes.

The hydraulic organ

4. A musical instrument which can be heard over a distance of sixty miles, as described by Mūrisṭus. The name Mūrisṭus has not yet been convincingly explained. Arabic text, ed. L. Cheikho, in *al-Mashriq*, IX (1906), pp. 21–3, German trans. E. Wiedemann and F. Hauser, in *Archiv für die Geschichte der Naturwissenschaften und der Technik*, VIII (1918), pp. 155–7; English trans. H. G. Farmer, *The Organ of the Ancients* (London, 1931), pp. 128–35. The translators have used additional manuscript material and included the passages referring to the attached diagram that are missing from Cheikho's edition; these passages have, however, not been translated here. In general, cf. E. Wiedemann, 'Zur Mechanik und Technik bei den Arabern', in *Sitzungsberichte der Physikalisch-medizinischen Sozietät in Erlangen*, XXXVIII (1906), pp. 1–56. See also chap. IX, no. 3.

The Greeks used to take this instrument to war with them, since their country was surrounded by enemies on all sides. When they wished to alert their friends, fetch troops and reinforcement in war or warn the inhabitants of the capital and elsewhere, they used to blow it. It is the great organ, designated as the one with the wide opening and the far-ranging sound; for its sound can be heard for sixty miles.

For the manufacture of such an instrument a copper vessel was used varying in size according to the desired range—wider or less wide, as mentioned above. The instrument that I manufactured for the King of the Inner Franks had a sound that was audible over the stated distance. Its volume was 1,000 *qisṭ* [*xestēs*],[2] its length 12 cubits and its circumference below 35 spans.

Its circumference below is very large and becomes narrower above, so that the opening above amounts to three spans. It has the shape of an oven. It is provided with a roof—that means a lid. Right at the top, a span beneath the upper end, three holes are pierced. They form a triangle and are equidistant from one another, hence they are each a third of the instrument's circumference distant from one another. Then one takes three large skins of cow's hide. They must be well tanned, so that they are soft, thin and watertight. For the opening of each hose a copper pipe of the same length as the instrument is fashioned, so that when the end of the pipe is inserted into the hole at the top of the instrument, it extends almost to the lower end of the instrument. These pipes must also be fashioned wide at the bottom and narrowing at the top, until they finally have the measurements I am about to describe here. Their upper end at the top of the instrument, at the hole, has an opening the size of a finger's joint, and its lower end the width of four open fingers.[3] The holes must have the corresponding size. The wide ends of the three pipes emerge from the holes at the top of the instrument each one and a half spans [?].

Then one takes all three skins and pulls their openings over the pipes that emerge at the top of the instrument, and ties them completely airtight. Then two wide holes are made in the rear parts of each skin, each of them being either four open fingers or four closed fingers wide. A pipe of a span's length is attached to each of these holes. The ends of the pipe must be narrow outside, each a finger joint wide. These pipes must be fitted very accurately so that no air can come out. Then one fashions for each of these pipes a Byzantine [*rūmī*] skin [a pair of bellows], this means a

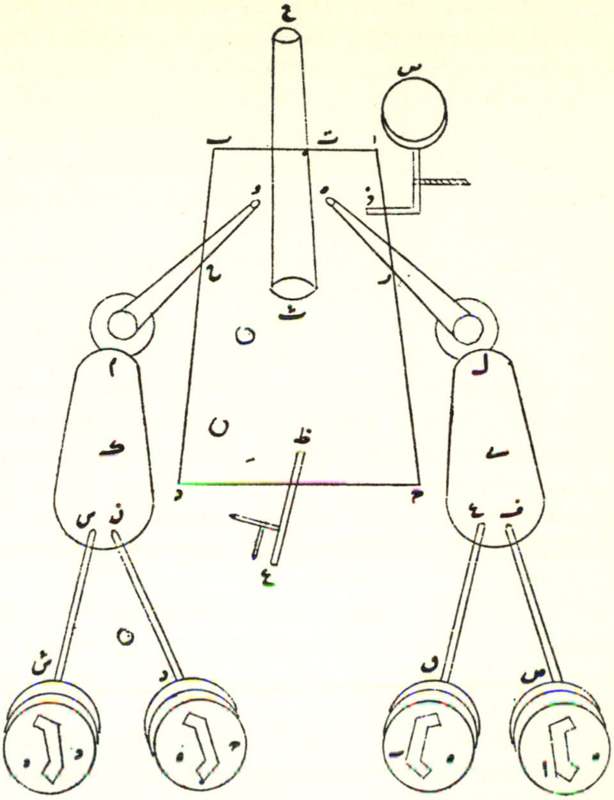

round skin, as used by goldsmiths for the manufacture of signet rings. These hoses must also be placed on the ends of the small pipes at the rear of the hoses. Through them, air penetrates into the hoses and then into the instrument. That is to be heeded.

Then a pipe is fashioned corresponding to the form of the instrument, one and a half spans wide below and four closed fingers above. It must be long enough to protrude by a third beyond the instrument at the top. Then a hole is pierced on the surface of the upper end of the instrument and this pipe is fitted in there in such a way that it juts out a span at the upper end of the instrument. That must then be sealed off most carefully with lead, so that no air can get out. The lower end of this instrument must be solid.

Then a place is picked a cubit below the upper end of the instrument for the entry of the water by making a hole there with a well-fitting stopper, on which a funnel-like vessel is set. At the lower end of the instrument a stopper is similarly fixed for the water to flow out, when one wants to let it out. Then water is poured into the instrument, in an amount soon to be stated by me. For it must reach the pipe fixed in the middle, from which the sound should emerge.

In order to be able to hear a sound, a pedestal is fashioned around the instrument. It should reach up to the skins, so that the skins can rest on it. It must be as wide as a couch, so that men can stand on it, who can insert the skins into the right pipes and then blow them up full of air. Then the air penetrates into the water, moves it, circulates in it and endeavours to emerge from it. It leaves the upper end of the pipe with a far-ranging, terrifying, powerful, heart-rending sound, audible over the distance already mentioned by us. The blowers must plug their ears with cotton, sealed, in addition, with wax, so that they should not lose their reason and that their hearing does not suffer any damage.

Besides, there is not only a single sound here, but different sounds, which I shall mention in turn, with God's help. Upon the pipe from which the air comes out, three or four pipes have been mounted, each of which has a whistle set on it, for producing other wonderful sounds. Similarly, different tones result when one blows hard, so that a lot of air passes through, or when one blows softly, so that little air passes through. By interrupting the air[flow] in different ways, all kinds of sounds, pleasant, moving ones, etc., are produced. However, originally this instrument was manufactured because of its far-reaching sound. That is to be heeded.

XI

THE OCCULT SCIENCES

According to the tenth-century encyclopaedist, Ibn Farīghūn, alchemy, the different kinds of magic and divination, physiognomy, dream interpretation and astrology can be classified as sciences about whose truth or untruth different opinions are held. We are inclined to regard all of them indiscriminately as unscientific. Yet, they varied considerably in historical significance. Alchemy was an important forerunner of chemistry, astrology an unfortunate deviation from astronomy, which did, however, presuppose a good knowledge of astronomy, while magic was largely pure phantasy demanding no scientific preparation of any kind. Besides, some occult sciences, astrology in particular, exerted an enormous influence on the political and cultural life of Islam while others were less widespread and influential. Furthermore, the attitude of educated men towards these sciences was not as unanimous as it is to a certain extent today. They were taken seriously as sciences in wide circles but they were also often strongly opposed. An animated discussion went on for centuries about the practical value of alchemy, and stimulated and aided by the classical tradition a fairly extensive and interesting literature concerning the true significance of astrology developed. Magic, in turn, could appeal to the authority of the Islamic religion, which acknowledged its reality, though it did not approve of it.

The oneirocritics of Artemidorus, the physiognomy of Polemo, the magical plant lore of the Geoponica, the basic works of classical astrology are all to be found in Arabic translation. Besides, forgers, who were particularly active in these disciplines, were always looking back to classical antiquity. They preferred using Greek names as authorities, much more so, it seems, than Indian, Persian or ancient Babylonian-'Chaldaean'. However, Hellenistic—or non-Hellenistic—origin is often hard to prove in detail. The late Hellenistic stage of alchemy, leading directly into the Islamic age, is practically lost to us, but the Greek connections of Muslim alchemy have been clarified in the splendid work by P. Kraus, *Jābir ibn Ḥayyān* (Cairo, 1942–3). Magic permitted its literary practitioners the greatest licence, though generally they, too, may have kept close to tradition; the German translation of the *Picatrix* by H. Ritter and M. Plessner (London, 1962) provides an insight into its source problems. The Ancient Orient had been the principal home of the occult sciences, and they continued to be cultivated by the local people and religious communities in their various national languages after the Muslim conquest. Much of the tradition preserved underground may have found its way into Arabic literature. However, for the most part, Greek literature can be assumed to have served as intermediary. In later times, it may be noted, translations of occult works from Arabic into Greek were not unusual.

From the astrological 'Pentateuchos' of Dorotheus

1. There exists a complete Arabic translation of the great astrological epic of Dorotheus of Sidon, of which only fragments have been preserved in Greek. Doubts as to the genuineness of the Arabic text have been allayed by the discovery of parallel passages in Arabic and Greek. However, while the Arabic translator 'took over all important statements of fact, he did so in the driest form imaginable, dispensing with all the poetical charm of the original' (J. Kraemer, in *Zeitschrift der Deutschen Morgenländischen Gesellschaft*, CVII [1957], p. 514). The history of the translation of the fifth book appears to differ from that of the first four books. It also seems likely that there was more than one Arabic translation. The existence of an intermediate Syriac translation is reflected in the preserved Arabic text. Thus, much research will be required before we can distinguish with some certainty between omissions of the Syriac and those of the Arabic versions.

The passages translated here from the Istanbul MS Yeni Cami 784, 1b, 31b and 49b–50a, are the short introduction to the whole work, a chapter from the second book about 'Mercury's stay in the house of another planet' and the first half of a chapter from the fifth book about 'partnership'.

My dear son, I would like to inform you and to provide you with clarity, so that you may be confident and your heart be set at rest through my knowledge and my words which I will expound to you here, concerning the stars which indicate to men all that happens to them from the time of the birth of a child until it leaves this world, God willing.

My dear son, I have crossed many countries and seen wonderful things which have happened in Egypt and in Babylon—which is where the Euphrates flows out. I have gathered the best of the remarks and the knowledge of those who lived before me, like a bee that collects its food from trees and all kinds of herbs and thus produces sweet honey.

When Mercury is in the house or field[1] of Saturn, man is dumb or affected with a speech defect or deaf. He is silent so that none can notice what goes on inside him. He is thoughtful and passionately interested in ferreting out everyone else's affairs. Some of them know the secrets of the books of adherents to the different religions. Some are familiar with the stars and others practise augury.

When Mercury is in the house or field of Jupiter, man is a dignified person, an orator, an administrator of the affairs of kings and noblemen, or else he educates men in speaking, litigation and pronouncing judgment. He is constantly in the service of capitals and kings.

When Mercury is in the field of Mars or in its house, man is foolish, frivolous [?] and untruthful. He is shameless, believes neither in God nor in good deeds and loves fornication. Some of them practise fraud and some participate in the sessions of sorcerers or converse with them or ferret out their calculations [?] He denies it when he has borrowed money, and everyone regards. him as without loyalty and of no repute.

When Mercury is in the house or field of Venus, man is cheerful, humorous and lively. Whatever he does, he does quickly and pushes on with it [??]. Some of them are scholars or poets or singers or jewellers [dyers ?]. Some can play backgammon and the like.

When Mercury is in a pole [*kentron*, *cardo*] outside the [sun's] rays, man is a poet, capable, devoted to acquiring money and in need of everybody's [help].

If you wish to become anyone's partner in an enterprise or in financial matters or in an affair where you require someone's partnership, then this must take place when the moon is in those signs [of the Zodiac] where, as I have mentioned, it is favourable for marriage, and the moon must be pure and free from the faults mentioned by me.

Then look, and if the ascendant and the moon are in Aries, a partnership will not be successful, since it will not be lasting, and a breach and dissension will soon occur between the two partners.

When the ascendant and the moon are in Taurus, one must not enter into partnership with a man of great importance, even if he has also connections with people of the lower classes; for quarrels will occur between the two partners, and the result of such an enterprise will not be a good one.

When the ascendant and the moon are in Gemini, the partnership will be successful. Both partners will derive benefit from it, and agreement and honesty will prevail between them.

When the ascendant and the moon are in Cancer, falsehood and deceit will infect both partners, and each of them will slander his partner.

When it[2] is in Leo, both partners will derive benefit and possess good repute.

When they are in Virgo, there will be sound benefit. Reasonable men will praise them [pl.], and they will be popular among men. Trade will bring them great profit, and both partners will have much success and joy from it.

When they are in Libra, no good results from such a partnership.

When they are in Scorpio, both partners will suffer from hostility and quarrels. Each of them will inwardly harbour deceit and slander against his partner.

When they are in Sagittarius, there will be success, except that each of them will feel greatly superior to his partner.

When they are in Capricorn, they will be infected with vivacity and joy.

When they are in Aquarius, damage and harm will befall both partners.

When they are in Pisces, they will be quite outstandingly successful.

These results I have mentioned here are, however, indicated by the ascendant and the moon only when planets of good and bad fortune are neither together with the ascendant and the moon nor look at them.

The influence of the stars on the character of the Eastern peoples

2. From ʿAlī b. Riḍwān's commentary on Ptolemy's *Tetrabiblos*, II, 3.65–6 (pp. 140_{25}–144_{8}, Robbins), according to the Arabic text of the Escorial MS 913, 54b–55a. In the introduction to his commentary, Ibn Riḍwān, an important Egyptian physician of the eleventh century, discusses the question whether or not the astronomer belonged to the Ptolemaic dynasty (cf. above, p. 30). He also attempts to prove the disputed authenticity of the attribution of the *Tetrabiblos* to him. The commentary closely follows Ptolemy's text. It is, throughout, dry and factual. Ibn Riḍwān remains unperturbed, even where Ptolemy discusses the astrological determination of national character, a subject very popular and hotly debated from ancient times, and touches on Ibn Riḍwān's Egyptian homeland and other Muslim countries. He appears completely convinced of the factuality of Ptolemy's statements and without objections to them, except where they refer to the changed religious situation.

The names of the countries are rather distorted in the manuscript. They are rendered here in their original forms. Ibn Riḍwān did not notice that later in the same chapter (II, 3.71, 72, 74) Ptolemy mentioned Arabia, since the name appears in an Arabic transliteration completely unrecognizable to an Arab.

For the medieval Latin translation of the commentary, the Venice edition of 1493 was consulted. Its text is presumably identical with those of the other editions inaccessible to me. In connection with the passage translated here, it contains only Ptolemy's text. It is shortened and has omissions. It is not known to me whether this was so in the original Latin translation or is due to the early printer. The Latin text is otherwise a very literal and correct rendering of the Arabic, though the place names, of course, remained largely unintelligible to the Latin translator.

Ptolemy: With Virgo and Mercury are connected [*assimilantur*] the area of Babylon, the Jazīrah [northwestern Mesopotamia] and Assyria—that means Mosul.[3] Hence they have developed especially into representatives of the mathematical sciences and the observation of the stars.

Commentator: They derive that from Mercury and their own magnanimity. This is still found among them today.

Ptolemy: With Capricorn and Saturn are connected the area of India, Ariana and Gedrosia. Hence the inhabitants of those countries have developed into dirty people of ugly build, their qualities of character those of wild beasts.

Commentator: These qualities of character are to be found among the inhabitants of India, ash-Shiḥr, parts of the Yemen, az-Zabaj [Java] and as-Sind and adjacent areas. Here we must ask ourselves: If those countries belong to Capricorn and Saturn, why then have they become so rich in perfume and incense. This question should be answered as follows: Saturn shares the management with the sun and Venus, when Saturn is connected with them in the condition in which his temperament is balanced [*eukratos*]. Hence those countries have become the birthplace of sweet smelling things, jewels and similar objects.

Ptolemy: The remaining parts of this quarter—that is to say, those adjoining the entire middle of the inhabited earth—are Idumaea, Deep [Coele-]Syria, the land of the Jews [Judaea], Phoenicia, Chaldea, Orchenia and Populated [Flourishing] Arabia. They are situated in the northwest of the whole quarter.

Commentator: Those countries belong to the corner [*gōnia*] which dominates the entire southeastern quarter. Idumaea is the Syrian coast and the region of Damascus. Deep [Coele-]Syria is the region of Aleppo. The land of the Jews is the region of Jerusalem, Tiberias and the Dead Sea [Zughar], Phoenicia is Syria, Chaldea Qinnasrīn, Orchenia the area adjoining Syria to the east and Populated Arabia the Yemen and the adjoining part of the Ḥijāz.

Ptolemy: They[4] also accept a connection with the triangle allocated to the northwestern area—that means the triangle of Aries, Leo and Sagittarius—and they are managed by Jupiter and Mars as well as Mercury. Thus it happened that the inhabitants of those regions move around more than others for trade; they have developed into commercially proficient, cunning and disdainful[5] people, people always out for deceit and cowards. In general, they are two-faced and -tongued owing to their connection with these stars.

Commentator: By 'they also accept' he means that although

they are managed by the triangle of Taurus and its masters, still they also occasionally accept management by the triangle of Aries and its masters, and Mercury shares the management with it [both of them ?] since the administration of the middle is his. The inhabitants of those lands have developed more than other people towards moving around for trade and being commercially proficient and cunning, since the sun obliges them to magnanimity, Saturn to cunning, Jupiter to trade, Mercury to business acumen, Mars to disdain and Saturn furthermore to deceit as well. As regards cowardice, the constellation has been close to falling into the condition allotted to evening [*hesperios*], and this has necessitated their becoming two-faced and -tongued, and also because cunning and deceit joined to cowardice make anyone involved in them two-faced and -tongued.

Ptolemy: Those among them who live in the region of Deep [Coele-]Syria, Idumaea and Judaea,[6] are specially linked to Aries and Mars. Therefore they have mostly developed into rash people, men who do not know God and are swindlers.

Commentator: These three regions extend from the Euphrates to the provinces of Palestine joining Syria to the south. Since their management is especially incumbent on Mars, in partnership with Saturn, this has obliged them to be rash and deceitful. But by the remark that 'they do not know God' he means that they do not understand [do ?] good deeds pleasing to God, but commit murder and deceit and ignore God.

Ptolemy: The inhabitants of Phoenicia, Chaldea and Orchenia are connected with the sun and Leo.[6] Hence they have become good natured and compassionate, and they love astronomy and honour among all stars the sun in particular.

Commentator: Phoenicia is Syria, Chaldea Qinnasrīn and Orchenia the part of Syria lying on the Mediterranean [*sic*]. Their good nature comes from the sun, for when it is good, it improves the temperament [*krasis*] of the heart. Falsehood and deceit, on the other hand, come from the weakness of the animal power. Their compassion also derives from the sun. Love of astronomy derives from the fact that Mercury shares with the sun in their management. Sun worship is something that was customary under the old religious law.

Ptolemy: The inhabitants of Populated [Flourishing] Arabia are connected with Sagittarius and Jupiter. Thus it happened that the fertility of their land corresponds to its name—with this I mean populousness [civilization] and fertility. Also the quantity of incense and the practice of beautiful customs, friendliness [*audaces*] and leadership [*regnare desiderant*] on the part of its inhabitants.

Commentator: By those countries the Yemen is meant. Those countries are desert by nature, as is indeed the case with the lands of the Arabs. However, owing to the position of Jupiter's power, they could be populated and hence were called 'populated'. The large quantity of incense there comes from the fact that Jupiter shares the management of that region with Venus, Mercury and the sun. Thus it happened that the inhabitants of those lands are more inclined to beautiful customs, friendliness and leadership than the remaining Arabs.

The introduction of the 'Secret of Creation'

3. From the *Sirr al-khalīqah*, attributed to Balīnūs (Balīnās) (Apollonius of Tyana), according to the Istanbul MS Köprülü 872, 2b–3b, and J. Ruska, *Tabula Smaragdina* (Heidelberg, 1926), pp. 134 f., 138 f.

The descent and origin of the philosopher Balīnūs

Now I should like to acquaint you with my origin and my descent. I was a poor orphan, an inhabitant of Tyana. In my locality there was a statue of stone, standing on a wooden column. On the front of the statue was written: 'I am Hermes, the threefold sage. I have erected this sign in public, yet in my wisdom I have veiled it, so that only a sage like me can reach it.' Underneath it was written in the first language: 'He who wishes to know the secret of creation and the production of nature[7] should look under my feet.' People did not consider what he might have meant by it. They always looked under his feet and saw nothing.

Because of my youthful age I was of a weak nature. But when my nature grew stronger and I read what was written on the front of the statue, I noticed what had been in his mind. I dug under the column and came across an underground passage which was completely dark, since the light of the sun could not penetrate it, even when it rose directly above it. Winds blew in it incessantly. Since it was so dark down there, it was impossible for me to enter, for every light was extinguished because the winds were so many.

In the face of this I was perplexed and grew very depressed. While I reflected with an anxious heart how much trouble I had taken [in vain], my eyes closed. Now behold, an old man appeared to me, resembling me in form and figure, and said to me: 'Rise, Balīnūs, and enter the underground passage here, so that you may attain knowledge of the secrets of creation and arrive at the production of nature.' I replied: 'I can see nothing in the dark here and every light is extinguished for me, since the winds are so many.' However he said: 'Balīnūs, set your light in a clear vessel to keep the wind away from it, and it will not be able to get at it, and you will thereby lighten the darkness here.' Now I grew calm of mind; for I knew that I had attained my desire. I said: 'Who are you, my God-sent benefactor?' He replied: 'I am your perfect nature.'

Highly delighted, I awoke. I set my light in a clear vessel, as he had commanded me, and entered the subterranean passage. There I saw a man sitting on a golden throne and holding a tablet of green emerald in his hand. On the tablet the production of nature was written, and in front of him lay a book containing the secret of creation and knowledge of the causes of things. In all calm I took the tablet and the book and then left the subterranean passage. From the book I have learnt the secrets of creation and knowledge of the causes of things. From the tablet I have obtained the production of nature. Thus I have become very famous as a sage. I have made amulets and miracles. I have understood the mixtures and compositions of the natures as well as their contradiction and harmony.

The Tabula Smaragdina

4. From *Sirr al-khalīqah*, MS Köprülü 872, 212b; Ruska, pp. 112 f., 120, 158 ff.

. . . An emerald tablet on which was written in the first language:

This is an indubitable, certain, correct truth. The highest stems from the lowest and the lowest from the highest. The performance of wonders stems from one, just as all things stem from one substance according to a single procedure. How wonderful is his work! He is the head of the world, its chief. His father is the sun, his mother the moon. The wind has borne him in its belly, the earth has nourished him. Father of amulets, guardian of the treasury of wonders, perfect in powers, substratum of lights, a fire that has become earth. Separate the earth from the fire, so that it may shine for you. What is fine is more noble than what is coarse in kindness and wisdom. He rises from the earth to heaven to draw the lights from the height and descends to earth possessed of the power of the highest and the lowest, since he brings with him the light of lights. Hence darkness flees from him. Power of powers, it overcomes all that is fine and penetrates all that is coarse. To the generation of the macrocosm correspond the generation of the microcosm and the operation. That is my pride. Hence I am called Hermes, the threefold sage.

The Book of the Monk

5. The preparation of the philosophers' stone, according to the *Kitāb ar-Rāhib*, attributed to Jābir, ed. P. Kraus, *Jābir ibn Ḥayyān, textes choisis* (Paris–Cairo, 1935), pp. 528–32.

Know, brother, that I have given this book the special title 'Book of the Monk', since it is my custom to attribute all knowledge to its possessor, if it is specially his own. If my knowledge and that of my blessed master were not so inseparably intermingled, my writings that derive from him would not circulate here without mention of this circumstance. However, through the knowledge he has deposited with me I have become part of him, as the son is part of his father, and I depend on him as the half on the double. In such cases there can be no difference between my knowledge, which I write down here, and the knowledge I have learned and taken over from him, since in the true sense it is all one and the same. Since he used to repeat the same idea in many kinds of words and expounded it to me from various points of view and developed it in different forms, his knowledge does not belong to one of us alone, with the exception of a few, very rare things, with which he pursued special purposes, as I have established in connection with the particular content of the 600 chapters of the *Kitāb aḍ-Ḍamīr* and other books of mine, for instance, *al-Imāmah*.

Since this kind of procedure is characteristic of that monk, and I have not heard it described in this manner by anyone else, I fell into doubt and feared that this would induce me to suspect my master. But when I came to him again and asked him concerning this subject, why he had not included it in the knowledge he had confided to me, he said: 'Jābir, how could my depositions on this subject remain hidden from you, since you have described them from a number of points of view?' I replied: 'I do not remember that, master.' Thereupon he referred me to the relevant books and said: 'The first is the *Kitāb at-Tajmīʿ* and the second *The United Procedures*, one of which describes the very same procedure.' Whereupon I returned to my books and studied them. I looked again at these two books and found that he was right. Now I knew that his knowledge does not omit anything pertaining to the subject, even though people of lower scientific rank think that his knowledge does not comprise everything. Nevertheless, I hold it right to describe the procedure in the words of that man and in the manner of his book, in order that my books here should be complete in every respect and an attacker have no chance of success. How then could that be possible, brother, yea, where could I find someone who could suppress even a little of these divine sciences expounded by me? When I say 'attacker' I mean in reality 'contradiction'. You must know that.

Know that I have studied with this monk for some time after my stay with my teacher Ḥarbī—God bless his spirit! I had always wished to see him, since I had heard that he had taken over the science from Maryānus. Khālid b. Yazīd had sent out people as observers and spies to find Maryānus till finally he was able to stop him on the way to Jerusalem, and every year he presented him with a great deal of gold. When Maryānus died, he was succeeded by that monk. When my teacher Ḥarbī died, I felt a great yearning for that monk and I was told that he was staying somewhere in the Syrian desert. So I set out to search for him and eventually found him and adopted from him this unusual treatment of the stone. He possessed much knowledge; however, in the whole of his knowledge I found only that one procedure remarkable. Hence I have confined myself to it and laid it down in this book, I swear, just as it is without any alteration, after I had tried it out myself and it had turned out to be correct.

When I encountered him, I asked him why he stayed in the desert and how he could remain there and work, since it was so difficult to obtain the required apparatus there, for he lived far from any civilization and had nothing on which to try out the drugs and no apparatus either. His answer was: 'The ferment I have with me suffices for me to be able to work continually, and if I wished, I could do so here in this place.' When I thereupon asked with what procedure and what apparatus, he laughed and said: 'In the shortest way and with the simplest apparatus.' I said: 'Instruct me in it, so that I may share your knowledge and can inform others of it in your name; for, although I have occupied myself with this science, I cannot dispense with a teacher in many respects.' He asked me: 'According to the method of the threefold sage Hermes?' and I replied: 'Which method, since I know most of them?' He said: 'His method as he describes it in his book to his son Ṭāṭ [MS: Bābā].' I said: 'I do not trust the words before I have seen the procedure; for I regard it as impossible that one can achieve this purpose through an ordinary procedure, which does not proceed according to the theory of scales and without sublimation and distillation, without oxidation and putrefaction.' He said: 'Let us go and I will show it to you.'

Thus he went with me to one of the caves to which he used to repair. There from inside it he brought out a piece of a pickaxe. With it he dug two [?] furrows resembling a fox's burrow, only they penetrated deeper into the ground, and he linked them by means of a long path in the rock. Then he took a piece of clay from the ground there, moistened it and kneaded it, gave it the shape of a censer and then let it dry. When it was dry, he set it as a lid over the excavated cavity. With a knife he cut it exactly until it fitted over the pit as well as the path. Then the monk [?][8] took freshly slaughtered meat, mixed it with all its juices and kneaded it with some of the oil which he used for his lamp for lighting at night, until it lay in that cavity like a little ball. On top of this he spread the prepared clay in the required amount, collected brushwood, laid it on top and kindled it. When it was aflame, he left it alone, and both of us went out of the cave. We sat down and conversed. I found his procedure strange and wondered at it. I did not know what he wanted to come out of it. I knew that the oil would burn those drugs and ingredients through the fire's heat and they would be fit only for sublimation, whereby their spirits would emerge, so that only the exterior materials would be tinctured.

Two hours after daybreak he said: 'Enter and let us see what has become of our stone through this procedure.' We entered. The fire was completely extinguished. He swept [the ashes of] the fire away with some grass and cleaned the place. Then he picked up the clay. It was burnt, which I had known in advance. It showed the gleam of the spirits which had let themselves be sublimated. I did not doubt that it was ruined. He picked it up and threw it away together with the ashes, which surprised me. When he had cleaned the place there, he went to the excavated path, and there lay something which in its form resembled an acorn. It sparkled and gleamed strongly. He took it, but it was not clean, since some of the filth and dirt and black of the oil adhered to it. Then he took out some mercury, spread it over the place, laid part of that acorn on top of it and covered it with the fine ash. Then he kindled a small fire over it, as is required to melt wax. When it became warm, I heard a powerful shaking in it, so that I feared that the mercury would fly in our face. I stood back, but he uncovered the place, and then it appeared that the mercury had turned into a fiery red bar, more beautiful than anything I had ever seen.

He said to me: 'This is my procedure, Jābir.' I learned it from him and knew that it constituted the best part of his knowledge. I swear that I have omitted nothing here. That you must know, and act correctly in accordance with it, God willing.

Since we have herewith reached the end of the monk's procedure, we will end the book and occupy ourselves with the things that follow on this.

Polemo on physiognomy

6. Aflīmūn, *Fī l-Firāsah*, ed. G. Hoffmann in R. Förster, *Scriptores Physiognomonici* (Leipzig, 1893), I, 121_{10}–123_{11}, 147_{14}–149_{7}, 167_{13}–169_{4}, 233, 273_{1-10}. Cf. also above, chap. II, no. 8, and, on the subject generally, Y. Mourad, *La Physiognomonie arabe* (Paris, 1939). See also E. C. Evans, 'Physiognomics in the Ancient World', in *Transactions of the American Philosophical Society*, n.s., LIX, 5 (Philadelphia, 1969), pp. 12 (Hadrian's eyes), 54 (scholars).

A blue-grey eye with dots around the pupil is the eye of a swindler and thief, who also possesses kindness and understanding appropriate for his situation.

From dots of this sort, when they surround the pupil and are small, and their owners have small eyes, it must be concluded that they are very dissolute, cunning and avaricious, have many bad thoughts and, besides, are smooth and talk glibly. One finds none more grasping and greedy [??]. Timidity and cowardice may keep them from bad things.

When both eyes are turned upwards, which makes them resemble the eyes of cows, it is a sign of stupidity, negligence and defective intelligence, since people with such eyes are gluttonous and addicted to sexual intercourse and drunkenness. When such eyes are greenish, this indicates murderous instincts, great pensiveness, aggressiveness and bloodthirstiness. If they are reddish and large, this indicates people who drink excessively, talk a great deal and are greatly addicted to women. Their speech is not free from obscenity, spite, quarrelsomeness and indolence.

If both eyes are turned downwards, the same conclusion must be drawn as in the case of people whose eyes are turned upwards. However, people with such eyes are angrier, ruder and unfriendlier [?], and nobody can dissuade them in any way from an opinion or notion since once they have made up their minds about something, it is embedded in their hearts as in iron.

Men with sparkling eyes are cunning, treacherous, little trustworthy and inclined to lewdness and other lusts. We wish to give information concerning such eyes and their qualities as well as about the corresponding clear, flashing eyes, whose owners are found to be decent, unless there are other negative signs. I have already advised the physiognomist not to draw any conclusion before examining all contradictory signs carefully. King Hadrian had such eyes, only they were full of a beautiful light, blue-black and sharp; nobody has ever possessed a more luminous eye.

We want to mention the physiognomics of joints, limbs, breath, and voice, etc. I have already remarked that a single sign is not sufficient and does not justify any conclusion, unless other signs are also taken into account. If all signs agree and confirm one another, one must draw the necessary conclusion. The signs provided by the eyes must be regarded as the most significant, original and reliable, since the eyes are the door of the heart and the storehouse of the thoughts. Upon the eyes there follow the eyebrows, the forehead, the nose, the mouth, the chin and the head; after the eyes, they give the most correct information and show most surely what goes on in the heart.

The physiognomic signs of the face and the cheeks

Very fleshy cheeks indicate drunkenness and laziness.

Thin cheeks demand the conclusion that we are dealing with a swindler with an evil mind.

Chubby cheeks demand the conclusion that their possessor is envious and impudent, especially where they are not placed close to the eyes [?].

Round cheeks demand the conclusion that their possessors are cunning and at the same time cowardly.

Long cheeks demand the conclusion that they imply useless garrulity and impudence.

A very fleshy face indicates that its possessor acts like women do and loves rest.

A rather thin face indicates greed, perseverance [?] and faithlessness.

A small face demands the conclusion that its possessor deals with small matters.

A large face demands the conclusion that its possessor is quick of movement and little desirous of learning.

When a twitching of the lips which extends to the area between eyes and cheeks appears in an ugly face, it demands the conclusion that such people are stupid, unintelligent and crazy. When the same signs occur in a beautiful and cheerful face, it demands the conclusion that its possessor is lewd and lecherous.

The features of the scholar

A man who loves scholarship has a well-proportioned, straigh figure, reddish-white complexion, wavy, reddish-brown hair which is smooth and not curly or thick. He possesses a well-proportioned figure and strong shoulder blades and has neither too much nor too little hair on his body. His tendons and thighs are full, his shanks strong, his upper arms full and strong, his posterior is smooth and broad. He possesses a wide, not a pointed forehead, is not very corpulent and has moist blue-grey eyes with an admixture of cheerfulness [?].

Physiognomist and philosopher

7. The famous anecdote about Zopyrus and Socrates, according to Ibn Juljul, *Ṭabaqāt al-aṭibbā'*, ed. Fu'ād Sayyid (Cairo, 1955), p. 17. It was extremely popular in Arabic where it was applied to Hippocrates, whose name looks very similar to that of Socrates in Arabic script.

There is an attractive story about Hippocrates, which we would like to mention in order to show his great virtue.

The physiognomist Aflīmūn [Polemo] states in his *Physiognomy* that he can infer a man's character from his constitution. One day Hippocrates' pupils assembled and discussed whether they knew of any contemporary more virtuous than the virtuous Hippocrates. They could name none, and somebody had the idea of testing on Hippocrates the claims advanced by Aflīmūn regarding physiognomy. They had a picture of Hippocrates painted and brought it to Aflīmūn and asked him politely to look at the individual portrayed and deduce his character from his constitution. He looked at it, compared the individual parts of the body with one another and pronounced his verdict as follows: 'The man here loves fornication.' 'Liar!' they said, 'that is a portrait of the wise Hippocrates.' Yet Aflīmūn insisted that his science must be true. 'Ask him yourselves,' he said. 'That man would not agree to an untruth.' Thereupon they again went to Hippocrates and told him the story, what they had done and what Aflīmūn had told them. Hippocrates replied: 'Aflīmūn is right. I love fornication, but I control myself.'

XII

LITERATURE AND ART

The great works of Greek literature remained unknown to the Arabs, and the great monuments of ancient artistic creativity suffered rapid or slow decay. The little that was known of Homer, Hesiod, Pindar, the tragedians, Aristophanes, etc., was known indirectly, for instance, through the works of Aristotle and Galen and gnomic literature. However, some forms of Greek literature persisted and re-emerged in Arabic guise. The historical novel of the Muslims resembles the Hellenistic novel in certain respects. The moralizing, instructive and entertaining writings of a Jāḥiẓ have their fairly exact counterpart in Greek literature. After G. E. von Grunebaum's study of 'Greece in the Arabian Nights' (*Medieval Islam* [Chicago, 1946], p. 294 ff.; German trans. [Zurich–Stuttgart, 1963], pp. 376 ff.) it is no longer possible to doubt the importance of the Greek heritage in this kind of fiction. Famous themes developed by the creative phantasy of the Greeks reached the Arabs either through literary channels, in which case they were transmitted fairly accurately, as, for instance, the Alexander legend, or else they passed through a popular intermediate stage and preserved only a remote, if unmistakable, resemblance.

As we have seen, gnomic literature made the popular wisdom of classical antiquity available to the Muslims and acquainted them with the names of some of its great poets. More than that, it occasionally inspired poets in Islam to transmute its themes into Arabic verse. Muslim literary critics have called attention to this fact, although their comparisons sometimes appear a little forced. It also preserved the memory of Greek humour in the form of jokes. A kind of middle-class and scholarly milieu was as characteristic of Islamic civilization as it was of classical antiquity, and we may assume that Greek humour struck a familiar chord among Muslims. We have much more material on humour in Islam than on humour in antiquity. Since the subject tends to be unusually conservative, much of the former may have been inherited from the latter, even if parallels from Greek literature are not always available.

In Islam as in medieval Europe, the architectural wonders of the classical world attracted less literary interest than they deserved, but it was sometimes impossible to repress admiration, despite uncertainty as to the history of the monuments and frequent attribution to them of supernatural origins. Byzantine painting, so faithful to life, was praised in early Arabic literature (cf. chap. II, no. 10), and the relevant passages were preserved by later writers. The ancient custom of decorating public baths with (sometimes improper) murals was continued together with the institution itself, and it is occasionally mentioned in literature. The idea that Arab painting on the whole follows a pre-Islamic Greek tradition has been most expertly propounded and illustrated by R. Ettinghausen in the chapter entitled 'Byzantine Painting in Islamic Garb' in his *Arab Painting* (Lausanne–Paris, 1962), pp. 67 ff. The few reproductions of murals and book illustrations included here show the direction which this tradition took in Islam.

Legendary themes

1. 'The Trojan Horse'

From the *Kitāb Luṭf at-tadbīr fī ḥiyal al-mulūk* by Abū ʿAbdallāh al-Khaṭīb, Istanbul MSS Topkapusarai, Ahmet III, 2633, 6b–7b, and Reïs el-küttap 1005, 19a–21a; ed. A. ʿAbd al-Bāqī (Baghdād, 1964), pp. 27 f. Cf. F. Rosenthal, in *Journal of the American Oriental Society*, LXXXI (1961), pp. 11 f.

The story goes that one of the Greek kings undertook an expedition against Africa [read: Phrygia]. He crossed the sea to reach them and besieged one of their cities for a long time. They resisted him at the gates of the city.

Among the Greek king's companions was a man named Achilles who excelled all in bravery. He had quarrelled with the king about something and hence kept away from the battle. Among the inhabitants of the African city was a man named Hector who was very brave. He slew every Greek who took the field against him. The King of the Greeks heard of it. It occurred to him to apply a ruse against Achilles. One of his friends was told: 'If you were to take the field against Hector on Achilles's horse, we could hope that you would slay him and liberate us from him.' His friend let himself be deceived by this. He put on Achilles's armour as well as the ensign by which he was known. Then he took the field against Hector, but the latter slew him. Thereupon the Greeks informed Achilles that Hector had slain his friend. He became violently angry, called for his weapons and his horse, took the field against Hector, fought with him and slew him. This greatly weakened the inhabitants of Africa.

Achilles spoke to the king: 'Since the people have killed my friend, the only thing that can satisfy me is to annihilate them. Therefore let me make a plan.' The king gave him permission to do so. Thereupon he ordered the artisans to fashion a big, hollow horse and coat it with gold and a mosaic in various colours. They made it so big that its belly could hold a hundred men. He also had a cart made for it on which it could be drawn, and a secret door by which the men could enter. Then Achilles said to the king: 'Direct to the inhabitants of the city assuring words which will not let them fear treason from you. Then leave them, and let them think that you are returning to your homeland. Sail with your ships so far out to sea that they can no longer see you there. But at night return with a number of your most valiant companions as fast as possible so that you reach the people by sunrise. Leave the horse behind. I intend to go in with a hundred of the most reliable of your men.'

The king sent messengers to the inhabitants of the city, and they accepted the truce. He tried to arouse their interest [in the horse], accepted a present they offered him and said to them: 'I did not intend to move from here until I had destroyed your city. Therefore I had this horse fashioned so that it should take the place of our native idols. However, I cannot take it with me now. So guard it for us.'

Achilles entered the horse together with a hundred of the bravest Greeks. When the King of the Greeks had left and disappeared from view on the sea, the inhabitants of the city came out, walked round the horse and admired it. Finally they pulled it away on the cart in order to bring it into the city. But the city gate was too narrow for it. So they widened it and eventually brought the horse into the city. They walked round it and drank wine. They had not noticed that the horse had an entrance. At last night fell and the wine began to have its effect. When it became morning and the people, either drunk or feeling entirely safe, had dispersed, the King of the Greeks went forth against them in fast ships with the bravest of his soldiers. He reached them towards morning. The city gate had collapsed. Achilles and his companions came out of the horse's belly, turned against them, smote them with their swords and prevented them from defending the gate. Thus the King of the Greeks could penetrate into the city and destroy it completely.

2. 'The Cranes of Ibycus'

From Abū Ḥayyān at-Tauḥīdī, *Kitāb al-Imtā' wa-l-mu'ānasah*, ed. A. Amīn and A. az-Zain (Cairo, 1939–44), II, pp. 153 f. The king's name is not clearly transmitted, but it was surely not Polycrates.

Another night the wazīr said: 'I would like to hear about the true nature of chance. It is something confusing that can even shake the intention of a determined man. I would also like to hear an interesting story about it.' I replied: 'There are many stories about it, and it is simpler to tell stories about chance than to explore its true nature.' He called on me to tell such a story, and I said:

'During the last few days Abū Sulaimān al-Manṭiqī as-Sijistānī told us that the Greek King Theodorus [?] wrote a letter to the poet Ibycus and asked him to visit him, together with his philosophical knowledge. Whereupon Ibycus put all his money into a large bag and set out on the journey. In the desert he met robbers who demanded his money and made ready to kill him. He conjured them by God not to kill him but to take his money and let him go. But they did not wish to do so. Desperately he looked to right and left to seek aid but found nobody. Thereupon he turned his face to the sky and gazed into the air. Seeing cranes circling in the air, he called out: "O flying cranes, I have none to help me. May you then seek atonement for my blood and avenge me!" The robbers laughed and said to one another: "He has the least sense a man can have, and it is no sin to kill someone who has no sense."

They killed him, took his money, divided it among themselves and returned to their homes. When news of the death of Ibycus reached his fellow citizens, they were sad and took the matter very seriously. They followed his murderer's tracks, but all their attempts were in vain and led to no result.

'The Greeks, among them Ibycus's fellow citizens, visited their temples for the recitation of hymns, learned discussions and sermons. People from all directions were present. The murderers came too, and mixed with the crowds. They seated themselves next to one of the pillars of the temple, and while they were sitting there, some cranes flew past cawing loudly. The robbers turned their eyes and faces to the sky to see what was the matter there, and behold, there were cranes cawing, flying about and filling the air. They laughed and said in jest to one another: "There you have the avengers of the blood of foolish Ibycus!" Someone nearby overheard this remark and informed the ruler, who had the men arrested and tortured. They confessed to having killed him, and he had them executed. Thus the cranes became avengers of his blood. If only they had known that he who seeks to catch them is on the lookout' [cf. Qur'ān 89. 14/13].

Abū Sulaimān commented to us: 'Though Ibycus turned to the cranes, he meant by that the Master and Creator of the cranes.'

3. 'The Golden Egg'

From ath-Tha'ālibī's collection of proverbs, *Thimār al-qulūb* (Cairo, 1326/1908), p. 394; ed. M. Abū l-Faḍl Ibrāhīm (Cairo, 1384/1965), pp. 498 f.

'The golden egg' is proverbial for something valuable to which one has become accustomed and whose source is then cut off.

The origin of the proverb was the custom of the Greeks [*ar-Rūm*] to pay the Persian kings an annual tribute of a thousand golden eggs, each of them weighing a hundred *mithqāl* [423 grams]. When Alexander came to power, a messenger from Darius, the son of Darius, came to him in order to demand the tribute, but Alexander replied: 'Tell him that the hen which used to lay the golden eggs has died.' This remark became proverbial. The event caused bad blood between Darius and Alexander, and in the end Darius was killed by Alexander.

This proverb has been used by a poet in a satirical poem on a governor [*ḥākim*]:

You for whom education was of advantage and
Would procure the highest positions,

Have thereby lost what
You inherited from mother and father.

Many a country estate that would
Shield you from the degradation of begging,

You have wasted, not on singing girls
Nor for love of the daughter of the grape,

But as a result of events, need,
Misfortunes and calamities.

How often did you say, when you sold it
And were filled with grief:

Our hen is lost,
That used to lay the golden eggs for us.

4. 'The Hostage'

From Abū l-Ḥasan b. Abī Dharr, *Kitāb as-Saʿādah wa-l-isʿād*, 25 f. Minovi. On this motif, cf. C. Brockelmann, *Geschichte der arabischen Litteratur*, *Suppl.*, I. p. 61; R. Sellheim, *Die klassisch-arabischen Sprichwörtersammlungen* (The Hague, 1954), pp. 41–3.

Tradition says that an-Nuʿmān b. al-Mundhir appointed two fixed days in the year, one of them called 'noble day' and the other 'day of misfortune'. He showed favour to everyone who met him on the 'noble day' and gave him presents. On the other hand, he killed everyone who met him on the 'day of misfortune'.

Now someone once appeared before him on the day of misfortune, and an-Nuʿmān asked him whether he did not know what sort of day it was. When the man replied that he knew it well, an-Nuʿmān enquired what had induced him to go out on this day. 'To avoid the shame of not having fulfilled a promise that has fallen due,' was the reply. 'Kill him,' said an-Nuʿmān. But the man entreated: 'Let me redeem my promise, and after that I will come back to you.' Thereupon an-Nuʿmān asked whether he could provide a surety. He referred him to an-Nuʿmān's secretary, and when they asked the secretary whether he would stand surety, he agreed to do so. 'If he does not return, I kill you,' threatened an-Nuʿmān. The secretary replied: 'As it please the king,' and an-Nuʿmān let the man go. He went and returned very soon. 'What induced you to come back, since you knew that I would kill you?' asked an-Nuʿmān, and the man replied: 'I wished to protect faithfulness against the shame of deceit and a broken promise.' Then an-Nuʿmān turned to his secretary and asked him what had induced him to stand surety for the man, since he knew that he would kill him if he did not come back. He replied: 'He asked me for protection, and I did not want to deny it to him lest otherwise one could say: "There is no nobility anymore." ' Then an-Nuʿmān said to the man: 'I forgive you so that one cannot say "There is no mercy anymore." '

Greek wisdom in Arabic verses

5. Some verses from the *Risālah al-Ḥātimīyah* by Muḥammad b. al-Ḥusain al-Ḥātimī, comparing verses by al-Mutanabbi' with alleged sayings of Aristotle. The text of the Istanbul MS Aya Sofya 3582, ed. with a German trans. by O. Rescher, in *Islamica*, II (1926), pp. 439–73, has been compared with the Istanbul MS Fatih 5323 (at the end), the edition by F. E. Boustany (Beirut, 1931, reprinted from *al-Mashriq*) and the text as quoted in Usāmah b. Munqidh, *al-Badīʿ fī naqd ash-shiʿr*, ed. A. A. Badawī, Ḥāmid ʿAbd-al-Majīd and I. Muṣṭafā (Cairo, 1380/1960), pp. 264 ff. The verses quoted here are Rescher's nos 11, 12, 13, 19, 20, 26, 58, 73, 74 and 75. Cf. also chap. IV B, no. 14.

Aristotle says: Substantial souls refuse to have anything to do with baseness, and they regard it as their true life if they should perish through this. Common souls behave in the opposite way.

Al-Mutanabbi' says:

The love the coward feels for the soul
brings him to fear.
The love the brave man feels for the soul
brings him to fight.

Aristotle says: Through the harmony of the humours and the equality of the bases of sense perception one can distinguish things from their opposites.

Al-Mutanabbi' says:

Wherefore does the eye serve him of worldly disposition
If light and darkness seem the same to him?

Aristotle says: He who does not love you for your own sake is he who is far from you, even if it is you who keep far from him.

Al-Mutanabbi' says:

When you leave people in whose power it was
That you leave them not, it is they who leave.

Aristotle says: The love that consists of the harmony of spirits, we do not forbid, but we forbid the union of bodies, since it belongs to the nature of the wild beasts.

Al-Mutanabbi' says:

Not everyone who loves is chaste like me when he is
Alone with his beloved and serves her [by protecting her]
when the horses meet [in battle].

Aristotle says: He who outwardly with chaste limbs keeps away from injustice but with his senses remains close to it is unjust.

Al-Mutanabbi' says:

It is no use holding the eyes' gaze lowered
If the heart's gaze is not lowered.

Aristotle said one day when he saw a beautiful boy and caused him to speak and found that he knew nothing: 'A pretty house, if only it were inhabited!' [Cf. Ibn Duraid, in *Orientalia*, n.s., XXVII (1958), p. 32.]

Al-Mutanabbi' says:

A beautiful face does no honour to a youth
If his actions and his character are not beautiful.

Aristotle says: The death of the soul is its life and its nonexistence its existence, since it attains its world after death.

Al-Mutanabbi' says:

As if you intended to become rich through poverty
And through death in battle to live eternally.

Aristotle says: He who does not know his illness cannot heal it.

Al-Mutanabbi' says:

Many a man knows me not and knows not of his ignorance,
Just as he knows not that I know that he knows me not.

Aristotle says: Poverty of the soul is worse than material poverty.

Al-Mutanabbi' says:

> My life is wretched when my honour is wretched.
> It is not wretched when food is wretched.

Aristotle says: If you perish in the course of an important affair, it is just the same as if you perish in the course of an unimportant affair.

Al-Mutanabbi' says:

> The death one suffers through a miserable affair tastes
> just the same
> As that suffered through an important affair.

Classical jokes

6. Jokes of *Rīsīmus*, whose name is probably to be interpreted as Zosimus, from al-Jāḥiẓ, *Kitāb al-Ḥayawān* (Cairo, 1323–5/1905–7), I, pp. 140 f.; ed. 'Abd-as-Salām M. Hārūn (Cairo, n.y. [1938–45]), I, pp. 53 f. Cf. G. E. von Grunebaum, in *Journal of the American Oriental Society*, LXII (1942), p. 284.

The cock-lover reports that al-'Utbī told him the following: Among the Greeks there lived a mad man named Zosimus, of whom there are wonderful anecdotes. The sages have handed down more than eighty of his anecdotes which, moreover, count among the most outstanding of their kind. One of these anecdotes is as follows:

Whenever he left his house at sunrise and walked to the bank of the Euphrates in order to relieve himself, he laid a stone under the door and the doorpost so that the door should not be slammed, whereby on his return after relieving himself he would not have the trouble of opening the door and pushing it back. Now he never found the stone in its place on his return, and the door was slammed. Thereupon he lay in hiding one day to see who was responsible for it. While he was waiting, a man came and removed the stone and, after he had removed it from its place, the door slammed. Zosimus asked the man what he had to do with that stone and why he removed it. The man replied: 'I did not know that it belonged to you.' 'But you did know,' replied Zosimus, 'that it did not belong to you.'

Somebody asked Zosimus why he instructed people in the art of poetry, though he was not a poet himself. He replied: 'Zosimus is like a whetstone that sharpens but does not cut' [*Gnom. Vat.*, no. 356 Sternbach (*Wiener Studien*, XI, 48)].

Someone saw him eat in the street and asked him why he ate in the street. He replied: 'When Zosimus is hungry in the street, he eats in the street' [Diog. Laert., VI, 58].

Someone bellowed at him rudely, attacked him and insulted him. However, he restrained himself politely and did not reply to him. When asked why he avoided taking revenge, although he had the opportunity to do so, he replied: 'Do you then consider it right, if an ass kicks you, to kick back.' 'No,' was the answer. 'And if a dog barks at you, to bark back at him?' 'No.' 'Now,' said Zosimus, 'the fool is either an ass or a dog, since he is either malicious or stupid and mostly combines both qualities' [Plutarch, *De lib. educ.* 10C; *Peri askēseōs*, in *Rhein. Mus.*, n.f., XXVII (1872), p. 528].

7. Jokes of Stratonicus, from Ibn Hindū, *al-Kalim ar-rūḥānīyah* (Cairo, 1318/1900), p. 124, with additions from MS Aya Sofya 2452. The first three jokes are also found in Abū Sulaimān al-Manṭiqī as-Sijistānī, *Ṣiwān al-ḥikmah*, and Ibn Duraid, cf. F. Rosenthal, in *Orientalia*, n.s., XXVII (1958), p. 51, with Greek parallels for the first and third remarks.

Stratonicus was told that somebody insulted him behind his back. He replied: 'If he were to whip me in my absence, it would not hurt me.'

When he saw how someone was taken to prison because of a crime, he said: 'You there! The pleasure your crime brought you is not worth this disgrace.'

He saw an ignorant physician and said: 'That is a skilful driver' —that means, he quickly dispatches his patients.

He went to a barber to have his hair and beard cut, and the barber did it badly and hurt him. When he had finished, he gave him three pennies. The barber drew his attention to the fact that he was entitled to only two pennies. He replied: 'I know that, but I gave you an extra penny because you did me the favour of letting me get away from you alive.'

He saw a little house with a big door and said: 'Where is the house in the door?'[1]

The ruins of Palmyra

8. From as-Silafī, according to MS photograph in Cairo, *Ta'rīkh* 3952, 451 f. (= MS Chester Beatty 3880, fol. 226a-b).

I have noted the preceding verses because of the author's unusual name [Abū l-Musayyab Wuhaib b. Mutarraf b. Mahyūf at-Tamīmī] and because of the place where the poet quoted them to me. Palmyra is an ancient place, situated between Damascus and ar-Raḥbah, of an architectural beauty the like of which is not seen elsewhere. The city is supposed to have been built by Solomon, the son of David, but God alone knows about this. When I saw Palmyra I spoke the following verses:

Many a place have I seen, but nought
Have I seen so beautifully founded and built as Palmyra.

A place entirely of chiselled stone:
When one looks at it, it fills one with awe.

According to the law [formation ?], cities resemble bodies
And Palmyra is truly head of all of them.

Painting in baths

9. From al-Ghuzūlī, *Maṭāli' al-budūr* (Cairo, 1299–1300), II, pp. 7 f.; English trans. Th. W. Arnold, *Painting in Islam* (Oxford, 1928), p. 88. The text at the end of the passage translated here is uncertain. Cf. also al-Mubashshir, p. 191, no. 110, and Ḥ. Zayyāt, in *al-Mashriq*, XLII (1948), pp. 321–7.

. . . In good baths you also find artistically painted pictures of unquestionable quality. They represent, for example, lovers and beloved, meadows and gardens and hunts on horseback or wild beasts. Such pictures greatly invigorate all the powers of the body, animal, physical and psychological.

The philosopher Badr-ad-dīn b. Muẓaffar, who was Kadi of Ba'labakk, has said in his *Mufriḥ an-nafs*: All physicians, philosophers and respectable men agree that the contemplation of artistic and beautiful pictures gladdens and delights the soul, removes melancholy thoughts and hallucinations from it and transmits matchless strength to the heart by keeping evil thoughts away from it. . . . If it is difficult to find beautiful forms [in nature], one should contemplate beautiful, artistically made pictures, as painted in books, temples or noble castles. To this idea the philosopher Muḥammad b. Zakarīyā' ar-Rāzī has already drawn attention, and he stressed the effect of its constant application on men whose minds harbour evil thoughts and corrupting hallucinations, which are contrary to the natural order of things. He says: When beautiful pictures also contain, apart from their subject, beautiful, pleasant colours—yellow, red, green and white—and the forms are reproduced in exactly the right proportions, they heal melancholy humours and remove the worries to which the human soul is prone, as well as gloom of spirits. For the mind is refined and ennobled by the contemplation of such pictures. The gloom in which it finds itself dissolves. . . . Consider only how the philosophers of old who, in the course of many years, invented the bath realized, thanks to their subtle mind and sound intellect, that a considerable part of the powers of a man who enters a bath relaxes. Their wisdom enabled them to discover through their intelligence how this can be accomplished swiftly, and they therefore had artistically made pictures, with beautiful, pleasing colours, painted in the baths. In addition, they were not content with a single subject but undertook a division into three, since they knew that the body possesses three sorts of spirits, animal, psychological and physical. Hence they arranged that each subject of a painting should serve to strengthen and increase one of the abovementioned powers. For the animal power they have depicted battles, fights, hunts on horseback and the chase of beasts. For the psychological power they have depicted love, themes of lovers and beloved, how they accuse one another or embrace, etc. And for physical power they have depicted gardens, trees pleasant to look at, a mass of flowers in charming colours. Such and similar pictures belong to first-class baths. If one asks a discerning painter why painters use only these three subjects for the painting of baths, he cannot give a reason for this; he would not remember those three qualities [of the mind] as the reason. This is due to the fact that the earliest beginnings lie so far back, and hence the cause is no longer known. [The philosophers] have not omitted anything that is correct, nor introduced anything meaningless.

NOTES

INTRODUCTION

1 Cf. C. J. Kraemer, *Excavations at Nessana*, Vol. II (Princeton, 1958), pp. 72, 112, 276.

2 'Der Orient und das griechische Erbe', in *Die Antike*, IV (1928), pp. 226–65, reprinted in Schaeder's *Der Mensch in Orient und Okzident* (Munich, 1960), pp. 107–60.

3 The language of the excerpts preserved in ar-Rāzī's *Ḥāwī* will perhaps make it possible to establish the date more reliably.

4 Cf. M. Grignaschi's discussion of the correspondence of Aristotle and Alexander, in *Bulletin d'Études Orientales* (*Institut Français de Damas*), XIX (1965–6 [1967]), pp. 1–83, and, in particular, F. Sezgin's passionate defence of this point of view in his *Geschichte des arabischen Schrifttums*, of which Vols III and IV (Leiden, 1970–1) are so far the volumes most pertinent.

5 H. W. Bailey, *Zoroastrian Problems* (Oxford, 1943), pp. 80 f., has a brief survey on the relations between Greek and Sassanian literature as seen by Iranists. For Arabic translations from Middle Persian, cf. the famous essay by C. A. Nallino, *Tracce di opere greche giunte agli Arabi per trafila pehlevica*, reprinted in his *Raccolta di scritti* (Rome, 1948), VI, pp. 285–303.

6 Cf. H. S. Nyberg's article on the Mu'tazilah in the *Encyclopaedia of Islam* and in the *Shorter Encyclopaedia of Islam* (Leiden, 1953).

7 Cf. R. Paret, *Der Islam und das griechische Bildungsgut* (Tübingen, 1950).

8 Cf. F. Rosenthal, *Knowledge Triumphant* (Leiden, 1970).

9 Cf. F. Rosenthal, 'State and Religion According to Abū l-Ḥasan al-'Āmirī', in *Islamic Quarterly*, III (1956), p. 45, n. 1.

10 Cf. the basic work of G. Bergsträsser, *Ḥunain ibn Isḥāq und seine Schule* (Leiden, 1913). Recent times have seen the publication of an increasing number of monographs on the terminology of individual translations. In particular, a comparative glossary is now considered indispensable for any scholarly edition of a translated text. For a double translation of Proclus, *De aeternitate mundi*, cf. F. Rosenthal, in *Journal of the American Oriental Society*, LXXXI (1961), p. 9 f. A Muslim and a Christian translation existed, for instance, for the silent philosopher, Secundus. For a threefold translation of Pseudo-Aristotle, *De mundo*, cf. S. M. Stern, in *Le Muséon*, LXXVII (1964), pp. 187–204, and LXXVIII (1965), pp. 381–93.

11 'Recenti studi sulla tradizione greca nella civilità musulmana' in *La Parola del Passato*, LXV (1950), pp. 147–60. Cf. also R. Paret, *Byzantion*, XXIX–XXX (1959–60), pp. 384–446.

12 *Das Problem der islamischen Kulturgeschichte* (Tübingen, 1959), chaps V and VI.

13 Among specialized surveys, mention may be made of J. van Ess, 'Jüngere orientalistische Literatur zur neuplatonischen Überlieferung im Bereich des Islam', in *Parousia* (*Festgabe für Johannes Hirschberger*) (Frankfurt/Main, 1965), pp. 333–50, or ʿA. Badawi, *La Transmission de la philosophie grecque au monde arabe* (Paris, 1968). For Hellas and Rome in Muslim historiography, cf. A. Dietrich in the *Festschrift* for H. Heimpel (Göttingen, 1971), pp. 81–101. The work done by Walzer, summed up in his *Greek into Arabic* (Oxford, 1962), has been of fundamental importance for this introduction, as well as for the present book as a whole.

14 Cf. J. Kraemer, 'Arabische Homerverse', in *Zeitschrift der Deutschen Morgenländischen Gesellschaft*, CVI (1956), pp. 259–316, and 'Zu den "Arabischen Homerversen" ', in *ibid.*, CVII (1957), pp. 511–18; M. Ullmann, 'Die arabische Überlieferung der sogenannten Menandersentenzen' (Wiesbaden, 1961, *Abhandlungen für die Kunde des Morgenlandes*, XXXIV, p. 1).

15 A strong case has now been made for the decisive role of Porphyry in the Arabic Plotinian tradition, cf. S. Pines, 'Les Textes arabes dits Plotiniens et le courant "Porphyrien" dans le Néoplatonisme grec', in *Le Néoplatonisme* (Royaumont Conference, 1969) (Paris, 1971) pp. 303–17.

16 Cf. G. E. von Grunebaum, *Modern Islam* (Los Angeles, 1962), pp. 20 f.

I. TRANSLATION TECHNIQUE AND TEXTUAL CRITICISM

1 The *Intermediate Works* are the collection of scientific treatises by Theodosius, Autolycus, Euclid, Archimedes, Aristarchus, Hypsicles and Menelaus, to be studied in between Euclid's geometry and Ptolemy's *Almagest*.

2 For this Syriac translation, cf. A. Périer, *Yaḥyā ben 'Adī* (Paris, 1920), pp. 27 f., A. Baumstark, *Geschichte der syrischen Literatur* (Bonn, 1922), p. 341, and R. Walzer, *Greek into Arabic* (Oxford, 1962), pp. 69, 81. So far the only evidence for the existence of such a translation appears to be the rather uncertain statement in the *Fihrist*.

II. BIOGRAPHY AND CULTURAL HISTORY

1 This is more likely than the frequently preferred reading 'Pelusian'.

2 The Arabic text says '19', a mistake easily made in Arabic writing. The modern numbering of the chapters counts the chapter referred to as the seventh, rather than the eighth, cf. the German translation of the *Almagest* by K. Manitius (Leipzig, 1912–13), I, p. 184.

3 'Two' is apparently meant here. The ruler was, in fact, Nabonassar. The very natural substitution of the famous Nebuchadnezzar is already found in the seventh-century Syriac author, Severus Sēbōkht, cf. F. Nau, in *Revue de l'Orient Chrétien*, XV (1910) p. 249.

4 Cf. *al-Fihrist*, ed. G. Flügel (Leipzig, 1871), p. 267; (Cairo, 1348), p. 374.

5 The 'nine hundred years' appears to go back to the statement concerning 'Nebuchadnezzar'.

6 The text is corrupt. The translation here is probably quite incorrect, cf. C. A. Nallino, *Raccolta di scritti* (Rome, 1944), V, pp. 263 f.

7 M. Plessner refers me to the possibility that Ghūrus may be (Anaxa)goras, and Mīnus (Anaxi)menes.

8 Concerning the legendary history of the origin of medicine, cf. Isḥāq b. Ḥunain's short 'Chronology of Physicians', ed. F. Rosenthal, in *Oriens*, VII (1954), pp. 55–80, and *id.*, in *Journal of the American Oriental Society*, LXXXI (1961), p. 10 f.

9. The name could also be read Hermippus, etc. It is uncertain who is meant here.

10 This appears to refer to a part of the Mediterranean.

11 Actually: to demonstrative science, to the science of logical demonstration.

12 This uncertain name, occasionally mentioned by Galen (Galen, Kühn, XIX, 58; *Scripta Minora*, ed. I. Müller, II, Introduction, p. lxiv) is closest to the Arabic consonant skeleton. The obvious emendation to Numisianus is not really supported by the text.

13 Galen, Kühn, XIII, 599, XIX, 15 f. However, the following data are not found in Galen's preserved works.

14 Part of the Arabic Plotinus tradition goes under the name of 'the Greek old man (or teacher)', cf. F. Rosenthal, in *Orientalia*, n.s., XXI–XXIV (1952–5), and below, chap. IV, C, no. 4.

15 Like the preceding Eudemus, he is said to have been a pupil of Aristotle. He is also mentioned in the same capacity in al-Mubashshir's biography of Aristotle. The name would hardly be Aeschylus.

16 The Arabic version of the *Tabula Cebetis* was already published in the seventeenth century, together with that of the 'Golden Words', by J. Elichmann (Leiden, 1640).

17 Perhaps the Mūrisṭus dealt with in chap. X, no. 4.

18 Cf. F. Rosenthal, in *Orientalia*, n.s., XXVII (1958), p. 35 f.

19 The reading Gregorius is indeed found in al-Mubashshir.

20 A saying attributed to him here appears in a Syriac version in E. Sachau, *Inedita Syriaca* (Vienna, 1870), p. v.

21 In connection with the famous sayings attributed to him, cf. *Orientalia*, n.s., XXVII (1958), p. 53, and Diog. Laert., VII, 23; Maximus Confessor 940D.

22 The text describes him as a famulus of Socrates.

23 Cf. al-Mubashshir, p. 195, no. 147.

24 In connection with the material attributed to him, cf. Maximus Confessor 824C.

25 Cf. F. Rosenthal, in *Atti del Convegno Internazionale sul Tema Plotino e il Neoplatonismo in Oriente e in Occidente* (Rome, 5–9 Oct. 1970) (forthcoming).

26 Here a famous anecdote about Bion (Diog. Laert., IV, 50) is transferred to him. Ibn Hindū, *al-Kalim al-rūḥānīyah* (Cairo, 1318/1900), p. 117, has Crates.

27 Under this name sayings attributed to Aristotle (Diog. Laert., V, 20) and to Anacharsis (*Gnom. Vat.*, no. 22 Sternbach [*Wiener Studien*, IX, 187]) are found.

28 Cf. al-Mubashshir, p. 179, no. 55.

29 Cf. Diog. Laert., II, 69 (Aristippus); Antonius Melissa 933D. In Ḥunain the saying attributed to him goes under the name of Diogenes.

30 Cf. Plutarch, *Apopth. Laconum* 210F, 234E; Maximus Confessor 748A.

31 The text connects him with Secundus the Silent, who has a chapter of his own further on. Accordingly, the name ought to be Hadrian, but it is difficult to see how *Hadrianus* could become *'rwn*.

32 That is, probably, Musonius, cf. al-Mubashshir, p. 186, no. 89.

33 Cf. *Orientalia*, n.s., XXVII (1958), p. 53, and al-Mubashshir pp. 175 f., no. 18.

34 Cf. chap. XII, no. 6.

35 Cf. Plutarch, *Apopth. Laconum* 215D. Agis occurs earlier in a different spelling and is credited with another equally famous saying. Duplications of this sort are not unknown in this work.

36 Cf. B. E. Perry, *Secundus the Silent Philosopher* (Ithaca, 1964).

37 The sequence of names here leaves no doubt that this is the commentator on Aristotle who is frequently quoted but cannot yet be identified with any certainty. One of the sayings attributed to him occurs in Greek tradition under the name of Apollonius of Tyana (*Philostrati Opera*, ed. Kayser, I, 352), and *'llynws* is indeed extremely close to Apollonius. Cf. F. Rosenthal, in Stern, Hourani and Brown, eds, *Islamic Philosophy and the Classical Tradition: Essays Presented . . . To Richard Walzer* (Oxford, 1972), pp. 337–49.

38. The expression is apparently not used here with the meaning of 'adherents of the Ismā'īlī-Shī'ah', but refers to people who use philosophical speculation to explain Muslim theological problems. On Empedocles in the history of Muslim philosophy and religion, cf. S. M. Stern, in *Encyclopaedia of Islam*,[2] *s.v. Anbaduklīs.*

39 Cf. Pseudo-Plutarch, *Placita philosophorum*, I, 3, cf. the edition of the Arabic translation by H. Daiber, pp. 111, 133 f. (Dissertation Saarbrücken, 1968).

40 See chap. IV, B, no. 13. For the *Epistle to the tyrant of Sicily*, see F. Rosenthal, in *Journal of the American Oriental Society* (1974 or 1975).

41 Similarly, about the Chinese, ath-Tha'ālibī, *Laṭā'if*, trans. C. E. Bosworth (Edinburgh, 1968), p. 141. For pictures within pictures, cf. P. P. Soucek, in *Islamic Art in the Metropolitan Museum* (New York, 1972), pp. 9–21.

42 The Arabic, here and later, suggests that Jesus was killed and his corpse exhibited on the cross.

43 The reading 'Bīrī' is quite uncertain. The later Persian fractions *dahōye* and *shashōye* are also of uncertain reading; a correction to *dahōtah* and *bistōtah* was suggested long ago (*Zeitschrift der Deutschen Morgenländischen Gesellschaft*, XXXVI [1882], pp. 339–41). As to

the dating, note that ʿAbd-ar-Raḥmān b. Muḥammad b. al-Ashʿath was killed in 704 during an insurrection that lasted approximately three years. Our report also appears in exactly the same form in al-Balādhurī, *Futūḥ al-buldān*, ed. de Goeje (Leiden, 1866), pp. 300 f.; ed. al-Munajjid (Cairo, 1956), pp. 368 f.

44 Note that Aristotle invites al-Ma'mūn in this way to accept the teaching of the Muʿtazilites regarding the oneness of God and, consequently, the divine attributes, including the createdness of the Qur'ān.

45 'Assertoric figures' is the correct translation, according to M. Plessner, in *Bulletin of the School of Oriental and African Studies*, XXXI (1968), p. 619, who refers to N. Rescher, *Studies in the History of Arabic Logic*, XXIV (Pittsburgh, 1963). This expression is not used in the Arabic translation of the *Analytica Priora* itself, but appears in the Arabic chapter headings.

III. THE CLASSIFICATION OF THE SCIENCES AND METHODS OF RESEARCH AND TEACHING

1 That is, astronomy in contrast with astrology.

2 Literally: the science (concerned with the transportation) of loads.

3 Here the Arabic is *ṣināʿah*, a word which has caused us many difficulties during the present work, though it is an extremely common and lucid word. It means 'craft' or 'art' and is frequently used in contrast with theoretical knowledge, *ʿilm* 'science'. Generally, Islamic thinkers have decided to regard *ʿilm* as theoretical and *ṣināʿah* as practical knowledge. This was expressed, for example, by the late Jurjānī (in his commentary on the introduction to az-Zamakhsharī's Qur'ān commentary) as follows:

> *ʿIlm*, which is not connected with an activity, is cultivated for its own sake and called *ʿilm*. If, on the other hand, it is connected with an activity, it is pursued for the sake of that activity and called *ṣināʿah* in the linguistic usage of the élite. The latter is divided into two parts, (1) what can be attained exclusively by means of speculation and as the result of inductive reasoning, as, for example, medicine, and (2) what can be attained only through persistent activity, for example, tailoring. This latter subdivision is specially *ṣināʿah* in the linguistic usage of the common people.

Whatever the truth of this, in linguistic usage *ṣināʿah* is often not essentially different from *ʿilm*. While in German, we have therefore mostly (though not invariably) used the translation 'Wissenschaft' for *ṣināʿah*, English 'craft' or 'art' is often suitable and has been used, as has been 'calling' (chap. IV, B, no. 7), although at times 'science' may have slipped through on the basis of the German text, or have been considered preferable for some reason or other.

4 G. Levi Della Vida suggests reading 'Arsacids'.

5 Cf. G. Weil, in *Encyclopaedia of Islam*², *s.v. arūḍ*, as well as Weil's *Grundriss und System der altarabischen Metren* (Wiesbaden, 1958).

6 Cf. A. J. Wensinck *et al.*, *Concordance et indices de la tradition musulmane* (Leiden, 1936 ff.), II, 376a26–8.

7 This is a reference to the frequent verses of the Qur'ān which state that God made the sun and moon 'do forced labour', that He has made everything in the world 'subservient' to man, etc. Cf. Qur'ān 3.191/188.

8 The editor, A. ʿA. Ghurāb, suggests 'pharmacology'. This is not impossible but seems unlikely here.

9 Cf. above, n. 5.

10 For this important term in Arabic linguistics and literary criticism, cf. G. E. von Grunebaum, in *Encyclopaedia of Islam*², *s.v. bayān.*

11 *Philosophia kai onomazetai kai hyphestēke* (Elias *in Cat.*, 108 Busse).

12 The Greek text of Elias has the inverted order: *ē kath' heautēn hyphestēke . . . ē pros hēmās . . .*

13 For this specific use of the word for 'ornamentation,' cf. S. D. Goitein, *A Mediterranean Society* (Berkeley-Los Angeles-London, 1971), II, p. 467.

14 *Ithbātāt*. The Arabic text and the Hebrew translation do not agree. Possibly, 'among Ṣābians, Magians, Jews and Christians in their temples', omitting *ithbātāt* (*isbātāt?*).

15 Following the Hebrew translation, which also contains the necessary reference to jurisprudence omitted in the Arabic text.

16 Normally the expression used here refers to meteorology, while here it denotes metaphysics. Cf. M. Plessner, in *Tarbiz*, XXIV (5715/1954), p. 68.

IV. PHILOSOPHY

1 Arabic *taṣawwur* and *taṣdīq* are rendered here by 'perception' and 'apperception'.

2 Cf. R. Walzer, *Galen on Jews and Christians* (London, 1949), p. 67.

3 In connection with this passage S. Pines has referred to Stobaeus, *Florilegium*, II, 134 Wachsmuth-Hense ('Un texte inconnu

d'Aristote', in *Archives d'histoire doctrinale et littéraire du Moyen Age*, XXIII [1956], p. 6).

4 The following passage has been excellently translated and studied by S. Pines in the article cited in the preceding note.

5 'Fire, heat', according to Zurayk's edition.

6 Cf. H. Ritter and R. Walzer, *Uno scritto morale inedito di al-Kindī*, Mem. R. Accad. Naz. dei Lincei, serie VI, vol VIII, fasc. 1, (Rome, 1938).

7 The following military ranks are designated by Arabic words which are clear as such, but their Greek equivalents are still to be determined. The translation of *aṣḥāb al-liqā'* is doubtful, probably 'masters of battle' in the sense required here of commander in chief.

8 Ibn Hindū has this saying in the chapter devoted to Anacharsis, but only in the unreliable printed edition (*al-Kalim ar-rūḥānīyah*, 126), and not in the Aya Sofya manuscript.

9 For a variant, cf. Abū Ḥayyān at-Tauḥīdī, *Kitāb al-Imtā*ᶜ, II, p. 45, who has also other sayings such as no. 28 (*Imtā*ᶜ, II, p. 37) and no. 98 (*Imtā*ᶜ, III, pp. 130 f.).

10 In Ḥunain this saying is attributed to a philosopher whose name appears to be Philoxenus.

11 The *Ṣiwān al-ḥikmah* attributes this saying to the same authority (Solon ?) to whom Ibn Duraid's saying no. 72, Rosenthal, belongs.

12 One group of Mubashshir manuscripts has Ptolemy, but according to the *Ṣiwān al-ḥikmah* Timon is the correct form.

13 Apparently the reading is *ijālah* (*iḥālah*), to be understood as *ijālat* (*iḥālat*) *ar-ra'y*.

14 This saying appears in a Syriac version in E. Sachau, *Inedita Syriaca* (Vienna, 1870), p. vii.

15 Reference may be made here to the saying in *Gnom. Vat.*, no. 6 Sternbach (*Wiener Studien*, IX, 180 f.), which is not an exact parallel but to some degree similar. The following saying (no. 61) corresponds fairly closely to *Gnom.Vat.*, no. 7, if the 'rhetorician' of the Greek text is substituted for 'wealth'.

16 The accuracy of this translation also appears to be confirmed by Ḥunain's text.

17 The Syriac version of this saying appears in E. Sachau, *Inedita Syriaca* (Vienna, 1870), pp. 78 f.

18 The correct form of this name is found in Ibn Hindū, pp. 95 f.

19 In the Arabic text, the first syllable of the name is missing. This suggests a Syriac original.

20 The spelling Musonius is found in the Aya Sofya manuscript of Ibn Hindū (to p. 124_{11} of the printed edition). One group of manu-

scripts has at the end: 'but the memory of ugliness remains.'

21 What follows is a lengthy extract from the pseudo-Aristotelian *Liber de pomo*. Its Persian version was published by D. S. Margoliouth, in *Journal of the Royal Asiatic Society*, 1892. For the Arabic original, cf. J. Kraemer, in *Studi orientalistici in onore di Giorgio Levi Della Vida* (Rome, 1956), I, pp. 484–506; for the Latin version, which differs considerably, cf. M. Plezia's edn (Warsaw, 1960).

22 In the *Liber de pomo*, the form of the name is Sīlūn (Milon according to Kraemer, *op. cit.*, pp. 497, 501).

23 One group of manuscripts has 'of their wise sayings'.

24 The same name appears together with Ql'yws (Philolaus ?) in Ammonius' work on the views of the philosophers (*fī ārā' al-falāsifah*), as quoted in al-Bīrūnī's *Chronology*. The quotation is missing in E. Sachau's edition. It was published by Ḥ. Taqizadeh, in *Bulletin of the School of Oriental Studies*, VIII (1935–7), pp. 947–54; cf. the Russian translation of the *Chronology* [Tashkent, 1957], p. 206. According to S. M. Stern, a manuscript of the work of Ammonius, containing this passage, has been preserved in Istanbul.

25 Read, with some manuscripts, *wa-qaṣṣara . . . fāza*.

26 Hardly the Niṭāfūrus of Ḥunain (chap. III, no. 8).

27 There are Greek parallels to the second sentence (Diog. Laert., I, 91; *Gnom. Vat.*, no. 370 Sternbach [*Wiener Studien*, XI, 53]); but the point here is the relationship between the two sentences.

28 For the vinegar worm in Arabic literature cf., for example, ath-Tha'ālibī, *Thimār al-qulūb* (Cairo, 1326/1908), p. 344.

29 Since the Greek text is based on a play of words (*hypomnēmata-mnēmata*), the original Arabic translation, on which al-Mubashshir drew directly or indirectly, must have had 'graves' (*qubūr*) instead of 'bonds' (*quyūd*). The two words look quite alike in Arabic script.

30 One group of manuscripts has in the fifth place: 'When you judge, be just!' (9) and (10) would then count as one item.

31 A slightly different and more detailed Syriac version attributed to Aristippus is found in E. Sachau, *Inedita Syriaca*, p. 79. Instead of 'without words' one group of MSS has a wrong 'through words'.

32 The manuscripts have 'whoever does not know' which makes no sense in this context, but is reminiscent of Sophocles.

33 The following extracts from Plutarch represent a comparatively free rendering of the already free Syriac rendering of the Greek text. The Syriac translation of *De capienda ex inimicis utilitate* was published by E. Nestle together with an English translation (London, 1894). The Syriac text of *De cohibenda ira* is found in P. Lagarde, *Analecta Syriaca* (Leipzig–London, 1858), pp. 186–95.

34 Apparently to be read in this way.

35 This paragraph which deviates greatly from the Greek text shows particularly clearly the dependence of the Arabic on the Syriac; cf. the German translation of the Syriac by J. Gildemeister and F Bücheler, in *Rheinisches Museum*, n.s., XXVII (1872), p. 521.

36 Al-Mubashshir is likely to have thought of 'ruin of fate [*dahr*]' rather than of 'waste of time'. In any case, this is a misunderstanding, since 'ruin of the mind [*dhihn*]' appears in Ḥunain where this saying is quoted after no. 4 and like no. 4 might have been ascribed to Erasistratus. That is presumably the original text.

37 On Stoicism in Islam, cf. F. Jadaane, *L'Influence du Stoïcisme sur la pensée musulmane* (Beirut, 1967).

38 Something seems to be missing here.

39 These three words and the following sentence appear only in part of the manuscript tradition.

40 The apparent meaning of the passage. The Arabic text is corrupt.

V. NATURAL SCIENCE

1 The Syriac text tells us that it is wind enclosed in the clouds that constitutes the second alternative, but no complete restoration of the Arabic text is possible.

VI. MEDICINE

1 Both M. Ullmann, *Die Medizin im Islam Handbuch der Orientalistik*, Ergänzungsband VI (Leiden–Cologne, 1970), and F. Sezgin, in Vol. III of his *Geschichte des arabischen Schrifttums* (Leiden, 1970), have used this source of information very extensively.

2 The original word order of the Arabic translation is still preserved, for example, in the *Ṣiwān al-ḥikmah*: '. . . and I swear by Asclepius and by the creator of healing and every treatment.' Here we have a very good example of how it was occasionally possible to soften the pagan character of a Greek text by slight changes.

3 For *ṣināʻah*, cf. n. 3 of chap. III.

4 In 948–9, Constantine VII Porphyrogenitus was Emperor of Byzantium. His predecessor as well as his successor was called Romanus.

5 Cf. p. 39.

6 The Greek tradition has both Chalcis and Colchis.

7 Latin: *et species opinionum eorum sunt infinitae: quidem enim. . . .*

8 The quotation is interrupted here by a remark of ar-Rāzī, as frequently happens in the *Ḥāwī*.

9 Here follows a remark of ar-Rāzī. However, it may not extend over the entire paragraph of the text, and part of the paragraph may go back to Rufus.

10 The Latin text (457–9 D.-R.) introduces another paragraph covering the following two pages of the Arabic text (I, 78 f.) with '*dixit Rufus*'. This reference to Rufus is not found in the printed Arabic text. But it is not impossible that we have here, in fact, a quotation from Rufus.

11 Thus according to the Latin. The Arabic text is obviously wrong in omitting the words 'in Egypt'.

12 'Not' is possibly a mistake in the Arabic text. Since the black mouth thrush had just been described as a fatal disease, some reader may perhaps have regarded it as senseless that a treatment for it should nevertheless have been indicated, and he therefore added the negation.

13 This paragraph follows a quotation from Rufus, *Concerning the Drinking of Milk*, but it belongs here, as is shown also by *Ḥāwī*, XIX, 372, where the same fragment recurs introduced by 'Rufus on the Treatment of Infants'.

14 Arabic *ta'b* is translated as *labor* by the Latin. That is surely more appropriate than the above translation which was chosen in deference to modern ways of thinking.

15 The Arabic text appears to have here a transliteration of the Greek word *glaukōn*.

VII. GEOMETRY, ARITHMETIC AND OPTICS

1 Cf. Sabra, *op. cit.*, p. 3, n. 9.

2 The Arabic text requires correction according to the Latin text.

VIII. GEOGRAPHY AND ASTRONOMY

1 The Arabic text has: '. . . relates on the authority of Khālid al-Marwarrūdhī, a number of . . . coppersmiths, he ordered instruments. . . .'

2 Apparently this refers to the capital of the plain of Sinjār, not the city of Mosul itself. Mosul, by the way, was 19 parasangs distant from the city of Sinjār, according to Arab geographers.

3 The text of the manuscript suggests something like 'the treachery of those spread out'. The correction necessary to yield the sense adopted above would, it must be admitted, be substantial.

4 Or rather, as suggested in Jamil Ali's translation: the interests of (financial) supporters.

5 Perhaps more accurately: like the chord of a circle.

IX. MUSICOLOGY

1 *Ṣināʿah* (n. 3 of chap. III), also occasionally translated here as art.

2 Of course, the last paragraph does not belong to the Sarakhsī quotation, nor, in all probability, does the one before it.

X. MECHANICS

1 It seems that we have here an idea considered very important by the author who had already mentioned it before in the *Kitāb al-Baḥth*, cf. P. Kraus, *Jābir ibn Ḥayyān, textes choisis* (Paris–Cairo, 1935), p. 502.

2 According to W. Hinz, *Islamische Masse und Gewichte* (Leiden, 1955), p. 50, the Islamic *qisṭ* contains approximately between 1.2 and 2.4 litres.

3 Cheikho's text ascribes the bigger opening to the upper end, but Wiedemann-Hauser and Farmer rely on manuscript authority for the above translation.

XI. THE OCCULT SCIENCES

1 That is, one of the five unequal parts into which every sign of the Zodiac is divided, each of them belonging to a particular planet.

2 Read, as in the following, '[both of] them', that is, the ascendant and the moon.

3 This gloss is not found in the Latin translation.

4 The Arabic text has the singular, as does the original Greek, where, however, the subject is neuter in the plural.

5 Perhaps the Arabic translator intended a passive (*mutahāwan*) 'despicable'. However, only comparison with the Greek text would let one think of anything but the active (*mutahāwin*) 'disdainful, indifferent'.

6 'Judaea', as well as 'Leo' later on, were accidentally omitted in the manuscript used.

7 'The science of production [*ṣan'ah*]' is alchemy.

8 The text appears to be defective. As it stands, it could only mean: 'Then he took the stone as something freshly slaughtered.' Perhaps the intended reading is: 'Then he took the stone [and took] fresh slaughtered meat.'

XII. LITERATURE AND ART

1 This saying calls to mind Diogenes' witty remark concerning the small city with the big gates (Diog. Laert., VI, 57; *Gnom. Vat.*, no. 168 Sternbach [*Wiener Studien*, X, 37]).

INDEX

Entries for persons, places and countries and topics at times include derived forms without express indication; for example, Pythagoras, Pythagorean (noun and adjective), or tyrant, tyrannical, tyranny, tyrannis, etc. Topical entries are highly selective, and all relevant references to a particular subject are combined under one characteristic word. Proper names transliterated without vowels have not been included. The Arabic article *al-* has been ignored in the alphabetical order. As a further aid to the reader, biographical dates have been added in brackets, as well as short references to the literature, usually C. Brockelmann's *Geschichte der arabischen Litteratur* and its *Supplementbände* (Weimar–Leiden, 1898–1949), abbreviated as Br. S., G. Graf's *Geschichte der christlichen arabischen Literatur* (Vatican City, 1944–53), abbreviated as Graf, F. Sezgin's *Geschichte des arabischen Schrifttums* (Leiden 1967—), abbreviated as Sezgin, and the *Encylopaedia of Islam*, abbreviated as EI and EI².

gnomic literature, florilegia, aphorisms, wise sayings, 10–12, 25, 36, 41, 70, 73, 83, 118–44, 255, 261–3
Gnomologium Vaticanum, 124–6, 130, 133, 139–41, 264, 270, 274–5, 279
Gnosticism, gnosis, 2, 14, 99, 154
goats, 139, 201
God, 45, 58, 65–7, 93–4, 99, 114, 120, 130, 138–9, 141–2, 153–7, 159–60, 183, 230, 245, 258–9; First Cause, 98, 145, 151 ff.; First Mover, 145 ff., 150; First Principle, 98, 156; oneness, 30, 40, 49, 67, 151–4, 272; attributes, 40–1; divine body, 147; intellect, 98, 153; nature in human beings, 112, 120; virtue, 94, 98, 120; world, 154–5; *see also* good
de Goeje, M. J., 272
Goethe, J. W., 13
Goichon, A.-M., 76
Goitein, S. D., 273
gold, 49–50, 66, 73, 121–2, 128, 130–1, 178, 231, 247, 249, 251, 257; coins, 86, 178; egg, 259–60; smith, 65, 236; *Golden Words*, *see Chrysā Epē*
Goldziher, I., 27
González Palencia, Á., 54
good, goods, 48–9, 96–7, 99, 102, 120, 127, 147–8, 152–3, 156; good—evil, 69, 94, 115, 160; God's goodness, 153, 156; First (Pure) Good, 98–9, 145, 151–3
Gorgias, 134
grammar, xv, 16, 31, 33, 54, 56, 59, 73, 81, 226, 230
Greeks, Greek *passim*, Greece, 39, 43; character, 43; language, 2, 6–8, 16, 18–19, 28, 39, 43, 48, 100, 194–6, 229, 240, 278; religion, 39; script, 73; *see also* Byzantium
Green Sea, 34
Gregory, 37, 133, 270; (= ?) of Nazianzus 83; (at Alexander's funeral), 122
Grignaschi, M., 116, 267
Grube, E. J., 194
von Grunebaum, G. E., xvii, 255, 263, 268, 273

Ḥabash (9th cent.), 215–16 (Br. S. I 393)
ḥadīth, traditions of the Prophet, 56, 58, 63–4, 67, 69–70, 81
Hadrian (Emperor), 30–1, 34, 251–2, 271
hail, 161, 179
hair, 29, 36, 43, 107, 185, 199, 253; barber, 264; dyeing, 124
al-Ḥajjāj b. Maṭar (9th cent.), 32, 49, 206 (Br. S. I 363)
al-Ḥajjāj b. Yūsuf (d. 714), 47–8
al-Ḥakam al-Mustanṣir (reg. 961–76), 196
halo (of the moon), 180
Halper, B., 19, 43
happiness, bliss, 67, 84, 97, 99, 101, 103, 115–16, 138, 148, 157–8
Ḥarbī, 249 (P. Kraus, *Jābir*, II, 261)
Ḥarrān, 6, 51
Hārūn, ʻA. M., 263
al-Ḥasan b. Aḥmad b. ʻAlī al-Kātib (12th/13th cent.), 224 (Br. S. II 1035)
Ḥasdāy b. Shabrūṭ (10th cent.), 196 (M. Steinschneider, *Die ar. Literatur der Juden*, 115–17)
Ḥashwīyah, 64, 67
Hasmoneans, 59
al-Ḥātimī, Muḥammad b. al-Ḥusain (d. 998), 261 (Br. S. I 193)
Hauser, F., 235, 278
Hebrew, 15, 18, 72
Hector, 257
Heiberg, J. L., 206, 212
Hellenism, *passim*
Henry, P., 154
Hense, O., *see* Stobaeus
Heraclitus, 28, 138, 141, 155
Hermes (Trismegistos), 36, 246 248, 250

Ibn Rushd (Averroes, 1126–98), 145, 149 (EI² III 909–20)
Ibn Sahdā (ca. 800?), 20 (Br. S. I 371)
Ibn Shahrām, Abū Isḥāq (10th cent.), 49
Ibn Sīnā (Avicenna, d. 1037), 61, 76, 78, 163 (EI² III 941–7; R. Sellheim, in *Oriens* XI, 1958, 231–9)
Ibn Suwār, Abū l-Khair al-Ḥasan (942 till after 1017), 9, 22, 42 (Br. S. I 378; Graf II 156–7; B. Lewin, in *Lychnos* 1954–5, 267–84)
Ibn Tāwīt aṭ-Ṭanjī, 215
Ibn Turk (9th cent.), 206 (Br. S. I 383)
Ibn Zur'ah (943–1008), 9 (Graf II 252–6; EI² III 979–80)
'ibrah, 225
Ibrāhīm, M. Abū l-Faḍl, 259
Ibrāhīm b. Bakkūsh, *see* Ibn Bakkūsh
Ibrāhīm al-Marwazī (9th cent.), 51
Ibrāhīm b. aṣ-Ṣalt (9th cent.), 32 (Br. S. I 371)
Ibycus, 258–9
ice, 179
ideal state, 110, 114–16
idols, 39, 41, 50, 129, 257; *see also* angels; Ṣabians
Idumaea, 244
ighrīqī(yah), 39, 195–6
Ikhwān aṣ-ṣafā' (10th cent.), 55 (EI² III 1071–6)
'ilm, 5, 272; *'ilm al-akhlāq*, 82; *see* knowledge
imagination (as a power of the soul), 98, 115, 127
immortality, 118, 142, 262
India, 4, 14, 38, 59, 126, 240, 244
Indo-European, 7
infinity, 150, 209
insanity, *see* melancholia
intellect, reason, sense, mind, 40–1, 48, 63–4, 67, 72, 78, 91, 97–8, 100–1, 108, 115, 127–8, 131, 138, 146 ff., 153–5, 157, 162, 185, 266; intellectual, 28, 60, 69, 82; perception, 63, 95, 148–9, 164, 175–6; intelligibilia, 72, 115, 128, 152, 155, 164
Intermediate Works, 18, 269
Iraq, *see* Babylon
iron, 49, 66, 138, 147, 177, 231; smith, 225; dross, 202
irrational, *see* soul; roots, 65
'Īsā b. 'Alī, Abū l-Qāsim (d. 1001), 42 (EI² I 387)
Isḥāq b. Ḥunain (d. 910–11), 8, 32, 43, 269 (Sezgin III 267–8; EI² IV 110)
Isḥāq b. 'Imrān (d. before 907), 228 (Sezgin III 266–7)
'ishq, 106
ishrāqīyūn, 144
Islam, *passim*, political, 2–3, 13; language problem, 15–16; pre-Islamic, 30, 36, 39, 83, 145, 256; *see also* religion
Ismā'īlī Shī'ah, 271
Isocrates, 37, 127 (no. 27)
Israelites, *see* Jews
Isrā'īl (bishop, 9th cent.), 51
Iṣṭifan, *see* Stephen

Jābir b. Ḥayyān, 232, 240, 248–9, 251, 278 (EI² II 357–9; Sezgin IV 132–269; M. Ullmann, *Die Natur- und Geheimwissenschaften im Islam*, 198–208)
Jacobites, 9
Jadaane, F., 276
al-Jāḥiẓ (d. 868–9), 18, 44, 255, 263 (Br. S. I 239–47; EI² II 385–7)
al-Jauharī, 17
Java (az-Zabaj), 244
al-Jazīrah, 243
Jerusalem, 244, 249
Jesus, 25, 33, 45, 271; *see also* Christians
jewels, 73, 129, 131–3, 231, 241, 244, 247